Optimization and Machine Learning

SCIENCES

*Computer Science,*
Field Directors – Valérie Berthé and Jean-Charles Pomerol

*Operational Research and Decision*, Subject Head – Patrick Siarry

# Optimization and Machine Learning

## *Optimization for Machine Learning and Machine Learning for Optimization*

*Coordinated by*
Rachid Chelouah
Patrick Siarry

WILEY

First published 2022 in Great Britain and the United States by ISTE Ltd and John Wiley & Sons, Inc.

ISTE Ltd
27-37 St George's Road
London SW19 4EU
UK

www.iste.co.uk

John Wiley & Sons, Inc.
111 River Street
Hoboken, NJ 07030
USA

www.wiley.com

Library of Congress Control Number: 2021949293

British Library Cataloguing-in-Publication Data
A CIP record for this book is available from the British Library
ISBN 978-1-78945-071-2

ERC code:
PE1 Mathematics
 *PE1_19 Control theory and optimization*
PE6 Computer Science and Informatics
 *PE6_11 Machine learning, statistical data processing and applications using signal processing (e.g. speech, image, video)*

# Contents

**Chapter 4. Solving the Mixed-model Assembly Line Balancing Problem by using a Hybrid Reactive Greedy Randomized Adaptive Search Procedure** . . . . . . . . . . . . . . . . . . . . . . . 91
Belkharroubi LAKHDAR and Khadidja YAHYAOUI

# Introduction

**Rachid CHELOUAH**
*CY Cergy Paris University, France*

Machine learning is revolutionizing our world. It is difficult to conceive of any other information technology that has developed so rapidly in recent years, in terms of real impact.

The fields of machine learning and optimization are highly interwoven. Optimization problems form the core of machine learning methods and modern optimization algorithms are using machine learning more and more to improve their efficiency.

Machine learning has applications in all areas of science. There are many learning methods, each of which uses a different algorithmic structure to optimize predictions, based on the data received. Hence, the first objective of this book is to shed light on key principles and methods that are common within both fields.

Machine learning and optimization share three components: representation, evaluation and iterative search. Yet while optimization solvers are generally designed to be fast and accurate on implicit models, machine learning methods need to be generic and trained offline on datasets. Machine learning problems present new challenges for optimization researchers, and machine learning practitioners seek simpler, generic optimization algorithms.

*Optimization and Machine Learning,*
coordinated by Rachid CHELOUAH and Patrick SIARRY © ISTE Ltd 2022.

Quite recently, modern approaches to machine learning have also been applied to the design of optimization algorithms themselves, taking advantage of their ability to capture valuable information from complex structures in large spaces. Those capacities appear to be useful, especially for the representation and evaluation components. As large, complex structures are ubiquitous in optimization problems, and can be used as huge implicit datasets, the use of machine learning enabled the efficiency and genericity of optimization methods to be improved.

This book presents modern advances in the selection, configuration and engineering of algorithms that rely on machine learning and optimization. It is structured into two parts. Part 1 is dedicated to the most common optimization applications. Part 2 describes and implements several applications of machine learning.

Part 1 comprises four chapters which focus on real-world application of optimization algorithms.

Chapter 1 addresses the problem of vehicle routing with loading constraints and combines two combinatorial optimization problems: the capacity vehicle routing problem (CVRP) and the two-/three-dimensional bin packing problem (2/3D-BPP). The authors have studied real transport problems such as the transport of furniture or industrial machinery.

The main objective of Chapter 2 is to create the most appropriate scheduling solution that optimizes several QoS metrics simultaneously; thus, the authors adapt the widely used metaheuristic, "Genetic Algorithm" as an optimization method. The proposed scheduling approach is tested by simulating a healthcare IoT application, modeled as a workflow and several scientific workflow benchmarks. The results show the effectiveness of the proposed approach; it generates a scheduling plan that better optimizes the various QoS metrics considered.

Chapter 3 focuses on the grey wolf optimization (GWO) and its adaptation to a continuous search space. It begins by addressing the mathematical modeling of optimization in a binary discrete search space. Binarization modules are then provided, allowing continuous metaheuristics for the solution of feature selection problems in a binary search space. These binarization modules are then used to create the binary metaheuristic bGWO. Finally, an experimental demonstration shows the performance of bGWO in solving feature selection problems on 18 datasets from the UCI Machine Learning Repository

Chapter 4 addresses the type-2 mixed-model assembly line balancing problem with deterministic task times. To solve this problem, an enhancement of the greedy randomized adaptive search procedure – known as the reactive greedy randomized adaptive search procedure – is proposed. This reactive version is based on variation of the restricted candidate list parameter value, alpha. The proposed reactive GRASP is hybridized with the ranked positional weight heuristic to construct initial solutions. Results obtained by the proposed hybrid reactive GRASP are compared with those obtained by the basic GRASP, demonstrating the effect of the learning mechanism.

Part 2 comprises four chapters devoted to artificial intelligence and machine learning and their applications.

The main challenge of recommender systems comes from modeling the dependence between the various entities, incorporating multifaceted information such as user preferences, item attributes and users' mutual influence, which results in more complex features. To deal with this issue, the authors of Chapter 5 design stacked ensemble machine learning models for recommendations. Their recommender system incorporates a collaborative filtering (CF) module and a stacking recommender module. An interactive attention mechanism is then introduced to model the mutual influence relationship between aspect users and items. Experiments on real-world datasets demonstrate that the proposed algorithm can achieve more accurate predictions and higher recommendation efficiency.

In internal auditing, the ability to process all of the available information related to the audit universe or subject could improve the quality of results. Classifying the audit text documents (unstructured data) could enable the use of additional information to improve the existing structured data, creating better knowledge support for the audit process. A comparison of results of classical machine learning and deep learning algorithms, combined with advanced word embeddings to classify the findings of internal audit reports, is presented in Chapter 6.

The design of a control architecture is a central problem in a project to realize an autonomous mobile robot. In the absence of a generic solution, it is essential to come up with a new approach detailing the design process of an intelligent system that is capable of adapting to all changes in the navigation environment. Chapter 7 proposes to use the multiagent paradigm and fuzzy logic in the design of the control architecture for the autonomous navigation of the mobile robot in a constrained environment. The control architecture is designed to solve various problems created during navigation. It is made up of four agents: the perception of the agent, the feasibility of the agent, the locomotion agent and the fuzzy control agent.

Intrusion detection is a key concept in modern computer network security. It is aimed at analyzing the current state of a network in real time and identifying potential anomalies in the system, reporting them as soon as they are identified. This allows for the detection of previously unknown malware. Artificial neural networks are supervised machine learning algorithms inspired by the human brain. This kind of network is a popular choice among data mining techniques today and has already been proven to be a valuable choice for intrusion detection. In Chapter 8, the author builds a feed-forward neural network trained on the NSL-KDD dataset, in order to classify network connections as belonging to one of two possible categories: normal or anomalous. Its goal is to maximize the level of accuracy in recognizing new data samples.

# PART 1

# Optimization

# 1

# Vehicle Routing Problems with Loading Constraints: An Overview of Variants and Solution Methods

**Ines Sbai[1] and Saoussen Krichen[1]**

[1] *Université de Tunis, Institut Supérieur de Gestion de Tunis, LARODEC Laboratory, Tunisia*

This chapter combines two of the most studied combinatorial optimization problems, namely, the capacitated vehicle routing problem (CVRP) and the two/three-dimensional bin packing problem (2/3D-BPP). It focuses heavily on real-life transportation problems such as the transportation of furniture or industrial machinery. An extensive overview of the CVRP with two/three-dimensional loading constraints is presented by surveying over 76 existing contributions. We provide an updated review of the variants of the L-CVRP studied in the literature and analyze some of the most popular optimization methods presented in the existing literature. Alongside this, we discuss their variants and constraints, their applications for solving real-world problems, as well as their impact on the current literature.

## 1.1. Introduction

Although the vehicle routing problem (VRP) is the most studied combinatorial optimization problem, the challenge still remains to achieve

*Optimization and Machine Learning,*
coordinated by Rachid Chelouah and Patrick Siarry © ISTE Ltd 2022.

the most optimal and effective results (Sbai *et al.* 2020a). The VRP aims to minimize total traveling cost in cases where a fleet of identical vehicles is used to visit a set of customers. The VRP is used in many real-world applications, for example: pharmaceutical distribution, food distribution, the urban bus problem and garbage collection. The basic version of the VRP is known as the capacitated VRP (CVRP); each vehicle has a fixed capacity which must be respected and must not be exceeded when loading items. It is aimed at minimizing the total cost of serving all the customers. The CVRP can be extended to the VRP with time windows (VRPTW) by adding time windows to define the overall traveling time for a vehicle. It can also be extended to the VRP with pickups and deliveries (VRPPD) where orders may be picked up and delivered. Another variant of the basic CVRP is the VRP with backhauls (VRPB). Here, pickups and deliveries may be combined in a single route; all delivery requests therefore need to be performed before the empty vehicle can collect goods from customer locations. Two surveys, conducted by Cordeau *et al.* (2002) and Laporte (2009), provide further details.

Loading and transporting items from the depot to different customers are practical problems that are regularly encountered within the logistics industry. The loading problem can be extended to the BBP. When taking into account the number of dimensions that are relevant to the problem, packing problems are classified into 2D and 3D problems. The first related problem is the 2D-BPP (Zang *et al.* 2017; Wei *et al.* 2018; Sbai and Krichen 2019) where both items and bins are rectangular and the aim is to pack all items, without overlap, into the minimum number of bins. The second one is the 3D-BPP (Araujo *et al.* 2019; Pugliese *et al.* 2019); this consists of finding an efficient and accurate way to place 3D rectangular goods into the minimum number of 3D containers (bins), while ensuring goods are housed completely within the containers.

In recent years, some researchers have focused on the combined routing and loading problem. The combinatorial problem includes the 2D loading VRP, denoted as 2L-CVRP and the 3D loading VRP, denoted as 3L-CVRP. The purpose of addressing these problems is to minimize the overall travel costs associated with all the routes that serve each of the customers, as well as to satisfy all the constraints of the loading dimensions. The two problems are solved by exact and metaheuristic algorithms which are reviewed in detail in the sections that follow. For further information, we refer the reader to Pollaris *et al.* (2015) and Iori and Martello (2010), wherein detailed surveys are presented in relation to vehicle routing with packing problems.

This chapter is organized as follows: section 1.2 provides an overview of the literature concerning VRPs in combination with 2D loading problems and the existing variants and constraints. Section 1.3 focuses on VRPs with 3D loading problems and the existing variants and constraints. Finally, in section 1.4, we close with conclusions and opportunities for further research.

## 1.2. The capacitated vehicle routing problem with two-dimensional loading constraints

The 2L-CVRP is a variant of the classical CVRP characterized by the two-dimensionality of customer demand. The problem aims to serve a set of customers using a homogeneous fleet of vehicles with minimum total cost. The 2D loading constraints must be respected.

The 2L-CVRP is available in a set of real-life problems (Sbai *et al.* 2020b), for example household appliances and professional cleaning equipment. Table 1.1 presents a comparative study of the existing literature for the 2L-CVRP, which includes solution methods, variants and constraints.

| Author | Problem | Routing problem Solution methods | Loading problem Solution methods |
|--------|---------|----------------------------------|----------------------------------|
| Iori *et al.* (2007) | 2L-CVRP | Branch-and-cut TS | Branch-and-bound |
| Gendreau *et al.* (2008) | 2L-CVRP | | $LH_{2SL}, LH_{2U} L$ |
| Fuellerer *et al.* (2009) | 2L-CVRP | ACO GTS | LB, Branch and Bound |
| Zachariadis *et al.* (2009) | 2L-CVRP | | Bottom-Left Fill (L,W axis) Max Touching Perimeter |
| Leung *et al.* (2011) | 2L-CVRP | EGTS | Max Touching Perimeter No Walls Min Area |
| | | | Bottom-Left Fill(L,W axis) Max Touching Perimeter |
| | | | Max Touching Perimeter No Walls Min. Area |
| | | | LBFH GRASP-ELS PRMP |

| Duhamel et al. (2011) | 2L-CVRP | GRASP-ELS LS | Skyline heuristic |
|---|---|---|---|
| Zachariadis et al. (2013) | 2L-CVRP | | Open space based heuristic |
| Wei et al. (2015) | 2L-CVRP | VNS SA GA | ALWF |
| Wei et al. (2017) | 2L-CVRP | $SA_H$ LS | Bottom-Left Fill (L,W axis) Max. Touching Perimeter |
| Sbai et al. (2020b) | 2L-CVRP | | Max. Touching Perimeter No Walls Min. Area |
| Leung et al. (2013) | 2L-HFVRP | | Max. fitness value |
| Sabar et al. (2020) | 2L-HFVRP | MA | Bottom-Left Fill (L,W axis) Max Touching Perimeter |
| | | | Max. Touching Perimeter No Walls Min. Area |
| Cote et al. (2013) | S2L-CVRP S2L-CVRP 2L-CVRPTW | L-Cuts L-Cuts MA GA ILP GVNS | Max. fitness value Lower Bound |
| Cote et al. (2020) | | | L-cuts MA ALWF ILP GVNS BLH |
| Khebbache-Hadji et al. (2013) | 2L-CVRPTW | Insert-heur LNS | Best-Fit LS |
| Sbai et al. (2017) Attanasio et al. (2007) | 2L-CVRPTW | Touch-Per LS | VNS VNS LS |
| Song et al. (2019) | 2L-VRPMB | VNS VNS LS | Bottom-Left |
| Pinto et al. (2015) | 2L-VRPB | Scheduling based-model | Heuristics |
| Dominguez et al. (2016) | 2L-VRPB | | |
| Zachariadis et al. (2017) | 2L-SPD | | |
| Pinto et al. (2017) | 2L-VRPB | | |
| Pinto et al. (2020) | 2L-VRPMB | | |
| Zachariadis et al. (2016) | 2L-SPD | | |
| Malapert et al. (2008) | 2L-VRPPD | | |

**Table 1.1.** *Comparative study of the 2L-CVRP*

## 1.2.1. Solution methods

The 2L-CVRP is an NP-hard problem, it is solved by exact, heuristic and metaheuristic algorithms:

Iori *et al.* (2007) use the first exact algorithm for solving small-scale instances of the 2L-CVRP and only for the sequential variant. They proposed a branch-and-cut approach for the routing problem and branch-and-bound for the packing problem.

Gendreau *et al.* (2008) use a Tabu search (TS) metaheuristic algorithm. They considered two loading heuristics for the sequential and unrestricted case, known as the LH2S L and the LH2U L.

Zachariadis *et al.* (2009) propose another metaheuristic algorithm which integrates TS and guided local search, referred to as GTS. For the loading problem, they used five packing heuristics and three neighborhood searches to generate the initial solution, namely: customer relocation, route exchange and route interchange.

Fuellerer *et al.* (2009) present an algorithm based on ant colony optimization (ACO) while bottom-left-fill and touching perimeter algorithms are proposed for solving the packing problem.

Leung *et al.* (2011) propose an extended guided Tabu search (EGTS) algorithm for the routing problem and a lowest line best-fit heuristic (LBFH) to solve 2D-BPP.

Duhamel *et al.* (2011) use the greedy randomized adaptive search procedure and the evolutionary local search algorithm, denoted GRASP-ELS.

Leung *et al.* (2013) study the heterogeneous fleet vehicle routing problem (2L-HFVRP). They propose six packing heuristics to check the feasibility of loading (presented in Table 1.1) and simulated annealing with a heuristic local search (SA-HLS) for the routing problem.

Zacharidis *et al.* (2013) present a static move description algorithm.

Dominguez *et al.* (2016) study the 2L-CVRP with a heterogeneous fleet using the multi-start biased randomized algorithm and the touching perimeter algorithm for the packing problem.

Wei *et al.* (2015) propose a variable neighborhood search (VNS) approach for solving the 2L-CVRP and adapt the skyline heuristic to examine loading constraints.

Wei *et al.* (2017) propose the simulated annealing (SA) algorithm to solve 2 |SO| L, 2 |SR| L, 2 |UO| L and 2 |UR| L versions of the 2L-CVRP.

Sbai *et al.* (2017) propose a new heuristic based on an adaptive genetic algorithm (GA) for solving the 2L-CVRP, considering only the unrestricted loading case.

Sabar *et al.* (2020) present a heterogeneous fleet 2L-CVRP, denoted as 2L-HFVRP. They propose a two-stage method: the routing stage and the packing stage. The problem is solved using MA for the routing stage and five heuristics (presented in Table 1.1) for the packing stage.

Coté *et al.* (2020) introduce a stochastic variant of the 2L-CVRP, known as the S2L-CVRP, where the size of some items is uncertain at the time the vehicle routes are planned. They use a lower bounding functional, called L-cuts, to solve the problem.

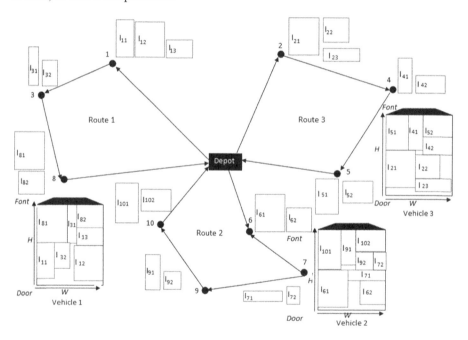

**Figure 1.1.** *An example of a 2L-CVRP solution*

### 1.2.2. *Problem description*

2L-CVRP is defined (Gendreau *et al.* 2008) on a complete undirected graph $G = (V, E)$, where $V = \{0, ..., n\}$ is the vertex set and $E = \{ (i, j) \mid i, j \in V, i \neq j\}$ is the edge set characterized by a cost $c_{i\ j}$. A set of v homogeneous vehicles are located at the depot, each one is identified by $D$, $W$ and $H$ representing the weight capacity, the width and the height, respectively. Let $A = W*H$ denote the loading area. The demand of client $i$ $\{1, ..., n\}$ consists of $m_i$ items of total weight $d_i$: item $I_{il}$ $\{l=1, ..., m_i\}$ has width $w_{il}$ and height $h_{il}$. Let $a_i = \sum_{i=1}^{mi} W_i\, h_{il}$ $(i = 1, .,.,.,n)$ denotes the total area of the client $i$ demand. Figure 1.1 illustrates an example of 2L-CVRP solution.

### 1.2.3. The 2L-CVRP variants

In the literature, several variants of the 2L-VRP have been defined, such as the 2L-CVRP with time constraints, the 2L-CVRP with backhaul constraints and the 2L-CVRP with pickup and delivery constraints. Some constraints are related to the loading configuration: (1) oriented loading, where items cannot be rotated; (2) sequential loading, where items should be loaded in reverse according to customer visits; (3) unrestricted loading, allowing items to be reloaded during the routing process; and (4) non-oriented or rotated loading, allowing items to be rotated 90° inside the vehicle. Four versions of the 2L-CVRP (2|SO|L, 2|SR|L, 2|UO|L and 2|UR|L) are designed.

### 1.2.3.1. The 2L-CVRP with time constraints

For the 2L-CVRP with time windows (2L-CVRPTW), a time window is assigned to each customer during which the customer demand is met. Attanasio *et al.* (2007) consider a variant of the 2L-CVRP where each shipment must take place within a multi-day time window (TW). They propose a cutting plane framework in which a simplified integer linear program (ILP) is solved. Items are allowed to be rotated and sequence-based loading is assumed.

Khebbache-Hadji *et al.* (2013) consider the weight limit of the vehicles as an additional constraint. The authors propose a memetic algorithm (MA) for both the routing and packing problems. Sbai *et al.* (2017) use a new heuristic based on an adaptive GA to solve the 2L-CVRP and designed an adaptive least wasted first (ALWF) heuristic to check the feasibility of the loading problem. Sbai *et al.* (2017) present an adaptive GA for solving the 2L-CVRP with time windows; the results improved the quality of the proposed solutions. Guimarans *et al.* (2018) propose a hybrid simheuristic algorithm to solve a version of the 2L-CVRP with stochastic travel times.

Song *et al.* (2019) consider the multi-objective VRP with loading and time window constraints, presented as a mixed integer linear programming (MILP) model. A generalized variable neighborhood search (GVNS) algorithm is designed to solve the MILP.

### 1.2.3.2. *The 2L-CVRP with backhaul*

In 2L-CVRP with backhaul (2L-CVRPB), a vehicle can deliver (linehaul), then collect goods from customers (backhaul) and bring back items to the depot. All linehaul must be done before the backhaul. Once customer demands are designed as a set of 2D rectangular weighted items, the problem is considered as a 2L-VRPB.

Pinto *et al.* (2015) studied the VRP with mixed backhaul using an insert heuristic and a bottom-left heuristic (BLH) for the packing aspect. Also, Dominguez *et al.* (2016) proposed a hybrid algorithm: the biased-randomized heuristic and a large neighborhood search metaheuristic framework to solve the 2L-VRPB.

In the same case, Zachariadis *et al.* (2017) described a local search (LS) approach for solving the 2L-VRPSDP and the 2L-VRPCB. Pinto *et al.* (2017) proposed a VNS algorithm for solving the 2L-VRPB.

### 1.2.3.3. *2L-CVRP with pickup and delivery constraints*

In the 2L-CVRP with pickup and delivery constraints, delivery items are unloaded and additional pickup items are loaded onto the vehicle. Likewise, the VRP with pickup and delivery (PD) and 2D loading constraints is only researched in two works. The first one is proposed by Malapert *et al.* (2008) for solving the 2L-VRPPD. The second one is introduced by Zachariadis *et al.* (2016), the VRP with simultaneous pickup and delivery (2L-SPD) with LIFO constraints using a local search algorithm.

## 1.2.4. *Computational analysis*

Gendreau *et al.* (2008) and Iori *et al.* (2007) generated the 180 2L-CVRP instances by extending the 36 well-known classical CVRP instances introduced by Toth and Vigo (2002). In particular, each customer is associated with a set of 2D items. In addition, the loading surface ($L$, $W$) is fixed as (40, 20) for all instances, and the available vehicle number is specified. According to the characteristics of the items demanded, five classes of the item demand characteristics introduced by Iori *et al.* (2007) are generated and available at http://www.or.deis.unibo.it/research.html.

For Class 1, each customer is assigned to one item of unit length and width so that packing is always feasible. Therefore, Class 1 can be regarded as a pure CVRP which is used to evaluate the performance of proposed algorithms, in terms of the routing aspect.

For Classes 2–5, customer demand $m_i$ is included at three given intervals. The unrestricted and sequential versions share the same test data, but sequential 2L-CVRP should account for additional unloading constraints when examining the feasibility of routes.

## 1.3. The capacitated vehicle routing problem with three-dimensional loading constraints

The 3L-CVRP integrates two of the most studied optimization problems: the CVRP and the 3D-BPP. The problem aims to minimize total traveling cost while respecting the three-dimensionality constraint of customer demands. The 3L-CVRP has many transportation applications (Ruan *et al.* 2013), such as the distribution of kitchen components, mechanical components, household appliances, soft drinks and staple goods. Table 1.2 presents a comparative study of the existing literature for the 3L-CVRP, including solution methods, variants and constraints.

### 1.3.1. *Solution methods*

Gendreau *et al.* (2006) study the first work reporting a combination of CVRP and 3D loading; they proposed a TS algorithm for both the routing and loading problem. They presented sequence-based loading, stacking and vertical stability constraints and a fixed vertical orientation of the items in the vehicles. The work is motivated by a real furniture distribution decision in Italy. Aprile *et al.* (2007) developed an SA to solve the 3L-CVRP.

Tarantilis *et al.* (2009) combine the TS and guided LS (GLS) to solve the 3L-CVRP black box feasibility. Fuellerer *et al.* (2010) addressed the 3L-CVRP with large-size instances and to solve the problem they used the ACO for the routing, and Ren *et al.* (2011) proposed a branch-and-bound for the routing sub-problem and a container loading algorithm to verify the packing of an item into the corresponding vehicle. Massen *et al.* (2012) presented a column generation-based heuristic method for vehicle routing problems with black box feasibility (VRPBB).

Bortfeldt (2012) proposes a TS and tree search algorithm (TRSA) where the first one is for the routing problem and the second one for the packing problem. Zhu *et al.* (2012) studied the 3L-CVRP using a TS algorithm.

Wisniewski *et al.* (2011) describe a TS and a first-improvement LS for the routing problem. On the other hand, the loading is efficiently done by a randomized bottom-left based algorithm. Miao *et al.* (2012) solve the 3L-CVRP problem using GA and TS (GATS) for the routing and packing sub-problem, respectively.

Ruan *et al.* (2013) propose a bee mating optimization (HBMO) for the routing problem and six loading heuristics (Back-Left-Low, Left-Back-Low, Max-Touching-Area-W, Max-Touching-Area-No-Walls-W, Max-Touching Area-L and Max-Touching-No-Walls-L algorithms) for 3D loading.

Ceschia *et al.* (2013) address the 3L-CVRP with sequence-based loading and a heterogeneous vehicle fleet. They proposed an LS approach that combines SA and large neighborhood search (LNS) to solve the problem in one stage. They consider stacking and stability constraints, orientation constraints, the maximum reach length of a worker or forklift as well as the possibility of split deliveries.

Tao and Wang (2015) propose a simple TS algorithm for the routing problem and a least waste algorithm for the packing problem.

Junqueira *et al.* (2013) propose an ILP exact method to solve small-scale instances of the 3L-CVRP (number of customers <15). They assume a homogeneous vehicle fleet, sequence-based loading, stacking constraints, orientation constraints and stability constraints. The authors take into account the unloading pattern of the items at customer sites to be solved.

Hokima *et al.* (2016) propose two branch-and-cut algorithms for the 3L-CVRP variant with only an LIFO constraint but no fragility and stability constraints. In addition, the authors propose an iterated local search (ILS) method for the routing sub-problem.

Vega *et al.* (2020) propose a hybrid heuristic that combines a greedy randomized adaptive search procedure (GRASP) heuristic and a Clarke and Wright savings (CWS) algorithm.

### 1.3.2. *Problem description*

The 3L-CVRP is defined as follows (Gendreau *et al.* 2006). Let $G = (V, E)$ be a complete graph, where $V = \{0, 1, ..., n\}$ is a set of $n + 1$ vertices and $E$ the complete set of edges connecting each vertex pair.

Vertex 0 corresponds to the depot, while vertices $\{1, ..., n\}$ are the $n$ customers to be served. Each edge is denoted by $(i, j)$ and has an associated routing cost $c_{ij}$ *where* $(i, j = 0, ..., n)$.

It is also given a fleet of v homogeneous vehicles, each one is characterized by four variants $D$, $W$, $H$ and $L$ presented the capacity, the width $W$, the height $H$ and the length $L$, respectively. Each vehicle has an opening on the rear for the loading/unloading operations. We suppose the opening to be as large as the vehicle ($W * H$).

The demand of customer $i$ consists of a set of $m_i$ *items* whose total weight is $d_i$ $(i = 1, ..., n)$. Each item $k$ of customer $i$ is denoted by $I_{ik}$ and is a 3D cuboid, having width $w_{ik}$, height $h_{ik}$ and length $l_{ik}$ $(i = 1, ..., n, k = 1, ..., m_i)$.

The total demand asked by a customer $i$ is denoted by $\sum_{k=1}^{mi}( i = 1, ..., n)$.

The 3L-CVRP calls for finding a set of at most $v$ routes where minimizing the total travel cost with ensuring that the constraint 3D of each item is respected. A 3D loading is feasible if it does not exceed the vehicle weight capacity D and if there exists a placement of the items in the vehicle volume that satisfies both the classical 3D-BPP constraints (items do not overlap and are completely contained by the bins/vehicles) and a series of operational constraints. Figure 1.2 illustrates an example of 3L-CVRP solution.

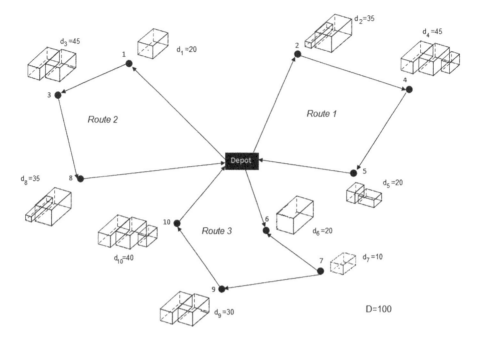

**Figure 1.2.** *An example of a 3L-CVRP solution*

### 1.3.3. *3L-CVRP variants*

The most studied 3L-CVRP variants are 3L-CVRP with time windows, 3L-CVRP with backhauls and 3L-CVRP with pickup and delivery. The 3L-CVRP is integrated with 3D-BPP constraints such as last in-first out (LIFO); rotation of items; vertical stability; fragility and weight limit.

#### 1.3.3.1. *3L-CVRP with time windows*

Moura (2008) presented three objectives organized as follows, to minimize the number of vehicles and the total distance and to maximize the volume used, respectively. Moura and Oliveira (2009) developed a sequential approach (using LS and GRASP heuristics) and a hierarchical approach (using constructive; post constructive; and local search phase) to solve the 3L-CVRPTW. The objectives are to minimize the number of vehicles and the total route time. In the hierarchical approach, the loading problem is seen as a sub-problem of the routing problem.

Bortfeldt and Homberger (2013) described two steps: the first one is to pack items into vehicles with respect to the capacity of each vehicle and the second one consists of designing a route sequence.

Zhang *et al.* (2017) proposed a hybrid approach by combining TS and the artificial bee colony (ABC) algorithm to solve a VRP with pallet loading and time window constraints.

The problem considers the LIFO constraint; fragility and orientation are not considered. Moura *et al.* (2019) presented a MILP model. The model allows all boxes to rotate in 3D and they may also have fixed or limited orientation. The boxes could be loaded in multiple layers formed by different sized and shaped boxes.

Vega *et al.* (2019) studied VRP with 3D loading constraints and additional constraints such as time windows and capacity constraints. They proposed a nonlinear mixed integer program (NLMIP). Pace *et al.* (2015) considered a constraint of a heterogeneous fleet of vehicles for the 3L-CVRPTW. Iterated local search (ILS) and simulated annealing (SA) are proposed to solve the problem.

### 1.3.3.2. *3L-CVRP with backhaul*

The combination of VRP with backhauls and loading constraints is a recently studied problem. Bortfeldt *et al.* (2015) proposed a large neighborhood search and a variable neighborhood search (LNS-VNS) for solving the 3D VRP with backhaul in both routing and a packing procedure in addition, a tree search heuristic (TSH) is considered for loading items. Koch *et al.* (2018) addressed the CVRP with time windows and 3D loading constraints (3L-VRPSDPTW). They used a large neighborhood search to solve the problem. Reil *et al.* (2018) extended the last approach proposed by Bortfeldt *et al.* (2015) for the VRPBTW with 3D loading constraints by considering various types of backhauls. Koch *et al.* (2020) proposed a TS for the routing problem and a set of loading heuristics for the loading problem for solving the 3L-CVRP with mixed backhauls (3L-VRPMB).

### 1.3.3.3. *3L-CVRP with pickup and delivery*

Bartok and Imreh (2011) used a simple local search method for solving the 3L-VRPPD. Mannel and Bortfeldt (2016) discussed several 3L-VRPPD variants and hybrid approaches based on LNS and tree search heuristics are proposed for packing boxes.

### 1.3.3.4. *3L-CVRP with split delivery*

Yi and Bortfeldt (2016) addressed the 3L-SDVRP with the same packing constraints as the 3L-CVRP in Gendreau formulation. Only inevitable splits are allowed, that is serving a customer in two or more routes is only permitted if not all boxes can be packed into a single loading space. A hybrid heuristic is developed that can be considered as a preliminary variant of the algorithm presented here.

Li *et al.* (2018) proposed a novel data-driven three-layer search algorithm to solve the 3L-SDVRP. They minimize the number of vehicles used as a first priority and the total travel distance as a second priority.

Bortfeldt and Yi (2020) studied two variants of the 3L-SDVRP. In the first, a delivery is only split if the customer demand cannot be carried by a single vehicle. In the second, splitting customer deliveries can be done any number of times. The authors proposed a hybrid algorithm consisting of an LS and a GA to solve the two variants.

Table 1.2 presents a comparative study of the existing literature on 3L-CVRP.

### 1.3.4. *Computational analysis*

The set of instances used for the 3L-CVRP is available at http://www.or.deis.unibo.it/research.html and was introduced by Gendreau *et al.* (2006). There are in total 27 3L-CVRP instances available on the web which provide an interesting test bed for the comparison of different heuristic and metaheuristic solutions. The vehicle characteristics are $W = 25$, $H = 30$ and $L = 60$, respectively. The demand of each customer is between 1 and 3. The capacity of vehicles is 0.75.

| Author | Problem | Routing problem Solution methods | Loading problem Solution methods |
|---|---|---|---|
| Gendreau et al. (2006) | 3L-CVRP | TS SA | TS SA |
| Apile et al. (2007) | 3L-CVRP | LS-GLS ACO | LS-GLS ACO |
| Tarantilis et al. (2009) | 3L-CVRP | Branch-and-bound black box algorithm TS | Branch-and-bound black box algorithm TRSA bottom-left |
| Fuellerer et al. (2010) | 3L-CVRP | TS TS | Deepest-Bottom-Left-Fill |
| Ren et al. (2011) | 3L-CVRP | | |
| Massen et al. (2012) | 3L-CVRP | GA HBMO P1R2 TS | heuristic and the Maximum Touching Area TS |
| Bortfeldt (2012) | 3L-CVRP | integer linear programming model | six heuristics P1R2 |
| Wisniewski et al. (2011) | 3L-CVRP | Branch-and-Cut | least waste algorithm |
| Zhu et al. (2012) | 3L-CVRP | GRASP-CWS | |
| Miao et al. (2012) | 3L-CVRP | GA | Branch-and-Cut |
| Ruan et al. (2013) | 3L-CVRP | LS, GRASP | GRASP-CWS GA |
| Bortfeldt and Homberger (2013) | 3L-CVRP | TS-ABC MILP | LS, GRASP |
| | 3L-CVRP | NLMIP LNS | TS-ABC MILP |
| Tao and Wang (2015) | 3L-CVRP | ILS and SA ILS | NLMIP LNS |
| Junqueira et al. (2013) | 3L-CVRP | | ILS and SA ILS |
| Hokima et al. (2016) | 3L-CVRP | LNS/VNS LNS | |
| Vega et al. (2020) | 3L-CVRPTW | TS TS LS LNS TS | TSH LNS TS TS |
| Moura (2008) | 3L-CVRPTW | Data-driven 3-layer | LS TSH TS |
| Moura and Oliveira (2009) | 3L-CVRPTW | GA-LS | Data-driven 3-layer |
| Zhang et al. (2017) | 3L-CVRPTW | | GA-LS |
| Moura et al. (2019) | 3L-CVRPTW | | |
| Vega et al. (2019) | 3L-HCVRP | | |
| Ceschia et al. (2013) | 3L-HFCVRPTW | | |
| Pace et al. (2015) | CVRP with pallet loading and axle weight constraints | | |
| Pollaris et al.(2017) | | | |
| Bortfeldt et al. (2015) | 3L-VRPB | | |
| Koch et al. (2018) | 3L-VRPBTW | | |
| Reil et al. (2018) | 3L-VRPBTW | | |
| Koch et al. (2020) | 3L-VRPMB | | |
| Bartok and Imreh (2011) | 3L-VRPPD | | |
| Mannel and Bortfeldt (2016) | 3L-VRPD | | |
| Yi and Bortfeldt (2016) | 3L-SDVRP | | |
| Li et al. (2018) | 3L-SDVRP | | |
| Bortfeldt and Yi (2020) | 3L-SDVRP | | |

**Table 1.2.** *Comparative study of the 3L-CVRP*

## 1.4. Perspectives on future research

In this review, the last decade of publications related to the combination VRP with 2/3D loading problems with additional variants and constraints has been surveyed. A comparative study of the existing optimization methods such as exact, heuristic and metaheuristic is described. These promising research areas give the opportunity for solving real-world problems in transportation. Given the importance of this problem, it still remains a challenge. However, future research could extend on the 2L-CVRP with multi-objective optimization. In addition, the 2L-VRP has been studied on the static case in which all information is known at the time of the planning routes. However, in most real-life applications, new customer requests can happen over time and thus trouble the optimal routing schedule that was originally invented. Therefore, the problem can be studied in the dynamic case.

## 1.5. References

Aprile, D., Egeblad, J., Garavelli, A.C., Lisi, S., Pisinger, D (2007). Logistics optimization: Vehicle routing with loading constraints. In *Proceedings of the 19th International Conference on Production Research*. Informs, Valparaiso, Chile.

Araujo, L.J., Ozcan, E., Atkin, J.A., Baumers, M. (2019). Analysis of irregular three-dimensional packing problems in additive manufacturing: A new taxonomy and dataset. *International Journal of Production Research*, 57(18), 5920–5934.

Attanasio A., Fuduli A., Ghiani, G., Triki, C. (2007). Integrated shipment dispatching and packing problems: A case study. *Journal of Mathematical Modelling and Algorithms*, 6(1), 77–85.

Bartok, T. and Imreh, C. (2011). Pickup and delivery vehicle routing with multidimensional loading constraints. *Acta Cybernetica*, 20, 17–33.

Bortfeldt, A. (2012). A hybrid algorithm for the capacitated vehicle routing problem with three-dimensional loading constraints. *Computers & Operations Research*, 39(9), 2248–2257.

Bortfeldt, A. and Homberger, J. (2013). Packing first, routing second: A heuristic for the vehicle routing and loading problem. *Computers & Operations Research*, 40(3), 873–885.

Bortfeldt, A. and Yi, J. (2020). The split delivery vehicle routing problem with three-dimensional loading constraints. *European Journal of Operational Research*, 282(2), 545–558.

Bortfeldt, A., Hahn, T., Mannel, D., Monch, L. (2015). Hybrid algorithms for the vehicle routing problem with clustered backhauls and 3D loading constraints. *European Journal of Operational Research*, 243, 82–96.

Ceschia, S., Schaerf, A., Stutzle, T. (2013). Local search techniques for a routing-packing problem. *Computers & Industrial Engineering*, 66(4), 1138–1149.

Christofides, N. and Beasley, J. (1984). The period routing problem. *Networks*, 14, 237–256.

Cordeau, J.F., Gendreau, M., Laporte, G., Potvin, J.Y., Semet, F. (2002). A guide to vehicle routing heuristics. *Journal of the Operational Research Society*, 53(5), 512–522.

Cote, J.F., Gendreau, M., Potvin, J.Y. (2013). *The Vehicle Routing Problem with Stochastic Two-Dimensional Items*. CIRRELT, Quebec.

Cote, J.F., Gendreau, M., Potvin, J.Y. (2020). The vehicle routing problem with stochastic two-dimensional items. *Transportation Science*, 54(2), 453–469.

Dominguez, O., Guimarans, D., Juan, A.A., de la Nuez, I. (2016). A biased-randomised large neighbourhood search for the two-dimensional vehicle routing problem with backhauls. *European Journal of Operational Research*, 255(2), 442–462.

Duhamel, C., Lacomme, P., Quilliot, A., Toussaint, H. (2011). A multi-start evolutionary local search for the two-dimensional loading capacitated vehicle routing problem. *Computers & Operations Research*, 38, 617–640.

Fekete, S.P. and Schepers, J. (2004). A general framework for bounds for higher-dimensional orthogonal packing problems. *Mathematical Methods of Operations Research*, 60(2), 311–329.

Fisher, M., Jakumar, R., van Wassenhove, L. (1981). A generalized assignment heuristic for vehicle routing. *Networks*, 11, 109–124.

Fuellerer, G., Doerner, K., Hartl, R., Iori, M. (2009). Ant colony optimization for the two-dimensional loading vehicle routing problem. *Computers & Operations Research*, 36, 655–673.

Fuellerer, G., Doerner, K.F., Hartl, R.F., Iori, M. (2010). Metaheuristics for vehicle routing problems with three-dimensional loading constraints. *European Journal of Operational Research*, 201(3), 751–759.

Gendreau, M., Iori, M., Laporte, G., Martello, S. (2006). A Tabu search algorithm for a routing and container loading problem. *Transportation Science*, 40(3), 342–350.

Gendreau, M., Iori, M., Laporte, G., Martello, S. (2008). A Tabu search heuristic for the vehicle routing problem with two-dimensional loading constraints. *Networks*, 51, 4–18.

Guimarans, D., Dominguez, O., Panadero, J., Juan, A.A. (2018). A simheuristic approach for the two-dimensional vehicle routing problem with stochastic travel times. *Simulation Modelling Practice and Theory*, 89, 1–14.

Hokama, P., Miyazawa, F.K., Xavier, E.C. (2016). A branch-and-cut approach for the vehicle routing problem with loading constraints. *Expert Systems with Applications*, 47, 1–13.

Holland, J.H. and Holland, J.H. (1975). *Adaptations in Natural and Artificial Systems: An Introductory Analysis with Applications to Biology, Control, and Artificial Intelligence*. The University of Michigan Press, Ann Arbor.

Iori, M. and Martello, S. (2010). Routing problems with loading constraints. *Top*, 18(1), 4–27.

Iori, M., Salazar, J.J., Vigo, D. (2007). An exact approach for the vehicle routing problem with two-dimensional loading constraints. *Transportation Science*, 41, 253–264.

Junqueira, L., Oliveira, J.F., Carravilla, M.A., Morabito, R. (2013). An optimization model for the vehicle routing problem with practical three-dimensional loading constraints. *International Transactions in Operational Research*, 20(5), 645–666.

Khebbache, S., Prins, C., Yalaoui, A. (2008). Iterated local search algorithm for the constrained two-dimensional non-guillotine cutting problem. *Journal of Industrial and Systems Engineering*, 2(3), 164–179.

Khebbache-Hadji, S., Prins, C., Yalaoui, A., Reghioui, M. (2013). Heuristics and memetic algorithm for the two-dimensional loading capacitated vehicle routing problem with time windows. *Central European Journal of Operations Research*, 21(2), 307–336.

Kilby, P., Prosser, P., Shaw, P. (1998). Dynamic VRPs: A study of scenarios. Technical Report, University of Strathclyde, Glasgow.

Koch, H., Bortfeldt, A., Wascher, G. (2018). A hybrid algorithm for the vehicle routing problem with backhauls, time windows and three-dimensional loading constraints. *OR Spectrum*, 40, 1029–1075.

Koch, H., Schlogell, M., Bortfeldt, A. (2020). A hybrid algorithm for the vehicle routing problem with three-dimensional loading constraints and mixed backhauls. *Journal of Scheduling*, 23(1), 71–93.

Laporte, G. (2009). Fifty years of vehicle routing. *Transportation Science*, 43(4), 408–416.

Leung, S., Zhou, X., Zhang, D., Zheng, J. (2011). Extended guided Tabu search and a new packing algorithm for the two-dimensional loading vehicle routing problem. *Computers & Operations Research*, 38(1), 205–215.

Leung, S., Zhang, Z., Zhang, D., Hua, X., Lim, M. (2013). A meta-heuristic algorithm for heterogeneous fleet vehicle routing problems with two-dimensional loading constraints. *Computers & Operations Research*, 225, 199–210.

Li, X., Yuan, M., Chen, D., Yao, J., Zeng, J. (2018). A data-driven three-layer algorithm for split delivery vehicle routing problem with 3D container loading constraint. In *Proceedings of the KDD'18: The 24th ACM SIGKDD International Conference on Knowledge Discovery & Data Mining*. ACM, London.

Malapert, A., Guéret, C., Jussien, N., Langevin, A., Rousseau, L.M. (2008). Two-dimensional pickup and delivery routing problem with loading constraints. In *First CPAIOR Workshop on Bin Packing and Placement Constraints (BPPC'08)*, Paris.

Mannel, D. and Bortfeldt, A. (2016). A hybrid algorithm for the vehicle routing problem with pickup and delivery and three-dimensional loading constraints. *European Journal of Operational Research*, 254(3), 840–858.

Massen, F., Deville, Y., Van Hentenryck, P. (2012). Pheromone-based heuristic column generation for vehicle routing problems with black box feasibility. In *International Conference on Integration of Artificial Intelligence (AI) and Operations Research (OR) Techniques in Constraint Programming*. Springer, Heidelberg.

Miao, L., Ruan, Q., Woghiren, K., Ruo, Q. (2012). A hybrid genetic algorithm for the vehicle routing problem with three-dimensional loading constraints. *RAIRO-Operations Research – Recherche Opérationnelle*, 46(1), 63–82.

Moura, A. (2008). A multi-objective genetic algorithm for the vehicle routing with time windows and loading problem. In *Intelligent Decision Support*, Bortfeldt, D.A., Homberger, P.D.J., Kopfer, P.D.H., Pankratz, G., Strangmeier, D.R. (eds). Gabler, Wiesbaden.

Moura, A. (2019). A model-based heuristic to the vehicle routing and loading problem. *International Transactions in Operational Research*, 26(3), 888–907.

Moura, A. and Oliveira, J.F. (2009). An integrated approach to the vehicle routing and container loading problems. *OR Spectrum*, 31(4), 775–800.

Pace, S., Turky, A., Moser, I., Aleti, A. (2015). Distributing fibre boards: A practical application of the heterogeneous fleet vehicle routing problem with time windows and three-dimensional loading constraints. *Procedia Computer Science*, 51, 2257–2266.

Pinto, T., Alves, C., de Carvalho, J.V., Moura, A. (2015). An insertion heuristic for the capacitated vehicle routing problem with loading constraints and mixed linehauls and backhauls. *FME Transactions*, 43(4), 311–318.

Pinto, T., Alves, C., de Carvalho, J.V. (2017). Variable neighborhood search algorithms for pickup and delivery problems with loading constraints. *Electronic Notes in Discrete Mathematics*, 58, 111–118.

Pinto, T., Alves, C., de Carvalho, J.V. (2020). Variable neighborhood search algorithms for the vehicle routing problem with two-dimensional loading constraints and mixed linehauls and backhauls. *International Transactions in Operational Research*, 27(1), 549–572.

Pollaris, H., Braekers, K., Caris, A., Janssens, G.K., Limbourg, S. (2015). Vehicle routing problems with loading constraints: State-of-the-art and future directions. *OR Spectrum*, 37(2), 297–330.

Pollaris, H., Braekers, K., Caris, A., Janssens, G.K., Limbourg, S. (2017). Iterated local search for the capacitated vehicle routing problem with sequence: Based pallet loading and axle weight constraints. *Networks*, 69(3), 304–316.

Pugliese, L.D.P., Guerriero, F., Calbi, R. (2019). Solving a three-dimensional bin-packing problem arising in the groupage process: Application to the port of Gioia Tauro. In *A View of Operations Research Applications in Italy*, Dell'Amico, M., Gaudioso, M., Stecca, G. (eds). Springer, Cham.

Reil, S., Bortfeldt, A., Monch, L. (2018). Heuristics for vehicle routing problems with backhauls, time windows, and 3D loading constraints. *European Journal of Operational Research*, 266(3), 877–894.

Ren, J., Tian, Y., Sawaragi, T. (2011). A relaxation method for the three-dimensional loading capacitated vehicle routing problem. In *2011 IEEE/SICE International Symposium on System Integration (SII)*, IEEE, 750–755.

Ruan, Q., Zhang, Z., Miao, L., Shen, H. (2013). A hybrid approach for the vehicle routing problem with three-dimensional loading constraints. *Computers & Operations Research*, 40(6), 1579–1589.

Sabar, N.R., Bhaskar, A., Chung, E., Turky, A., Song, A. (2020). An adaptive memetic approach for heterogeneous vehicle routing problems with two-dimensional loading constraints. *Swarm and Evolutionary Computation*, 100730.

Sbai, I. and Krichen, S. (2019). A hybrid PSO-LS approach for solving the two-dimensional bin packing problem with weight capacities constraint: A case study. In *Proceedings of the 9th International Conference on Information Systems and Technologies*. Association for Computing Machinery, NY, United States and Cairo, Egypt.

Sbai, I., Limem, O., Krichen, S. (2017). An adaptive genetic algorithm for the capacitated vehicle routing problem with time windows and two-dimensional loading constraints. In *Computer Systems and Applications (AICCSA), 2017 IEEE/ACS 14th International Conference*, IEEE.

Sbai, I., Krichen, S., Limam, O. (2020a). Two meta-heuristics for solving the capacitated vehicle routing problem: The case of the Tunisian Post Office. *Operational Research*, ISO 690.

Sbai, I., Limem, O., Krichen, S. (2020b). An effective genetic algorithm for solving the capacitated vehicle routing problem with two-dimensional loading constraint. *International Journal of Computational Intelligence Studies*, 9(1/2), 85–106.

Song, X., Jones, D., Asgari, N., Pigden, T. (2019). Multi-objective vehicle routing and loading with time window constraints: A real-life application. *Annals of Operations Research*, 291, 799–825 [Online]. Available at: https://doi.org/10.1007/s10479-019-03205-2.

Tao, Y. and Wang, F. (2015). An effective Tabu search approach with improved loading algorithms for the 3L-CVRP. *Computers & Operations Research*, 55, 127–140.

Tarantilis, C.D., Zachariadis, E.E., Kiranoudis, C.T. (2009). A hybrid metaheuristic algorithm for the integrated vehicle routing and three-dimensional container-loading problem. *IEEE Transactions on Intelligent Transportation Systems*, 10(2), 255–271.

Toth, P. and Vigo, D. (2002). The vehicle routing problem. *SIAM Monographs on Discrete Mathematics and Applications*. SIAM, Philadelphia [Online]. Available at: http://www.lavoisier.fr/livre/notice.as p?id=OS6WSLARK6SOWC.

Vega-Mejia, C.A., Montoya-Torres, J.R., Islam, S.M.N. (2019). A nonlinear optimization model for the balanced vehicle routing problem with loading constraints. *International Transactions in Operational Research*, 26(3), 794–835.

Vega-Mejia, C., González-Neira, E., Montoya-Torres, J., Islam, S. (2020). Using a hybrid heuristic to solve the balanced vehicle routing problem with loading constraints. *International Journal of Industrial Engineering Computations*, 11(2), 255–280.

Wei, L., Zhang, Z., Zhang, D., Lim, A. (2015). A variable neighborhood search for the capacitated vehicle routing problem with two-dimensional loading constraints. *European Journal of Operational Research*, 243(3), 798–814.

Wei, L., Zhang, Z., Zhang, D., Leung, S.C. (2018). A simulated annealing algorithm for the capacitated vehicle routing problem with two-dimensional loading constraints. *European Journal of Operational Research*, 265(3), 843–859.

Wei, L., Wang, Y., Cheng, H., Huang, J. (2019). An open space based heuristic for the 2D strip packing problem with unloading constraints. *Applied Mathematical Modelling*, 70, 67–81.

Wisniewski, M.A., Ritt, M., Buriol, L.S. (2011). A Tabu search algorithm for the capacitated vehicle routing problem with three-dimensional loading constraints. In *XLIII Simposio Brasilero de Pesquisa Operacional*, 15–18 August, Ubatuba.

Yi, J. and Bortfeldt, A. (2016). The capacitated vehicle routing problem with three-dimensional loading constraints and split delivery – A case study. In *Proceedings of the Operations Research*, Fink, A., Fügenschuh, A., Geiger, Martin J. (eds). Springer, Cham.

Zachariadis, E., Tarantilis, C., Kiranoudis, C. (2009). A guided Tabu search for the vehicle routing problem with two-dimensional loading constraints. *European Journal of Operational Research*, 195, 729–743.

Zachariadis, E., Tarantilis, C., Kiranoudis, C. (2013). Integrated distribution and loading planning via a compact metaheuristic algorithm. *European Journal of Operational Research*, 228, 56–71.

Zachariadis, E.E., Tarantilis, C.D., Kiranoudis, C.T. (2016). The vehicle routing problem with simultaneous pick-ups and deliveries and two-dimensional loading constraints. *European Journal of Operational Research*, 251(2), 369–386.

Zachariadis, E.E., Tarantilis, C.D., Kiranoudis, C.T. (2017). Vehicle routing strategies for pick-up and delivery service under two-dimensional loading constraints. *Operational Research*, 17(1), 115–143.

Zhang, D., Cai, S., Ye, F., Si, Y.W., Nguyen, T.T. (2017). A hybrid algorithm for a vehicle routing problem with realistic constraints. *Information Sciences*, 394/395, 167–182.

Zhou, S., Li, X., Zhang, K., Du, N. (2019). Two-dimensional knapsack-block packing problem. *Applied Mathematical Modelling*, 73, 1–18.

Zhu, W., Qin, H., Lim, A., Wang, L. (2012). A two-stage Tabu search algorithm with enhanced packing heuristics for the 3L-CVRP and M3L-CVRP. *Computers & Operations Research*, 39(9), 2178–2195.

# 2

# MAS-aware Approach for QoS-based IoT Workflow Scheduling in Fog-Cloud Computing

**Marwa MOKNI**[1,2] **and Sonia YASSA**[2]
*[1]MARS Laboratory LR17ES05, University of Sousse, Tunisia*
*[2]ETIS Laboratory CNRS UMR8051, CY Cergy Paris University, France*

Scheduling latency-sensitive Internet of Things (IoT) applications that generate a considerable amount of data is a challenge. Despite the vital computing and storage capacities, Cloud computing affects latency values due to the distance between end-users and Cloud servers. Therefore, this limitation of the Cloud has led to the development of the Fog Computing paradigm in order to build the new Fog-Cloud Computing architecture. In this chapter, we make use of the collaboration between Fog-Cloud Computing to schedule IoT applications, formed as a workflow, by considering the relationships and communications between IoT objects. The proposed scheduling approach is supported by a multi-agent system (MAS) to exploit each agent's independent functionalities. The main objective of our work is to create the most appropriate scheduling solution that optimizes several QoS metrics simultaneously; thus, we adopt the widely used metaheuristic "genetic algorithm" as an optimization method. The proposed scheduling approach is tested by simulating a healthcare IoT application modeled as a workflow and several scientific workflow benchmarks. The

*Optimization and Machine Learning,*
coordinated by Rachid CHELOUAH and Patrick SIARRY © ISTE Ltd 2022.

results demonstrate the effectiveness of the proposed approach; it generates a scheduling plan that better optimizes the various QoS metrics considered.

## 2.1. Introduction

The Internet of Things (IoT) holds a vast amount of interconnected objects (Davami *et al.* 2021). In some cases, IoT objects model automation routines (Smart Home, Healthcare, etc.) that involve execution within a strict response time and advanced programming skills. Notably, in human health monitoring, patients need to be provided with tools to easily monitor and control their surrounding IoT devices and model simple processes that automate daily tasks. To address this issue, we propose a self-management workflow modeling that monitors, controls and synchronizes the relationship between applications generated by IoT objects as an acyclic graph. At this point, workflow technology supplies orchestration sequences of activities to ensure the execution of IoT applications, without any errors or perturbations (Hoang and Dang 2017; Mokni *et al.* 2021). For this reason, the IoT-based workflow requires computing resources that meet its needs and optimize its execution. However, even though many existing studies propose a workflow model for IoT processes, IoT workflow scheduling is yet to be widely discussed. In this chapter, we focus on providing IoT processes that are coordinated by a workflow model. Given the nature of IoT applications (Matrouk and Alatoun 2021), stringent latency needs make the processing of IoT workflows at the Cloud computing level a performance bottleneck. Fog computing is a paradigm, proposed by Cisco (2015), that creates a cooperative architecture with Cloud computing, in which they complement each other. The collaboration between Fog and Cloud services is a suitable solution for producing an optimal IoT-based workflow scheduling plan that may require both reduced latency and significant computing capacity (Saeed *et al.* 2021). From Cisco's perspective, Fog computing (Chen *et al.* 2017) is considered a local extension of cloud computing from the network core to the network edge. Fog computing nodes are installed under the cloud computing layer, close to end-users. This highly virtualized platform provides computing, storage and networking services between endpoints and traditional cloud servers, accessible through users' mobiles. However, with the increasing complexity of workflows, networks and security requirements, scheduling algorithms are becoming more and more challenging because they have to manage several contradictory parameters that concern distinct actors with different interests. For example, the reduction in the workflow execution cost will increase the overall execution time and can lead to the use of less reliable machines. Generally, workflow scheduling in the Fog-Cloud computing environment is an Np-Hard problem (Helali and Omri 2021) that requires more than simple rules to be solved. Therefore, in this chapter, we propose an IoT-workflow scheduling approach based on a genetic algorithm (GA) (Bouzid *et al.* 2020), which aims to create a multi-objective optimization solution that optimizes more than one QoS metric. The critical issue surrounding distributed infrastructures, such as Cloud computing, is implementing techniques and methods that adapt to changes in states and behaviors following high-level user directives. Self-management, self-detection and autonomy techniques that meet these requirements can be based on multi-agent systems (MAS). Indeed, an SMA (Mokni *et al.* 2018) is a very well-adjusted paradigm for simulating phenomena in which the interactions between different entities are complex, with the need to negotiate user access, develop intelligent services, and efficiently exploit Cloud computing and Fog computing resources. In this context, we are interested in modeling an SMA around three layers: the IoT layer, the Fog computing layer and the Cloud computing layer. The key contributions of this work are:

– proposing a workflow modeling for IoT processes;

– developing a multi-objective scheduling solution based on the GA;

– modeling an MAS to enhance scheduling approach entities.

The remainder of the chapter is organized as follows: section 2.2 presents work related to existing scheduling approaches. The problem formulation is provided in section 2.3. The proposed model, its design and implementation are described in section 2.4. Section 2.6 describes the experimental setup and presents the results of the performance evaluation. Section 2.7 presents the conclusion and future works.

## 2.2. Related works

Workflow scheduling problems attract much interest from researchers, are adopted in various computing environments (e.g. Cloud computing, Fog computing and Cloud-Fog computing) and serve several domains, such as science, bioinformatics and the IoT. The approach presented in Saeedi *et al.* (2020) proposes a workflow scheduling approach in Cloud computing based on the Particle Swarm Optimization algorithm. Authors aim to satisfy both user and cloud provider's conflicting exigence by reducing the makespan, cost and energy consumption, and maximizing the reliability of virtual machines. The results obtained demonstrate that the developed algorithm outperforms the LEAF, MaOPSO and EMS-C algorithms, in terms of makespan, cost and energy consumption. In Sun *et al.* (2020), a workflow scheduling approach based on an immune-based PSO algorithm is proposed, which intends to generate an optimal scheduling plan in terms of cost and makespan, respectively. The proposed approach yields a scheduling solution with minimum cost and makespan compared with PSO results. In Shirvani (2020), a scientific workflow scheduling approach is proposed, based on the discrete PSO combined with a Hill Climbing local search algorithm. The approach aims to create a scheduling solution that minimizes makespan and the total execution time, balancing exploration and exploitation. Energy consumption in Cloud computing was addressed in Tarafdar *et al.* (2021), where the authors proposed an energy-efficient scheduling algorithm for deadline-sensitive workflows with budget constraints. Results show that the proposed approach succeeded in minimizing energy consumption and deadline violation by adopting Dynamic Voltage and Frequency Scaling (DVFS), in order to adjust the voltage and frequency of the virtual machines executing the tasks in the workflow. In Nikoui *et al.* (2020), a scientific workflow scheduling approach was developed in a Cloud computing environment that aimed to minimize the total execution time and the makespan by applying the hybrid discrete particle swarm optimization (HDPSO) algorithm. The authors proved the efficiency of the parallelizable task scheduling on parallel computing machines to minimize execution time. Another workflow scheduling approach proposed in Gu and Budati (2020) intended to reduce the energy consumption caused by the immense scale of workflow applications and the massive amount of resource consumption. The authors developed the proposed scheduling approach based on the bat algorithm. Aburukba *et al.* (2020) developed an IoT request scheduling approach in Fog-Cloud computing that aimed to minimize the latency value. The GA adopted results in a reduced latency compared with various algorithms. Kaur *et al.* (2020) proposed a prediction-based dynamic multi-objective evolutionary algorithm, called the NN-DNSGA-II algorithm. They incorporated an artificial neural network with the NSGA-II algorithm to schedule scientific workflow in Cloud computing, taking into account both resource failures and the number of objectives that may change over time. The detailed results show that the proposed method significantly outperforms the non-prediction-based algorithms in most test instances. The experimental results demonstrate that the proposed approach provides a low response time and makespan compared with CPOP, HEFT and QL-HEFT. Also, a Workflow Scheduling Approach was proposed in Setlur *et al.* (2020), combining the HEFT algorithm with multiple Machine Learning techniques, ranging from Supervised Classification like Logistic Regression, Max Entropy Models for the replication count for each task. The proposed approach improves upon metrics like Resource Wastage and Resource Usage in comparison to the

Replicate-All algorithm. Hoang and Dang (2017) proposed a task scheduling concept based on region to satisfy resource and sensitive latency requirements and utilize appropriate cloud resources for heavy computation tasks. In Abdel-Basset *et al.* (2020), an IoT task scheduling problem in Fog computing is addressed. The authors proposed a scheduling approach based on the marine predator's algorithm (MPA), aiming to improve the different QoS metrics. In Aburukba *et al.* (2021), an IoT scheduling approach based on the weighted round-robin algorithm is proposed in Fog computing. The developed approach is based on smart city application and intends to assure effective task execution according to the processing capacity available.

As summarized in Table 2.1, proposed scientific workflow scheduling approaches were developed in the Cloud environment to optimize one or two QoS metrics, without considering the amount of latency. Otherwise, scheduling approaches for IoT tasks in hybrid Fog-Cloud computing are proposed to maximize the utilization of Fog resources than those of Cloud computing to minimize cost and latency. Otherwise, the authors do not consider the heterogeneity, the relationship between IoT tasks or the high dynamicity of computing infrastructures.

This chapter presents the MAS-GA-based approach for IoT workflow scheduling in Fog-Cloud computing, which aims to optimize makespan, cost and latency values. The proposed approach is based on a MAS, taking into account the different QoS metrics. A multi-objective optimization method is adopted to create the IoT workflow scheduling solution by developing the GA.

## 2.3. Problem formulation

The workflow scheduling problem on distributed infrastructures revolves around three main entities:

– workflow tasks to be executed;

– resources to be allocated;

– quality of service metrics to be optimized.

Formally, the workflow scheduling problem consists of two sides: a supplier of $m$ virtual machines $(VMs)$ and a user workflow that consists of n tasks. The tasks must be mapped on the virtual machines by respecting precedence constraints between tasks and optimizing the different QoS metrics.

| Work | Fog-Cloud | Cloud | Fog | Metaheuristic | IoT | Workflow | Dynamicity | Makespan | Cost | Latency |
|---|---|---|---|---|---|---|---|---|---|---|
| Saeedi et al. (2020) | | ✓ | | ✓ | | ✓ | | ✓ | ✓ | |
| Sun et al. (2020) | | ✓ | | ✓ | | ✓ | | ✓ | ✓ | |
| Shirvani (2020) | | ✓ | | ✓ | | ✓ | | ✓ | | |
| Tarafdar et al. (2021) | | ✓ | | ✓ | | ✓ | | | | |
| Nikoui et al. (2020) | ✓ | | | | ✓ | | | | | ✓ |
| Gu and Budati (2020) | | ✓ | | ✓ | | ✓ | | | | |
| Aburukba et al. (2020) | ✓ | | | ✓ | ✓ | | ✓ | | | ✓ |
| Kaur et al. (2020) | | | ✓ | ✓ | ✓ | | | | | ✓ |
| Setlur et al. (2020) | | | ✓ | ✓ | ✓ | | | ✓ | ✓ | |
| Hoang and Dang (2017) | | ✓ | ✓ | ✓ | | | | | | ✓ |
| Abdel-Basset et al. (2020) | | | ✓ | ✓ | ✓ | | | | | ✓ |
| Aburukba et al. (2021) | | | ✓ | ✓ | ✓ | | | | | ✓ |
| MAS-GA-based approach | ✓ | ✓ | ✓ | ✓ | ✓ | ✓ | | ✓ | ✓ | ✓ |

**Table 2.1.** *Comparison of existing scheduling approaches*

### 2.3.1. *IoT-workflow modeling*

In this chapter, we model a workflow application as a directed acyclic graph (DAG) noted by G (T; A). T is the set of workflow tasks $T = (T_1; ...; T_n)$, where each task $T_i \in T$ consists of the set of instructions needed to execute an IoT application. All tasks forming the IoT-workflow G are characterized by an $Id$ (an identifier to distinguish the task), a Computing Size $CS_i$ representing the number of instruction lines, a Geographic Position $GP_i$ (namely, a longitude and latitude value to specify its position) and a set of predecessor tasks. Every task $T_i$ in G can only be executed after all of its predecessor's tasks have been executed. The set of T tasks is interrelated by a precedence constraint, where a task $T_i$ is connected to its successor task $T_j$ with an Arc $A_{ij}$, characterized by a Communication Weight $CW_{ij}$, which represents the amount of data that must be transferred from $T_i$ to $T_j$.

### 2.3.2. *Resources modeling*

A computing infrastructure (Cloud computing and Fog computing) holds a set of resource nodes $N = (N_1, ..., N_k)$. Each $N_j$ is characterized by a Utilization Threshold $UT_j$, a Geographical Area $GA_j$ and set of virtual machines $VM(VM_1, ..., VM_h)$. Every $VM_i$ residing on $VM$ is characterized by a computing capacity expressed in the number of instructions processed per second (MIPS), a bandwidth, that is the amount of data that may be transmitted per second, and a price per unit of time.

### 2.3.3. *QoS-based workflow scheduling modeling*

Multi-objective optimization is a critical issue for all real-world problems, such as the workflow scheduling problem in the Cloud-Fog computing environment. Generally, the workflow scheduling problem is characterized by a set of complex and conflicting objectives. The group of objectives is depicted in a set of QoS metrics that must be optimized; namely, (1) makespan, which is used to evaluate workflow planning algorithms; (2) cost, which is the total cost of execution of a workflow; (3) response Time, which is the data transfer time via the network and the demand time in the Fog layer. These metrics are defined respectively by the following equations [2.1], [2.2] (Yassa *et al.* 2013), and [2.3]:

– The makespan metric:

$$Makespan = max(DF(T_i)) \qquad [2.1]$$

where,

- $T_i$ is a task of the workflow;

- $DF(T_i)$ is the date of the end execution of the task $T_i$.

– The cost metric:

This metric represents the total cost of execution of a workflow. It is given by the following equation:

$$Cost = \sum_{i=0}^{n} \sum_{j=0}^{m} (DF(T_i) * U_j) + \sum_{i=1}^{n} \sum_{j=1}^{m} (Cw_{ij} * TRC_{ij}) \qquad [2.2]$$

where:

- $DF(T_i)$ represents the date of the end execution of the task $T_i$;

- $U_j$ is the unit price of a $vm_j$ that process the task $T_i$;

- $Cw_{ij}$ is the communication weight between $T_i$ and $T_j$;

- $TRC_{ij}$ is the cost of communication between the machine where $T_i$ is mapped and another machine where $T_j$ is affected.

– The response time metric:

The response time represents the data transfer time via the network and the elapsed time in the Fog layer. In this work, we calculate it as the sum of the requested Transfer Time $TT$ from the $CTA$ to the Fog Agent, between Fog Agents, between Fog Agent and Cloud Agent and from Fog Agent to $CTA$. The propagation Time $PT$ represents the time a signal takes to propagate from one point to another. In our case, we use Wi-Fi technology as an internet medium between agents.

$$Response time = TT + PT \qquad [2.3]$$

where,

$$TT = Request_{size}/(VM Bandwidth(MB/s)) \qquad [2.4]$$

and

$$PT = Distance * Propagation\ Speed(s/m) \qquad [2.5]$$

with:

- $Request_{size}$ is the size of data that must be transferred;

- $VM Bandwidth(MB/s)$ is the amount of data that can be transferred per second;

- $Distance$ is the distance in meters, between two virtual machines;

- $PropagationSpeed(s/m)$ is the time elapsed to transfer the request per meter.

Therefore, the average latency relies on the distance value between each scheduling actor (users, Fog nodes and Cloud data center). Thus, we define the different Earth positions of users, Fog nodes and Cloud data centers. With this in mind, we adopted the Haversine formula, which determines the orthodromic distance (the shortest distance between two points on the surface of a sphere) between two points on the Earth's surface, which depend on their longitude and latitude. The following equation presents the Haversine formula:

$$d = 2R(\sqrt{\sin^2(\frac{\Phi_2 - \Phi_1}{2}) + \cos(\Phi_1)\cos(\Phi_2)\sin^2(\frac{\lambda_2 - \lambda_1}{2})}) \qquad [2.6]$$

where:

- $R$ is the radius of the sphere;

- $\Phi_1$, $\Phi_2$ are the latitude of points 1 and 2, respectively;

- $\lambda_1$, $\lambda_2$ are the longitude of points 1 and 2, respectively.

## 2.4. MAS-GA-based approach for IoT workflow scheduling

In this section, we present the main concepts, definitions and notations related to the proposed approach.

### 2.4.1. *Architecture model*

The proposed approach is modeled around three layers. The user layer consists of an IoT system with three levels that communicate with one other to connect the tangible world of objects to the virtual world. As illustrated in Figure 2.1, an IoT level holds a set of IoT devices connected to a workflow management layer; this layer involves establishing communication with the hardware level and the software level via the network, as well as extracting services from IoT objects to form a workflow. This layer is managed by a Manager Agent that communicates with the scheduler level, driven by a set of Contractual Agents. The Fog layer presents the Fog computing infrastructure consisting of interconnected resource nodes $N = (N_1, ..., N_k)$. Each Fog node is supervised by a Fog agent that communicates with other Fog agents to maximize Fog resources. The fog environment adopted in this work consists of node sets that can reside on a factory floor, along a railroad track, or in a vehicle. Any device with computer, storage and network connectivity can be a fog node, such as Wi-Fi Hot Spots, switches, routers and embedded servers. Fog nodes are stationed everywhere with a network connection (Cisco 2015). The Fog computing layer collaborates with the Cloud computing layer, which is also equipped with a set of interconnected resource nodes and supervised by Cloud Agents.

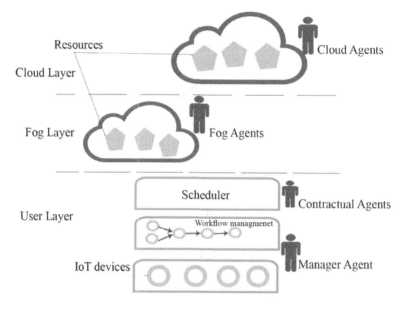

**Figure 2.1.** *Solution architecture. For a color version of this figure, see www.iste.co.uk/chelouah/optimization.zip*

## 2.4.2. *Multi-agent system model*

The MAS comprises agents located in a specific environment that interact, collaborate, negotiate and cooperate according to certain relationships. Each agent in the MAS has explicit information and plans that allow it to accomplish its goals. In this chapter, we model an MAS consisting of a set of agent types with a specific mission to meet. Each agent type presents a component in the approach proposed in the following section:

### 2.4.2.1. *Agent types*

– Manager Agent

The global workflow is managed by the first type of agent called a Manager Agent ($MA$). It is responsible for supervising the workflow execution by respecting the imposed deadline and budget. Firstly, the MA develops the Mixed Min-Cut Graph algorithm that partitions the global workflow in p sub-workflows to reduce overall workflow execution time by minimizing data movement and communication costs between tasks. Secondly, each generated sub-workflow is associated with a Contractual Agent as a reached contract. The MA specifies the sub-workflow characteristics, budget and deadline to respect.

– Contractual Agents

The MAS adopted in our work consists of a set of Contractual Agents $CTA(CTA_1...CTA_n)$ equal to the sub-workflow number. They collaborate between them to execute the global workflow in a minimum execution time. Each of them is responsible for affecting all sub-workflow tasks on the appropriate resources by communicating with the closer Fog Agent. The restrictions of a $CTA_i$ are a limited deadline and budget that must be respected.

– Fog Agent

The created MAS disposes of a set of Fog Agents $FA(FA_1, ..., FA_f)$, which represents the Fog resource providers in the Fog computing environment. Each $FA_i \in FA$ is responsible for creating a scheduling plan for a received sub-workflow by optimizing the QoS metrics.

– Cloud Agent

The Cloud Agent $CA_i \in CA(CA_1, ..., CA_c)$ manages a cloud data center, which is responsible for collaborating with FA to create the most suitable scheduling solution.

### 2.4.3. *MAS-based workflow scheduling process*

The MA launched the MAS-based workflow scheduling process while it is the supervisor of the global workflow execution process. After applying the partitioning algorithm MMCG (Italiano *et al.* 2011) on the workflow, the MA initiates p Contractual Agents (CTA) and affects each sub-workflow characteristic, the deadline and the budget constraints. Each created $CTA$

analyzes the received sub-workflow and makes resource requests $RR_i$, as indicated in formula [2.7], which will be sent to the closer Fog Agent $FA_i$.

$$RR_i = (idTasks;\ Precedence\ Constraints;\ QoSs; \\ computing\ Size(CS_i); deadline\ D_i;\ budget B_i) \qquad [2.7]$$

where:

– $Id\ Tasks$: represents a group of the unique identifier of each task in the sub-workflow;

– $Precedence\ Constraints$: represents the relationship between tasks that determine the order of scheduling which must be respected;

– $QoSs$: represents the different quality of service metrics that must be satisfied;

– $CS_i$: represents the Computing Size;

– $D_i$: represents the Deadline of the sub-workflow execution which is imposed by the Manager Agent;

– $B_i$: represents the budget of the sub-workflow execution which is imposed by the Manager Agent.

The $CTA$ agent disposes of a Knowledge Directory $KD$ (it is similar to the Directory Facilitator "DFAgentDescription" created by the JADE framework (Bellifemine *et al.* 2000), which provides a directory system that allows agents to find service provider agents by ID), which contains all Fog Agents information, and through it, the $CTA$ picks the closer Fog agent. After receiving the request $RR_i$ from the $CTA$, the $FA$ compares the computing size $CS_i$ of the received $RR_i$ with its Utilization Threshold $UT_i$. If $RR_i$ respects the $UT_i$, the Fog Agent proposes to the $CTA$, a scheduling solution on its resources created by the GA. Otherwise, in the context of maximizing the Fog resource utilization, the $FA_i$ must generate a scheduling solution on its resources to the sub-workflow tasks that respect its utilization threshold and create an $RR_j$ for the remaining tasks. The $RR_j$ is then sent to all Fog Agents in $FA_i$ in $KD$ to collaborate between them and find the appropriate scheduling plan on Fog resources. Thus, the $FA_i$ must define a Waiting Time (WT) for receiving a scheduling solution from Fog Agents. If the $WT$ exceeds without accepting any scheduling offer, the $FA_i$ sends the $RR_j$ to the Cloud Agent. The MA ends the process after receiving the global workflow scheduling plan from all $CTAs$. The proposed MAS-GA workflow scheduling approach steps are illustrated in algorithm 2.1.

---

**Algorithm 2.1:** MAS-GA-based algorithm

---

1   **Input:** G(T, A); $N^{Fog}N^{Cloud}$
2   **Output:** Scheduling solution
3   /* *Launch the partitioning algorithm*
4   SubWorkflows ← MMC(G)
5   $p$ ← the number of SubWorkflows
6   /* *Write p contractual agents*
7   **for** $p$ **do**
8   | Initiating $CTA$(SubWorkflow, $D$, $B$, $QoS$)

9   **for** *each CTA* **do**
10   | Create $RR_i$ = (idTasks; PrecedenceConstraints; QoSs; computingSize($CS_i$); deadline $D_i$; budget $B_i$)
11   | $FA$ ← Send($RR$)
12   | /* *Comparing the computing Size CS of received RR with Fog Node Utilisation Threshold UT*
13   | **if** $CS < UT$ **then**
14   | | Proposal ← MAS-GA($RR$, $N^{Fog}$)
15   | | $CTA$ ← Send(Proposal)
16   | **else**
17   | | SubWorkflows ← MMC(SubWorkflow)
18   | | **while** $CS < UT$ **do**
19   | | | /* *Creating scheduling plan to subworkflow tasks that respect the UT*
20   | | | Proposal ← GA-based(SubWorkflows, $N^{Fog}$)
21   | | /**Diffusing the rest of tasks to the closest Fog agents*
22   | | Define the waiting time $WT$
23   | | Define the closest distance $DS$
24   | | **while** $WT$ *not reached and FA.DS* $\in KD <= DS$ **do**
25   | | | Diffuse(SubWorkflows)
26   | | **if** *Proposal received* **then**
27   | | | $CTA$ ← Send(Proposal)
28   | | **else**
29   | | | /* *Sending proposal to the Cloud agent*
30   | | | $CA$ ←Send(SubWorkflows)
31   | | $CTA$ ← Send(Proposal)

---

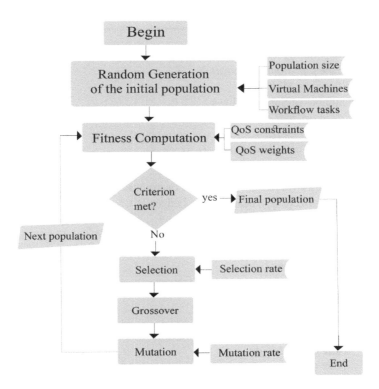

**Figure 2.2.** *GA flowchart*

## 2.5. GA-based workflow scheduling plan

The GA is one of the widely used metaheuristics to solve multi-objective optimization problems by optimizing the QoS metrics of the workflow scheduling solution. Figure 2.2 depicts the global GA flowchart. The GA starts by randomly creating the first population, which consists of a set of scheduling solutions. Based on the different QoS metrics, the GA evaluates each population individual (scheduling solution) by calculating the Fitness function $F$. Afterward, the GA applies the roulette wheel technique to select individuals most appropriate to reproduce a new generation and uses the crossover operator on each pair of individuals, called "parents", to produce two new individuals called "children". Then, the mutation operator is applied to the produced children. The GA is repeated until it converges to the most suitable scheduling solution or the maximum number of generations is reached. Figure 2.3 illustrates an example of the workflow scheduling process, which is the essential part of generating a population. The scheduling process selects the ready task (the task for which all of its predecessor tasks are already scheduled). It schedules it in a virtual machine that minimizes the fitness function. The process is repeated until all workflow tasks are scheduled.

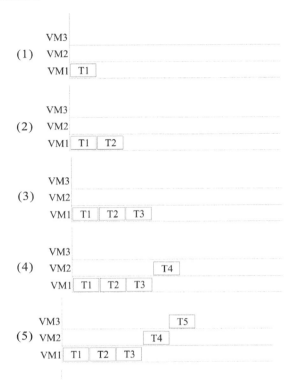

**Figure 2.3.** *Workflow scheduling process*

### 2.5.1. *Solution encoding*

The workflow schedule means that every workflow task must be scheduled on the appropriate resource without breaking the precedence constraint between them. Figure 2.4 illustrates an example of a workflow composed of five tasks, where $T_1$, $T_2$ and $T_3$ are the input tasks and can be executed in parallel since precedence constraints do not interconnect them. Then, tasks $T_4$ and $T_5$ are grouped in sequence and must respect the precedence constraint between them. For example, $T_4$ can only be started when all of its predecessors have been executed and have transmitted their data.

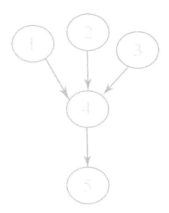

**Figure 2.4.** *Workflow example. For a color version of this figure, see www.iste.co.uk/chelouah/optimization.zip*

Figure 2.5 demonstrates an example of three VMs interconnected with a bandwidth speed and modeled as a non-directed graph.

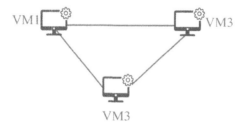

**Figure 2.5.** *Example of resources. For a color version of this figure, see www.iste.co.uk/chelouah/optimization.zip*

A scheduling solution based on a VM graph and the workflow must be created while considering all imposed objectives and constraints. An example of an encoding solution is presented in Table 2.2, where each workflow task is assigned to a resource.

| Task | T1 | T2 | T3 | T4 | T5 |
|---|---|---|---|---|---|
| Resource | VM1 | VM1 | VM1 | VM2 | VM3 |

**Table 2.2.** *Solution encoding*

### 2.5.2. *Fitness function*

The Fitness function $F$ is adopted to optimize several QoS metrics by assigning a weight $W_i$ to each of these metrics. Each weight defines the importance of the metric given by the user. The fitness function is illustrated in equation [2.8].

$$F = \sum w_i * QoS_i normalized \qquad [2.8]$$

As illustrated in equation [2.9], we adopt the normalization calculation to determine the fitness value of a solution. Indeed, the QoS metrics have different values and scales; moreover, specific metrics have to be maximized, and others minimized.

$$QoS_i normalized \begin{cases} \frac{QoS_i}{MaxQoS_i} & \text{if } QoS_i \text{ must be minimized} \\ 1 - \frac{QoS_i}{MaxQoS_i} & \text{if } QoS_i \text{ must be maximized} \end{cases} \qquad [2.9]$$

where:

$MaxQoS_i$ is the maximal value of $QoS_i$ founded during the previous iteration.

#### 2.5.2.1. *Crossover operator*

The crossover operator combines various parts of selected individuals to produce new individuals. Firstly, the crossover operator chooses two points at random from the scheduling order of the selected first parent (individual 1). Then, the positions of the tasks that are between these two points are permuted. The results of this step are two produced individuals, called children. An illustration of the crossover operator is shown in Figure 2.6.

### 2.5.3. *Mutation operator*

The mutation method used is the swap mutation. For a given individual, two randomly selected tasks will exchange their assigned resources. Figure 2.7 depicts an illustration of the swap mutation operation. In the chosen solution, the resources allocated to task 1 and task 4 are exchanged.

Before crossover

Parent1

| T1 | T2 | T3 | T4 | T5 |
|------|------|------|------|------|
| VM1 | VM1 | VM1 | VM2 | VM3 |

Parent2

| T1 | T2 | T3 | T4 | T5 |
|------|------|------|------|------|
| VM3 | VM3 | VM3 | VM1 | VM2 |

Crossover

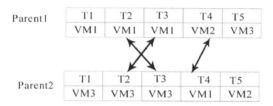

Parent1

| T1 | T2 | T3 | T4 | T5 |
|------|------|------|------|------|
| VM1 | VM1 | VM1 | VM2 | VM3 |

Parent2

| T1 | T2 | T3 | T4 | T5 |
|------|------|------|------|------|
| VM3 | VM3 | VM3 | VM1 | VM2 |

After crossover

Child1

| T1 | T2 | T3 | T4 | T5 |
|------|------|------|------|------|
| VM1 | VM3 | VM3 | VM1 | VM3 |

Child2

| T1 | T2 | T3 | T4 | T5 |
|------|------|------|------|------|
| VM3 | VM1 | VM1 | VM2 | VM2 |

**Figure 2.6.** *Illustration of crossover operator*

Before mutation

| T1 | T2 | T3 | T4 | T5 |
|------|------|------|------|------|
| VM1 | VM1 | VM1 | VM2 | VM3 |

Mutation

| T1 | T2 | T3 | T4 | T5 |
|------|------|------|------|------|
| VM1 | VM1 | VM1 | VM2 | VM3 |

After mutation

| T1 | T2 | T3 | T4 | T5 |
|------|------|------|------|------|
| VM2 | VM1 | VM1 | VM1 | VM3 |

**Figure 2.7.** *Illustration of mutation operation*

## 2.6. Experimental study and analysis of the results

To evaluate the proposed MAS-GA-based approach for IoT workflow scheduling, we were inspired by the characteristics of Amazon EC2 instances to define the Fog-Cloud compute resources used in our experiments. We have tested the proposed scheduling approach on a real case IoT workflow of the health monitoring process, as illustrated in Figure 2.8, compared with the Inspiral-15 scientific workflow benchmark shown in Figure 2.9. We have set four VMs as the number of resources on the Cloud environment and vary the Fog environment's number from 1 VM to 3 VMs. Figure 2.8 illustrates the health monitoring process that aims to monitor the health of patients in a hospital remotely. The process is managed by a workflow containing three main tasks. The first task, called "coordination node", receives data from sensors, stores it and generates diagnostic information. The second task is the "medical assistant node", which receives the diagnostic information from the previous node about whether to signal an emergency alert or not. The last task is a "hospital node" which makes the previous decision according to feedback received from the previous node. Furthermore, we executed the inspiral-15 workflow benchmark, a scientific workflow requiring necessary computing capacities to be completed. As illustrated by Figure 2.9, inspiral-15 holds 15 tasks that are structured in parallel and in sequence.

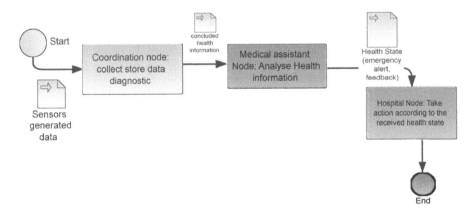

**Figure 2.8.** *Health monitoring process*

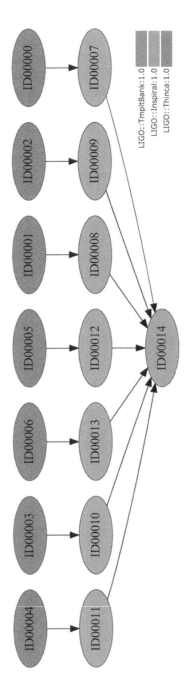

**Figure 2.9.** *Inspiral-15 workflow benchmark. For a color version of this figure, see www.iste.co.uk/chelouah/optimization.zip*

### 2.6.1. *Experimental results*

The experimentation results reveal that when we enhanced the resource number at the Fog layer, the collaboration between Cloud and Fog computing is improved. As demonstrated in Figure 2.10, the third result, while adopting the number of VMs on the Fog layer to 3, maximizes the number of tasks executed on the Fog layer compared to the Cloud layer, without ignoring the collaboration between them, which leads to minimizing the cost and latency, respectively. Otherwise, Cloud-Fog computing collaboration affects the makespan values, since the resources that reside in the Fog layer are less efficient than those in Cloud computing, making the workflow execution process slow. In Figure 2.11, the number of inspiral-15 scientific workflow tasks executed on the Cloud layer is greater than the number of tasks performed in the Fog layer, even when the number of Fog resources is increased; this is because scientific workflows like inspiral-15 require high computational capacity. Furthermore, the results obtained show that executing all of the inspiral-15 workflow tasks in the Cloud layer generates a makespan lower than that developed by the collaboration between Fog-Cloud computing and high cost and latency values. The inspiral-15 scheduling solution developed by Fog-Cloud is the cheapest and has the lowest latency value. Makespan, cost and latency are calculated by the average values taken from 10 execution times. Figure 2.13 demonstrates the average makespan when executing the healthcare workflow and the inspiral-15 workflow. In healthcare implementation cases, average makespan increases relatively by increasing the number of Fog VMs, contrary to the inspiral-15 workflow executing case; average makespan increases exponentially. Notably, the collaboration of Fog-Cloud computing affects the makespan results when performing a scientific workflow; this is because fog computing is characterized by resources with low efficiency. The results illustrated in Figure 2.14 demonstrate the required cost of scheduling the healthcare workflow and the inspiral-15 workflow; the cost decreased by augmenting the Fog VMs number. According to the results obtained, the explanation is that the Fog resources are cheaper than those of Cloud computing.

As in Figure 2.10, Figure 2.12 depicts the latency results. It is apparent that enhancing the collaboration between Fog-Cloud resources is a suitable method for reducing average latency when executing the healthcare workflow and the inspiral-15 workflow; this is because the proposed scheduling approach attempts to maximize utilization of Fog resources rather than those of Cloud computing. Finally, from the presented results we can extract that Fog-Cloud computing is suitable for exeuting an IoT-based workflow, since it optimizes the cost and latency simultaneously.

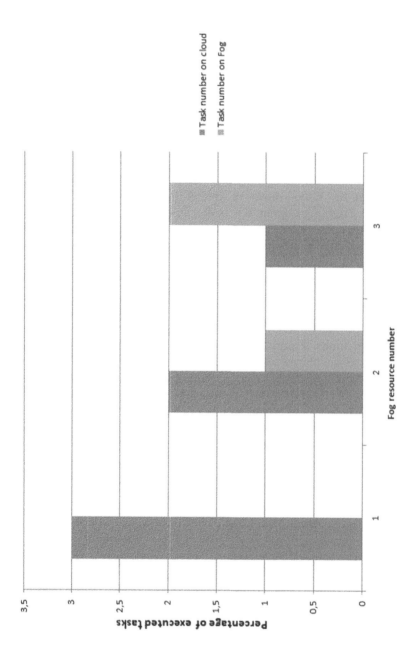

**Figure 2.10.** *Percentage of IoT workflow executed tasks on Fog computing and Cloud computing. For a color version of this figure, see www.iste.co.uk/chelouah/optimization.zip*

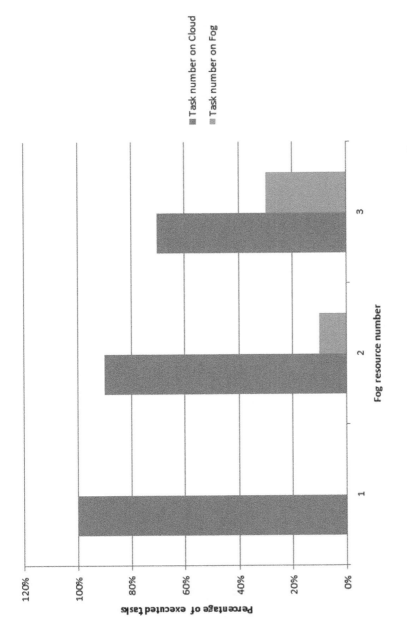

**Figure 2.11.** *Percentage of Inspiral-15 workflow executed tasks on Fog computing and Cloud computing. For a color version of this figure, see www.iste.co.uk/chelouah/optimization.zip*

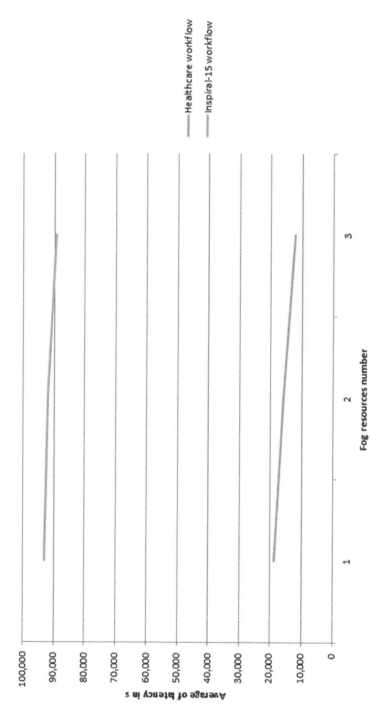

**Figure 2.12.** *Average of latency when executing the healthcare workflow and Inspiral-15 workflow. For a color version of this figure, see www.iste.co.uk/chelouah/optimization.zip*

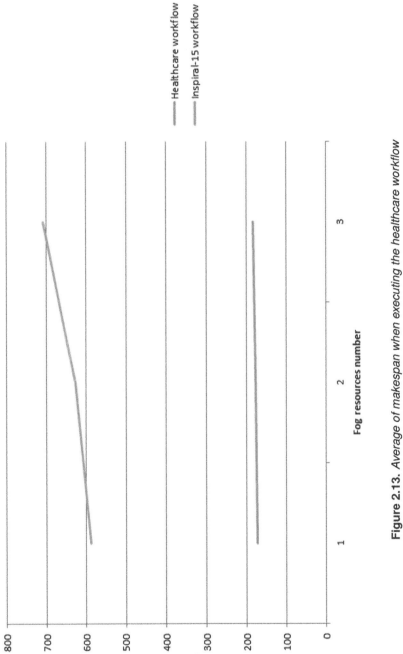

**Figure 2.13.** *Average of makespan when executing the healthcare workflow and Inspiral-15 workflow. For a color version of this figure, see www.iste.co.uk/chelouah/optimization.zip*

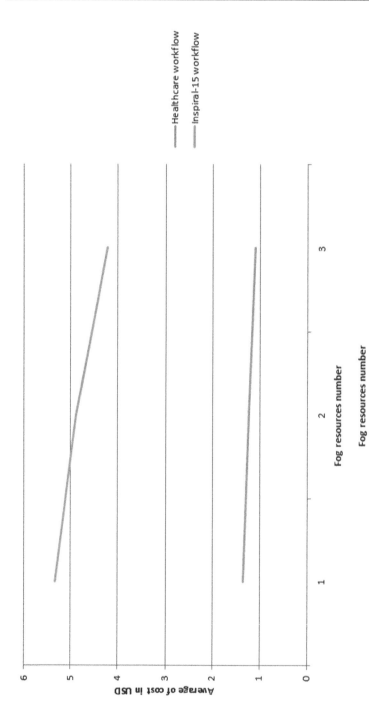

**Figure 2.14.** *Average of cost when executing the healthcare workflow and Inspiral-15 workflow. For a color version of this figure, see www.iste.co.uk/chelouah/optimization.zip*

Otherwise, Fog-Cloud computing affects the makespan when running a scientific workflow and an IoT workflow.

## 2.7. Conclusion

In this chapter, we have presented the MAS-GA-based approach for IoT workflow scheduling in Fog-Cloud computing environments. IoT workflow scheduling was proposed to create a multi-objective scheduling solution based on the widely used GA metaheuristic. We have tested and validated the efficiency of the proposed approach in creating the optimal IoT workflow scheduling solution, in terms of makespan, cost and latency when executing a real use case IoT workflow, by using various experiment scenarios on the WorkflowSim simulator. Experimental results demonstrate that the MAS-GA-based approach for IoT workflow scheduling in Fog-Cloud computing generates a scheduling solution that optimizes the cost and latency values when maximizing the workflow task number in Fog resources. Future work will expand the proposed model to include an agent negotiation mechanism, which may be helpful to achieve a scheduling solution that satisfies both the consumer and the resource provider.

## 2.8. References

Abdel-Basset, M., Mohamed, R., Elhoseny, M., Bashir, A.K., Jolfaei, A., Kumar, N. (2020). Energy-aware marine predators algorithm for task scheduling in IoT-based fog computing applications. *IEEE Transactions on Industrial Informatics*, 17(7), 5068–5076.

Aburukba, R.O., AliKarrar, M., Landolsi, T., El-Fakih, K. (2020). Scheduling internet of things requests to minimize latency in hybrid fog–cloud computing. *Future Generation Computer Systems*, 111, 539–551.

Aburukba, R.O., Landolsi, T., Omer, D. (2021). A heuristic scheduling approach for fog-cloud computing environment with stationary IoT devices. *Journal of Network and Computer Applications*, 102994.

Bellifemine, F., Poggi, A., Rimassa, G. (2000). Developing multi-agent systems with jade. *International Workshop on Agent Theories, Architectures, and Languages*, 89–103.

Bouzid, S., Seresstou, Y., Raoof, K., Omri, M., Mbarki, M., Dridi, C. (2020). Moonga: Multi-objective optimization of wireless network approach based on genetic algorithm. *IEEE Access*, 8, 105793–105814.

Chen, S., Zhang, T., Shi, W. (2017). Fog computing. *IEEE Internet Computing*, 21(2), 4–6.

Cisco (2015). Fog computing and the Internet of Things: Extend the cloud to where the things are. Wite Paper. 10032019 [Online]. Available at: https://www. cisco.com/c/dam/en_us/solutions/trends/iot/docs/computing-overview.pdf.

Davami, F., Adabi, S., Rezaee, A., Rahmani, A.M. (2021). Fog-based architecture for scheduling multiple workflows with high availability requirement. *Computing*, 15, 1–40.

Gu, Y. and Budati, C. (2020). Energy-aware workflow scheduling and optimization in clouds using bat algorithm. *Future Generation Computer Systems*, 113, 106–112.

Helali, L. and Omri, M.N. (2021). A survey of data center consolidation in cloud computing systems. *Computer Science Review*, 39, 100366.

Hoang, D. and Dang, T.D. (2017). FBRC: Optimization of task scheduling in fog-based region and cloud. *IEEE Trustcom/BigDataSE/ICESS*, 1109–1114.

Italiano, G.F., Nussbaum, Y., Sankowski, P., Wulff-Nilsen, C. (2011). Improved algorithms for min cut and max flow in undirected planar graphs. *Proceedings of the Forty-Third Annual ACM Symposium on Theory of Computing*, 313–322.

Kaur, A., Singh, P., Batth, R.S., Lim, C.P. (2020). Deep-Q learning-based heterogeneous earliest finish time scheduling algorithm for scientific workflows in cloud. *Software Practice and Experience*, February.

Matrouk, K. and Alatoun, K. (2021). Scheduling algorithms in fog computing: A survey. *International Journal of Networked and Distributed Computing*, 9, 59–74.

Mokni, M., Hajlaoui, J.E., Brahmi, Z. (2018). MAS-based approach for scheduling intensive workflows in cloud computing. *IEEE 27th International Conference on Enabling Technologies: Infrastructure for Collaborative Enterprises (WETICE)*, 27, 15–20.

Mokni, M., Yassa, S., Hajlaoui, J.E., Chelouah, R., Omri, M.N. (2021). Cooperative agents-based approach for workflow scheduling on fog-cloud computing. *Journal of Ambient Intelligence and Humanized Computing*, 1–20.

Nikoui, T.S., Balador, A., Rahmani, A.M., Bakhshi, Z. (2020). Cost-aware task scheduling in fog-cloud environment. *CSI/CPSSI International Symposium on Real-Time and Embedded Systems and Technologies (RTEST)*, 1–8.

Saeed, W., Ahmad, Z., Jehangiri, A.I., Mohamed, N., Umar, A.I., Ahmad, J. (2021). A fault tolerant data management scheme for healthcare Internet of Things in fog computing. *KSII Transactions on Internet and Information Systems (TIIS)*, 15, 35–57.

Saeedi, S., Khorsand, R., Bidgoli, S.G., Ramezanpour, M. (2020). Improved many-objective particle swarm optimization algorithm for scientific workflow scheduling in cloud computing. *Computers & Industrial Engineering*, 147, 106649.

Setlur, A.R., Nirmala, S.J., Singh, H.S., Khoriya, S. (2020). An efficient fault tolerant workflow scheduling approach using replication heuristics and checkpointing in the cloud. *Journal of Parallel and Distributed Computing*, 136, 14–28.

Shirvani, M.H. (2020). A hybrid meta-heuristic algorithm for scientific workflow scheduling in heterogeneous distributed computing systems. *Engineering Applications of Artificial Intelligence*, 90, 103501.

Sun, J., Yin, L., Zou, M., Zhang, Y., Zhang, T., Zhou, J. (2020). Makespan-minimization workflow scheduling for complex networks with social groups in edge computing. *Journal of Systems Architecture*, 108, 101799.

Tarafdar, A., Karmakar, K., Khatua, S., Das, R.K. (2021). Energy-efficient scheduling of deadline-sensitive and budget-constrained workflows in the cloud. *International Conference on Distributed Computing and Internet Technology*, 65–80.

Yassa, S., Sublime, J., Chelouah, R., Kadima, H., Jo, G.-S., Granado, B. (2013). A genetic algorithm for multi-objective optimisation in workflow scheduling with hard constraints. *International Journal of Metaheuristics*, 2, 415–433.

# 3

# Solving Feature Selection Problems Built on Population-based Metaheuristic Algorithms

**Mohamed Sassi**

*PJGN IT Director, Gendarmerie Nationale, France*

Machine learning classifiers require a large amount of data for the training, validation and testing phases. These data are generally high dimensional. However, the higher the dimension, the more the performance of the classifier deteriorates due to the huge quantity of irrelevant and correlated data and noise, without mentioning the curse of the dimension. The effect on machine learning algorithms is detrimental: overfitting, high complexity, high computational cost and poor accuracy. The corollary is that in order to obtain a better performance, an efficient feature selection process must be implemented. However, feature selection is also an optimization problem. Therefore, nature-inspired and population-based metaheuristics, such as the grey wolf optimization (GWO) algorithm, are one of the best solutions to this problem. This chapter allows us to demonstrate step by step, in a pedagogical way, the use of the GWO for the feature selection process applied on a KNN (k-nearest neighbor) classifier with very competitive results compared to the GA and PSO metaheuristics.

## 3.1. Introduction

The 21st century has seen an exponential increase in the amount of data, irrespective of the professional sectors: forensics, medicine, meteorology, finance, astrophysics, agronomy, etc. This huge mass of data results in errors within even the most sophisticated machine learning algorithms.

However this observation does not spell disaster, thanks to feature selection algorithms. These algorithms extract a subset of data containing the most meaningful information. Nevertheless, feature selection is an NP-difficult multi-objective optimization problem (Fong *et al.* 2014; Siarry 2014; Hodashinsky and Sarin 2019). Extensive research in this area has shown the superiority of metaheuristic algorithms in solving these problems compared to other optimization algorithms, such as deterministic methods (Sharma and Kaur 2021). Population-based swarm intelligence metaheuristics have been shown to be effective in this area.

Unfortunately we have found very few book chapters dedicated to the study of metaheuristics, and which actually describe the operation of metaheuristics for feature selection. Metaheuristics are powerful tools for these data processing steps.

In this chapter, we do not create a new metaheuristic. Our contribution is to explain, in an educational way, all the steps required to apply a modern metaheuristic in a continuous research space to feature selection. To do this, we rely on the work of Mirjalili and of Emary (Mirjalili *et al.* 2014; Emary *et al.* 2016).

This chapter is organized into eight sections as follows. Section 3.2 presents inspiration from the nature of the GWO algorithm. Section 3.3 develops a mathematical model of the GWO for optimization in a continuous search space. Section 3.4 allows us to assimilate the theoretical fundamentals of feature selection. Section 3.5 discusses the mathematical modeling of optimization in a binary discrete search space. Section 3.6 provides the binarization modules allowing continuous metaheuristics to be able to solve feature selection problems in a binary search space. Section 3.7 is the heart of this chapter because it uses the binarization modules of section 3.6 to create the binary metaheuristics bGWO. Section 3.8 will demonstrate, experimentally, the performance of bGWO in solving feature selection problems on 18 datasets from UCI reference datasets.

## 3.2. Algorithm inspiration

The grey wolf belongs to the *Canis lupus* (Canidae) family. Over the centuries, since their appearance about two million years ago, wolves have developed and perfected their hunting technique. Their existence on several continents is evidence that this hunting technique is optimal for finding the best prey; it thus inspired the GWO algorithm, which is based on the hierarchical organization of the pack as well as the four phases of the hunt.

### 3.2.1. *Wolf pack hierarchy*

The keystone of the grey wolf pack is its hierarchy, which is structured into four groups: Alpha, Beta, Delta and Omega (Figure 3.1).

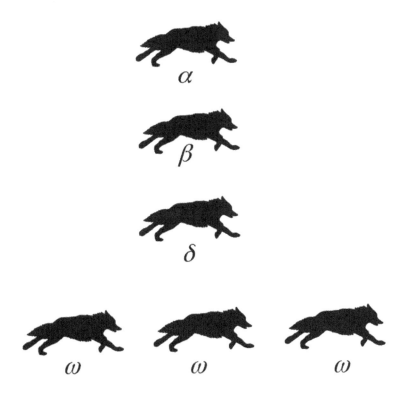

**Figure 3.1.** *Wolf pack hierarchy*

### 3.2.1.1. *Alpha wolf*

An Alpha male wolf pairs with an Alpha female wolf to form an Alpha pair. These Alpha wolves lead the pack, taking charge of hunting, meals, reproduction and defense. They therefore ensure the success of the pack.

### 3.2.1.2. *Beta wolf*

The Beta wolf assists the Alpha wolves. They will become the Alpha if the latter is no longer able to fulfill their role. On a daily basis, they assist the Alpha wolves in commanding and maintaining order in the pack.

### 3.2.1.3. *Delta wolf*

The Delta wolf is ranked lower than the Beta wolf. Much like the Beta, they help its Alpha and Beta superiors in day-to-day tasks and in maintaining discipline in the ranks.

### 3.2.1.4. *Omega wolf*

Omega wolves are at the bottom of the pack hierarchy. They obey and follow the Alpha, Beta and Delta and bear the brunt of any suffering within the pack. Aside from the Alpha, Beta and Delta, the rest of the wolves in the pack are all Omega.

The Alpha, Beta, Delta and Omega hierarchy is thus an expression of the methodical rigor of grey wolf pack life. Applying this methodical rigor is most crucial when the pack executes its hunting technique.

## 3.2.2. *The four phases of pack hunting*

The grey wolf pack hunts their prey by progressing through four phases, as illustrated in Figure 3.2:

1) search;

2) pursue;

3) surround and harass the prey until trapped or exhausted;

4) attack the prey.

The hierarchy of the pack and the four phases of its hunting technique constitute the two pillars of the GWO metaheuristic. These are modeled mathematically in the next section.

**Figure 3.2.** *Search, pursue, surround-harass and attack the prey (source: https://phys.org (ecologists larger group)). For a color version of this figure, see www.iste.co.uk/chelouah/optimization.zip*

## 3.3. Mathematical modeling

### 3.3.1. *Pack hierarchy*

Wolf agents Alpha, Beta and Delta (Figure 3.3) are the most important wolves in the pack and assume prime position when surrounding prey during hunting (Figure 3.4). They will therefore be respectively the first, second and third best solutions to the optimization problem. The Omega wolves alter their position based on the positions of the Alpha, Beta and Delta.

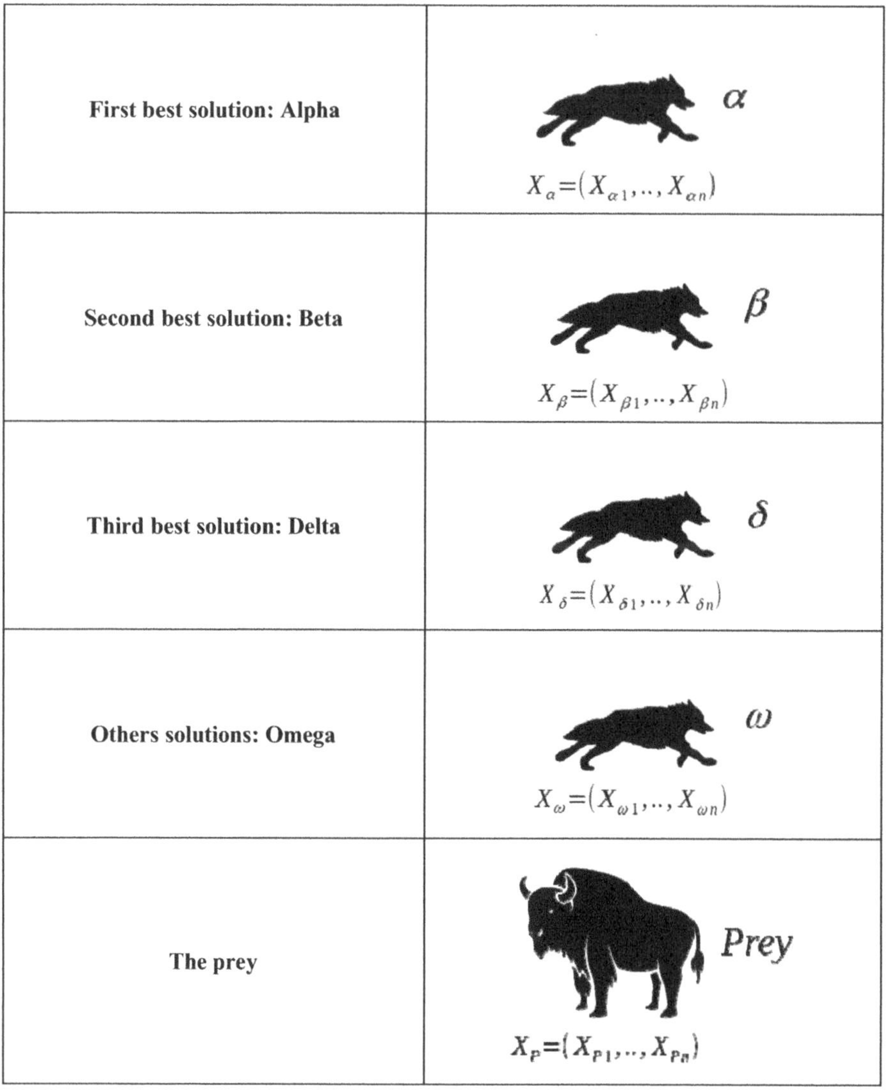
First best solution: Alpha
α
$X_\alpha=(X_{\alpha 1},..,X_{\alpha n})$
Second best solution: Beta
β
$X_\beta=(X_{\beta 1},..,X_{\beta n})$
Third best solution: Delta
δ
$X_\delta=(X_{\delta 1},..,X_{\delta n})$
Others solutions: Omega
ω
$X_\omega=(X_{\omega 1},..,X_{\omega n})$
The prey
Prey
$X_P=(X_{P1},..,X_{Pn})$

**Figure 3.3.** *Pack hierarchy modeling*

**Figure 3.4.** *Alpha, Beta, Delta and Omega Wolf positions around prey (source: https://phys.org (ecologists larger group)). For a color version of this figure, see www.iste.co.uk/chelouah/optimization.zip*

### 3.3.2. *Four phases of hunt modeling*

#### 3.3.2.1. *Search and pursue*

This phase involves searching for and then pursuit of the most promising areas in which to hunt for prey. It is the GWO exploration phase. As a result of these phases, the three best solutions will create the hierarchy of the pack: Alpha, Beta and Delta. They will lead the encirclement and harassment phases.

#### 3.3.2.2. *Encirclement and harassment*

The encirclement and harassment of prey by wolf agents are modeled by equations [3.1]–[3.5].

$$\vec{D} = \left| \vec{C}.\overrightarrow{X_p}(t) - \vec{X}(t) \right| \tag{3.1}$$

$$\vec{X}(t+1) = \overrightarrow{X_p}(t) - \vec{A}.\vec{D} \tag{3.2}$$

$- t$ indicates the current iteration;

$- \vec{X}(t)$ is the Omega wolf position at iteration $t$ ;

$- \vec{X}(t+1)$ is the Omega wolf position at the next iteration $t+1$;

– $\overrightarrow{X_p}(t)$ is the prey position;

– $\vec{A}$, $\vec{C}$ and $\vec{D}$ are vectors defined by equations [3.3], [3.5] and [3.1];

– $a$ is a coefficient that decreases linearly from 2 to 0 in terms of $t$ until maximum iteration $ItMax$.

Vectors $\vec{A}$, $\vec{a}$ and $\vec{C}$ are calculated as follows:

$$\vec{A} = 2\vec{a}.\overrightarrow{r_1} - \vec{a} \text{ with } r_1 \in [0;1] \tag{3.3}$$

$$a = 2 - t * \frac{2}{ItMax} \text{ with } \quad t \in [0; ItMax], a \in [0;2] \text{ and } \vec{a} = a.\overrightarrow{1} \tag{3.4}$$

$$\vec{C} = 2.\overrightarrow{r_2} \text{ with } r_2 \in [0;1] \tag{3.5}$$

Based on equations [3.1] and [3.2] in a search area of size $N$, wolf agents evolve in a hypercube around the prey (the best solution). Figures 3.5 and 3.6 graphically illustrate the hypercube created by a wolf around the prey before the attack with equations [3.1] and [3.2] for $N = 2$ and $N = 3$, respectively. In the attack equations [3.6]–[3.12], the position of the prey is represented by the three best solutions at the iteration $t$: Alpha, Beta and Delta. Therefore, three hypercubes will be created for each of them.

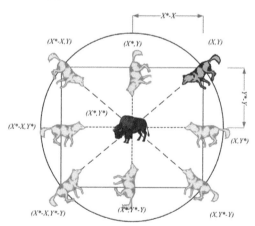

**Figure 3.5.** *Position of the wolf agent and its prey in a square with $N = 2$ (Mirjalili et al. 2014). For a color version of this figure, see www.iste.co.uk/chelouah/optimization.zip*

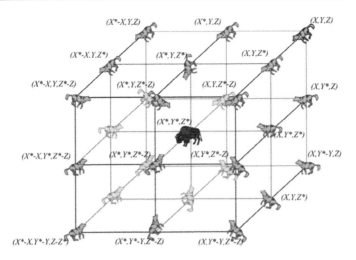

**Figure 3.6.** *Position of the wolf agent and its prey in a cube with N = 3 (Mirjalili et al. 2014) . For a color version of this figure, see www.iste.co.uk/chelouah/optimization.zip*

### 3.3.2.3. Attack

According to the social order established by the hierarchy of the pack, the Alpha, Beta and Delta wolf agents guide the attack. The postulate of the pack is based on the principle that the hierarchy has a better perception of the position of prey. Therefore, the Omega will update their position $\vec{X}$ from the encirclement areas around the prey, created by the positions of the Alpha, Beta and Delta: $\overrightarrow{X_\alpha}$, $\overrightarrow{X_\beta}$ and $\overrightarrow{X_\delta}$.

To do this, equations [3.1] and [3.2] are used with positions $\overrightarrow{X_\alpha}$, $\overrightarrow{X_\beta}$ and $\overrightarrow{X_\delta}$ to obtain $\vec{X_1}$, $\vec{X_2}$, $\vec{X_3}$ in the encirclement areas of the Alpha, Beta and Delta. $\vec{X_1}$, $\vec{X_2}$, $\vec{X_3}$ are provided by equations [3.6], [3.9] and [3.11]. The wolf agents will update their position $\vec{X}$ on the mean of $\vec{X_1}$, $\vec{X_2}$ and $\vec{X_3}$ with equation [3.12]. This update allows the pack to approach the best solutions.

$$\overrightarrow{D_\alpha} = \left| \overrightarrow{C_1} . \overrightarrow{X_\alpha} - \vec{X} \right| \tag{3.6}$$

$$\overrightarrow{X_1} = \overrightarrow{X_\alpha} - \overrightarrow{A_1} . \overrightarrow{D_\alpha} \tag{3.7}$$

$$\overrightarrow{D_\beta} = \left| \overrightarrow{C_2} . \overrightarrow{X_\beta} - \vec{X} \right| \tag{3.8}$$

$$\vec{X_2} = \vec{X_\beta} - \vec{A_2}.\vec{D_\beta} \tag{3.9}$$

$$\vec{D_\delta} = |\vec{C_3}.\vec{X_\delta} - \vec{X}| \tag{3.10}$$

$$\vec{X_3} = \vec{X_\delta} - \vec{A_3}.\vec{D_\delta} \tag{3.11}$$

$$\vec{X}(t + 1) = \frac{(\vec{X_1} + \vec{X_2} + \vec{X_3})}{3} \tag{3.12}$$

The vectors $\vec{A}$ and $\vec{C}$ are strategic random vectors for the GWO algorithm. Indeed, their stochastic nature supports the exploration phase. $\vec{A}$ is the vector that leads the exploration and exploitation phases. $\vec{C}$ stochastically models the obstacles between the wolf and the prey. $\vec{C}$ also plays a fundamental role in the exploration and exploitation phases. The closer $|\vec{C}|$ is to 2, the more complex it will be to attack the prey and therefore the more the wolf will have to explore other areas around the prey in order to access it. On the other hand, the closer $|\vec{C}|$ is to 0, the closer the wolf is getting to the area around the prey that favors exploitation.

For example, if $N = 2$, the equations [3.6] and [3.7] are calculated as follows:

$$\vec{D_\alpha} = |\vec{C_1}.\vec{X_\alpha} - \vec{X}| \Leftrightarrow \begin{cases} D_{\alpha x} = |C_{1x}.X_{\alpha x} - X_x| \\ D_{\alpha y} = |C_{1y}.X_{\alpha y} - X_y| \end{cases},$$

$$\vec{X_1} = \vec{X_\alpha} - \vec{A_1}.\vec{D_\alpha} \Leftrightarrow \begin{cases} X_{1x} = X_{\alpha x} - A_{1x}.D_{\alpha x} \\ X_{1y} = X_{\alpha y} - A_{1y}.D_{\alpha y} \end{cases}$$

By doing the same for $\vec{D_\beta}$, $\vec{D_\delta}$, $\vec{X_2}$ and $\vec{X_3}$ the next agent position is:

$$\begin{cases} X_x = \frac{X_{1x} + X_{2x} + X_{3x}}{3} \\ X_y = \frac{X_{1y} + X_{2y} + X_{3y}}{3} \end{cases}$$

### 3.3.3. Research phase – exploration

The search for prey requires wolves to occupy the search area by spreading out. When $|A| \geq 1$, the wolf agents are in the exploration phase which involves a random search for promising areas. The wolf agents change positions by dispersing and are therefore better placed to find new promising zones around prey.

$|C|$ is stochastic and randomly evolves from 0 to 2. If $|C| \geq 1$, it removes the wolf agents from the prey and promotes exploration.

### 3.3.4. Attack phase – exploitation

Attacking prey is the exploitation phase of the hunt when $1 > |A| \geq 0$. Indeed, in this interval, the wolf agents will progress toward the prey by getting closer to one another.

If $|C| < 1$, the wolf agents are brought closer to the prey after overcoming obstacles and this promotes exploitation.

Figure 3.7 graphically illustrates the evolution of A between exploration and exploitation phases and Figure 3.8 shows the position of the wolf in relation to the prey in the exploration and exploitation phase.

It can be noted that the first half of the iterations, when $t \in \left[ 0, \dfrac{ItMax}{2} \right]$, promotes the exploration with $2 \geq a \geq 1$, and the second half, when $t \in \left[ \dfrac{ItMax}{2}, ItMax \right]$, promotes the exploitation with $1 > a \geq 0$.

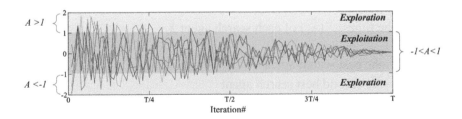

**Figure 3.7.** *Steering of exploration and exploitation phases with vector A during iterations (Faris et al. 2017) . For a color version of this figure, see www.iste.co.uk/chelouah/optimization.zip*

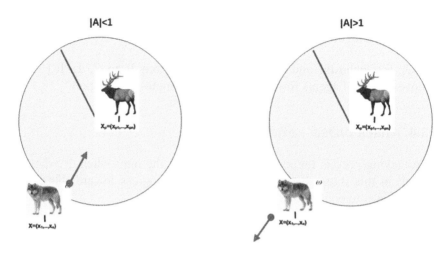

**Figure 3.8.** *Search exploration phase |A|≥1 and attack exploitation phase 1>|A|≥0. For a color version of this figure, see www.iste.co.uk/chelouah/optimization.zip*

### 3.3.5. *Grey wolf optimization algorithm pseudocode*

**Algorithm 3.1. GWO pseudo code**

**In**: Population size N, Number of iterations *ItMax*, fitness function *F*
**Out** : : $\overrightarrow{X_\alpha}$ and $F(\overrightarrow{X_\alpha})$

Initialization of the grey wolf population agents $\overrightarrow{X_i}\ i\ \in [\![1, N]\!]$
Initialize a, A, and C
Calculate the fitness $F(\overrightarrow{X_i})$ of each search agent $\overrightarrow{X_i}$
Define
　　　$\overrightarrow{X_\alpha}$=the best search agent
　　　$\overrightarrow{X_\beta}$=the second best search agent
　　　$\overrightarrow{X_\delta}$=the third best search agent
**While** (t < *ItMax*)
　　　**For** each search agent
　　　　　Update the position of the current search agent $\overrightarrow{X_i}$ with
　　　　　equations (6) to (12)

**End for**
Update a, A, and C with equations (3) to (5)
Calculate the fitness $F\left(\overrightarrow{X_l}\right)$ of all search agents $\overrightarrow{X_l}$
Update $\overrightarrow{X_\alpha}$, $\overrightarrow{X_\beta}$ and $\overrightarrow{X_\delta}$
t=t+1
**End while**

We now have all the elements allowing us to understand the mathematical modeling of the GWO algorithm. The understanding and mastery of the key points of this algorithm is an imperative for the remainder of this chapter. In the following section, we are going to approach the main topic of this chapter: feature selection. We must first know the theoretical fundamentals of feature selection and optimization in a binary discrete search space.

## 3.4. Theoretical fundamentals of feature selection

Machine learning classification algorithms are a component of artificial intelligence that require maximum reactivity to the data mass they need to process. They must therefore be reactive, accurate, adaptive and as light as possible. To do this, we must provide the algorithm with only the data necessary for its decision-making so as not to swamp it with redundant or irrelevant data. This is the purpose of feature selection. This section will provide the theoretical fundamentals of feature selection as well as the main advantages of feature selection for the machine learning classifiers.

### 3.4.1. *Feature selection definition*

Feature selection is the problem of how to choose the fewest features in the original dataset that are often high-dimensional (Almomani *et al.* 2019). It is therefore an extraction process that eliminates irrelevant and redundant features for a better understanding of datasets (Sharma and Kaur 2021). In practice, feature selection consists of exploiting *ad hoc* algorithms for processing a dataset with $N$ features as the input and providing at the output a subset of $p$ feature data with $p < N$. Figure 3.9 illustrates this process. But what are the methods to achieve it?

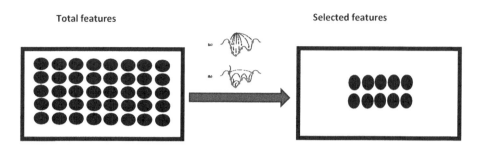

**Figure 3.9.** *Feature selection process. For a color version of this figure, see www.iste.co.uk/chelouah/optimization.zip*

### 3.4.2. *Feature selection methods*

There are two main feature selection algorithm families: chaotic and binary (Sharma and Kaur 2021). The binary feature selection is the most used in the literature thanks to its good performance and a better theoretical and practical control. It is therefore the binary selection that we will implement in this chapter.

The binary feature selection family has two predominant types of feature selection methods: the filter method and the wrapper method (Chandrashekar and Sahin 2014; Almomani *et al.* 2019; Sakr *et al.* 2019; Sharma and Kaur 2021).

### 3.4.3. *Filter method*

The filter method is independent of the optimization problem and classifier; its key advantage. It uses statistical algorithms that make it possible to calculate a weight for each feature by analyzing any attributes specific to the data. The weights will be compared to a threshold that will provide a feature classification. This ranking will make it possible to delete the feature superior to the threshold. However, this method provides much less precision than selection of the wrapper method. The most used filter methods in the literature are (Sakr *et al.* 2019):

– information gain;

– principal component analysis;

– characteristics correlation selection.

### 3.4.4. *Wrapper method*

The wrapper method uses the machine learning classifier to guide the metaheuristic to lead the feature selection process. This method is therefore *adherent* to the classifier. In addition, the wrapper method requires more calculation and processing time than the filtering method. However, its main advantage is that it provides better precision and thus better results in solving the feature selection problem. The literature confirms that wrapper methods outperform the filtering methods (Siarry 2014; Sakr *et al*. 2019; Sharma and Kaur 2021).

In addition, the use of population-based multiple solution metaheuristics provides better results than single solution metaheuristics (Sakr *et al*. 2019; Sharma and Kaur 2021). The GWO algorithm is therefore suitable for solving the feature selection problem.

Therefore, in this chapter, GWO will be integrated with the wrapper binary feature selection method (Emary *et al*. 2016). The binary feature selection can be done either by forward selection or by backward elimination.

### 3.4.5. *Binary feature selection movement*

The wrapper method allows two feature selection "moves": forward selection and backward elimination. The selection of forward or backward will depend mainly on the binary vector initialization method chosen.

#### 3.4.5.1. *Forward selection*

Forward selection consists of starting with a minimum of features and then inserting the features one after another during the selection process until an acceptable error rate is obtained.

#### 3.4.5.2. *Backward elimination*

Unlike forward selection, the backward elimination process starts with the maximum of features at the start and eliminates them one after another during the selection process, until an acceptable error rate is obtained.

The experimental results explained in section 3.8 demonstrate the qualities of these two selection movements.

### 3.4.6. *Benefits of feature selection for machine learning classification algorithms*

The benefits of feature selection on machine learning classification algorithms are multiple. We list the most important here:

– removal of redundant and irrelevant data;

– noise reduction;

– extraction from the curse of the dimension;

– decrease in classifier complexity;

– improvement in the quality of supervised learning;

– increased classification accuracy;

– decreased classifier response time;

– material resources saving when running the classifier: memory, CPU, GPU processors and energy.

In view of the benefits listed above, feature selection is a vital step in data processing before the learning phase of a classifier. Being a powerful algorithm for solving NP-hard multi-objective optimization problems, metaheuristics GWO has become one of the keystones in the process of creating a successful classifier. Indeed, feature selection is an NP-hard multi-objective optimization problem in a binary search space. So a modern and powerful metaheuristic like GWO is able to solve this problem. But before developing the binary GWO metaheuristics, we must first know the mathematical modeling of the problem of optimizing feature selection in a binary search space.

## 3.5. Mathematical modeling of the feature selection optimization problem

In this section, we detail the mathematical environment of the multi-objective feature selection optimization problem: binary discrete search space and objective functions to be minimized. Binary GWO metaheuristics will provide an acceptable solution to this problem within a reasonable time.

### 3.5.1. *Optimization problem definition*

Patrick Siarry (Collette and Siarry 2002) defines optimization as "the search for the minimum or the maximum of a given function". It is therefore a matter of searching in the search space for a data vector which minimizes or maximizes the objective function. The search space of interest to us is the discrete binary search space.

### 3.5.2. *Binary discrete search space*

The binary discrete search space is a search space whose vector components can only take the discrete values 0 or 1.

The mathematical representation of a binary vector in the binary search space $\mathcal{B}^N$ with $N$ features is $B_i = \left( b_i^1, ..., b_i^N \right)$.

The binary search space $\mathcal{B}^N$ is represented by a hypercube with $2^N$ vertices. The $2^N$ binary vectors of the search space $\mathcal{B}^N$ are positioned on the vertices. For example, for $N=3$, $\mathcal{B}^3$ is a cube with eight binary vectors positioned on the eight vertices as illustrated in Figure 3.10.

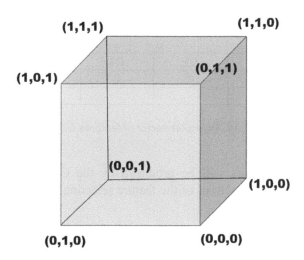

**Figure 3.10.** *Binary search space with N=3*

Therefore, there are $2^N - 1$ solutions for a problem of feature selection with $N$ features. The null vector is ignored because it means to select no features.

Thus, the space research $B^N$ exponentially increases with the size of $N$ features. But why would metaheuristics be more appropriate than other algorithms to solve the problem of feature selection? The reason is simple: it is not possible, unless you devote several hours or even several days, to use a deterministic method to solve the problem of feature selection (Zita *et al.* 2010; Sharma and Kaur 2021). What we need is an acceptable solution within a reasonable wait time. However, the literature abounds with articles demonstrating the effectiveness of population-based metaheuristics, such as GWO.

Before moving on to the next section, we need to understand how to translate a binary vector into a feature selection problem. To do this, let us take the example of a dataset with $N = 6$. The space research $\mathcal{B}^6$ consists of binary vectors $B_i = \left(b_i^1, b_i^2, b_i^3, b_i^4, b_i^5, b_i^6\right)$. There are therefore 63 possible solutions. Translating each vector into a feature selection solution in this search space is extremely simple: 0 means that the feature is not selected and 1 means the opposite. Take one of the vertices of the hypercube: $B_p = (0,1,0,0,1,0)$. This vector selects the two features D2 and D5 as illustrated in Figure 3.11.

| D1 | D2 | D3 | D4 | D5 | D6 |
|----|----|----|----|----|----|
| 0  | 1  | 0  | 0  | 1  | 0  |
| -  | D2 | -  | -  | D5 | -  |

Figure 3.11. *Selection vector of features D2 and D5*

These binary vectors will be produced by the GWO metaheuristic as input to the objective functions of the feature selection problem.

### 3.5.3. *Objective functions for the feature selection*

We have previously stated that a feature selection problem is a multi-objective problem, to be precise a bi-objective problem. Indeed, we must maximize the accuracy of the classifier and minimize the number of selected features. But before setting the two mathematical functions to be optimized, it is necessary to define the vocabulary making it possible to measure the quality of a classifier.

### 3.5.3.1. *Accuracy*

Accuracy measures the rate of good classifications. So the higher this rate is, the more the classifier will be able to give us a good answer.

### 3.5.3.2. *Error rate*

The error rate is the complement of accuracy. It measures the rate of bad classifications.

The accuracy and error rate are calculated from the number of true positive $TP$, true negative $TN$, false positive $FP$ and false negative $FN$. Their mathematical definition is respectively provided by the equations [3.13] and [3.17].

To define $TP$, $TN$, $FP$ and $FN$ let us take the concrete example of a CNN (convolutional neural network) classifier to detect dogs in pictures.

### 3.5.3.3. *True positive (TP)*

This is the number of pictures correctly classified containing a dog.

### 3.5.3.4. *True negative (TN)*

This is the number of pictures correctly classified without a dog.

### 3.5.3.5. *False positive (FP)*

This is the number of pictures without a dog but classified as containing a dog.

### 3.5.3.6. *False negative (FN)*

This is the number of images containing a dog but classified as not containing a dog.

The confusion matrix below illustrates the result of the CNN classification (source image: https://www.kaggle.com/).

| | Positive | Negative |
|---|---|---|
| **Predicted positive** | *TP*<br> | *FP*<br> |
| **Predicted negative** | *FN*<br> | *TN*<br> |

Let us now set the two mathematical functions to be optimized.

The function $A(B_i)$ is the classifier accuracy depending on the binary vector $B_i = \left(b_i^1, \ldots, b_i^N\right)$, and the function $D(B_i)$ is the number of selected features by the binary $B_i$ and $N$ is the feature size. The feature selection problem is defined by equations [3.13], [3.14] and [3.15]:

$$A(B_i) = \frac{TP(B_i) + TN(B_i)}{TP(B_i) + FN(B_i) + TN(B_i) + FP(B_i)} \qquad [3.13]$$

$$D(B_i) = \sum_{j=1}^{N} b_i^j \qquad [3.14]$$

The two objective functions $f1$ and $f2$ of the feature selection problem are provided by [3.15]. It is about maximizing these two functions.

$$\begin{cases} f1(B_i) = \max_{B_i} A(B_i) \\ f2(B_i) = \max_{B_i} \frac{(N - D(B_i))}{N} \end{cases} \qquad [3.15]$$

Being a two-objective optimization problem, it will be necessary to find the dominant solutions; the optimal solutions in the Pareto are on the Pareto border as illustrated in Figure 3.12.

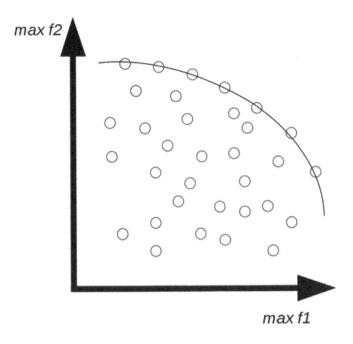

**Figure 3.12.** *Border of optimal dominant solutions with the Pareto meaning*

To solve this problem of feature selection, a uniobjective function is more suitable for GWO metaheuristics. To do this, it suffices to aggregate the two equations into one linked by a weighting coefficient: $\theta \in [0,1]$

$$f(B_i) = \theta A(B_i) + (1 - \theta)\frac{(N-D(B_i))}{N} \qquad [3.16]$$

The coefficient $\theta$ is used to assign a weight to each function in order to distribute the importance of the desired objective: do we want to promote the performance of the classifier or decrease the number of features? This coefficient is therefore not trivial to determine.

In addition, since the inherent nature of GWO is to minimize, it would be more expedient to take into account the error rate $\mathcal{E}(B_i)$ [3.17] instead of the accuracy $A(B_i)$ [3.13]. In the same way, instead of the removed feature rate $\frac{(N-D(B_i))}{N}$ we take the selected feature rate $\frac{D(B_i)}{N}$. This provides the new objective function [3.18]:

$$\mathcal{E}(B_i) = \frac{FP+FN}{TP+FN+TN+FP} \qquad\qquad [3.17]$$

$$f(B_i) = \theta\mathcal{E}(B_i) + (1-\theta)\frac{D(B_i)}{N} \qquad\qquad [3.18]$$

We now have the new uniobjective function to be minimized for our optimization problem. This uniobjective optimization problem is easier to implement in the wrapper feature selection method. We will detail in the next part how to adapt a metaheuristic, designed for optimization on a continuous search space, to a metaheuristic for optimization on a discrete binary search space.

## 3.6. Adaptation of metaheuristics for optimization in a binary search space

The literature provides several methods of binarizing a continuous metaheuristic (Crawford *et al.* 2017). There are mainly two groups:

– the two-step binarization allowing us to keep the strategy and the operators of a metaheuristic;

– binarization by transformation of continuous operators into binary operators.

The second group has been applied successfully to swarm intelligence metaheuristics such as Particle Swarm Optimization (PSO) (Afshinmanesh *et al.* 2005). However, this method cannot be generalized to other metaheuristics of the same family.

Our aim in this chapter is to maintain the excellent hunting strategy of the GWO with its main operators by integrating two new mathematic modules $M1$ and $M2$. These two modules will allow the GWO to adapt to optimization problems in a discrete binary search space.

The first module $M1$ with transfer functions carries out the transition from the continuous search space $\mathbb{R}^N$ to an intermediate probability space $[0,1]^N$. And the second module $M2$ with Boolean rules will make the final transition from intermediate space $[0,1]^N$ to binary space $\mathcal{B}^N$.

If we name $T$ the transfer function used in the module $M1$ and $R$ the logic rule used in the module $M2$, the transition from $\mathbb{R}^N$ to the two spaces $[0,1]^N$ and $\mathcal{B}^N$ can be summarized by the mathematical expression [3.19]:

$$\begin{cases} X_i \in \mathbb{R}^N, \ P_i \epsilon [0,1]^N \ and \ B_i \epsilon \ \mathcal{B}^N \\ X_i = \left(x_i^1, \dots, x_i^N\right) \overset{T}{\Rightarrow} P_i = \left(p_i^1, \dots, p_i^N\right) \overset{R}{\Rightarrow} B_i = \left(b_i^1, \dots, b_i^N\right) \quad [3.19] \\ p_i^d = T\left(x_i^d\right) \ and \ b_i^d = R\left(p_i^d\right) \ with \ d \in [\![1,N]\!] \end{cases}$$

### 3.6.1. *Module M1*

This step is similar to the process of normalizing continuous variables which allow, for each feature, the transition from $\mathbb{R}$ to $[0,1]$. This process uses S or V transfer functions. The most commonly used functions in the literature are listed in Table 3.1 and graphically represented by Figure 3.13.

Transfer functions are used to assess the probability that a component $b_i^d$ of a binary vector $B_i$ changes from 0 to 1 or vice versa. The transfer functions are defined mathematically by [3.20]:

$$T = \{(X, Y) \in \mathbb{R} \times [0,1] \mid Y = T(X)\} \qquad [3.20]$$

| S function transfer | V function transfer |
|:---:|:---:|
| $\dfrac{1}{1 + e^{-2(x)}}$ | $\dfrac{\lvert x \rvert}{\sqrt{1 + (x)^2}}$ |
| $\dfrac{1}{1 + e^{-(x)}}$ | $\lvert \tanh(x) \rvert$ |
| $\dfrac{1}{1 + e^{-\frac{(x)}{2}}}$ | $\left\lvert \dfrac{\sqrt{2}}{\pi} \displaystyle\int_0^{\frac{\sqrt{\pi}}{2}x} e^{-t^2}\, dt \right\rvert$ |
| $\dfrac{1}{1 + e^{-\frac{(x)}{3}}}$ | $\left\lvert \dfrac{2}{\pi} \arctan\left(\dfrac{\pi}{2}x\right) \right\rvert$ |

**Table 3.1.** *Most commonly used S and V transfer functions for feature section (Mirjalili and Lewis 2013; Mafarja et al. 2017)*

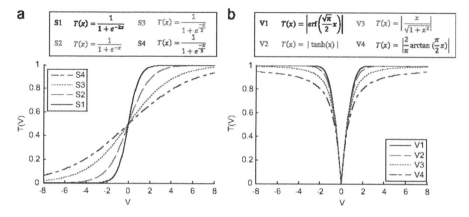

Figure 3.13. *S and V transfer function (Mirjalili and Lewis 2013). For a color version of this figure, see www.iste.co.uk/chelouah/optimization.zip*

We now know the transfer functions S and V allowing the first module to make the transition from space $\mathbb{R}^N$ to $[0,1]^N$. Now let us move on to the binarization module $M2$ allowing transition from $[0,1]^N$ to $\mathcal{B}^N$.

### 3.6.2. *Module M2*

The first module transforms a vector $X_i = (x_i^1, \dots, x_i^N)$ in $\mathbb{R}^N$ to a vector $P_i = (p_i^1, \dots, p_i^N)$ in $[0,1]^N$. The second module applies logical rules $R$ on the vector $P_i = (p_i^1, \dots, p_i^N)$. The result creates a binary vector $B_i = (b_i^1, \dots, b_i^N)$. The rules R are mathematically defined by [3.21]:

$$R = \{(X, Y) \in [0,1] \times \{0,1\} \mid Y = R(X)\} \qquad [3.21]$$

In the literature, binary metaheuristics applied to the feature selection (Crawford *et al.* 2017) mainly use the following rules:

– the change rate rule $R1$;

– the standard rule $R2$;

– the 1's complement rule $R3$;

– the statistical rule $R4$.

### 3.6.2.1. *Change rate rule* $R1$

The rule $R1$ is the simplest but is somewhat risky because it requires us to define by ourselves, in metaheuristics, a threshold probability or rate of modification $TM$. Unlike the standard rule $R2$ which is based on dynamic thresholds defined by $T$, the rule $R1$ is static.

For each component $b_i^d$ of the binary vector $B_i = (b_i^1, \dots, b_i^N)$, $b_i^d$ will take the value 1 only if the modification rate $TM$ is greater than $rand$ with $rand$ a random value between 0 and 1. The rule $R1$ is defined by equation [3.22].

$$R1: b_i^d = \begin{cases} 1 \ if \ rand \ \leq \ TM \\ b_i^d \ else \end{cases} \qquad [3.22]$$

This rule has been used in the bABC metaheuristics (Schiezaro and Pedrini 2013) with mixed results. As we specified above, this rule is too "simplistic" because it does not take into account the feedback between the metaheuristics, the objective function and the updating of the positions of the agents in the search space as the standard rule $R2$ does.

### 3.6.2.2. *Standard rule* $R2$

The standard rule $R2$ exploits the dynamism of the S transfer function to provide the value $p_i^d$, making it possible to measure the probability of $b_i^d$ to be 0 or 1.

This rule will be applied to each bit $b_i^d$ of the binary vector $B_i = (b_i^1, \dots, b_i^N)$. The obtained probability values will be compared to a random value $rand \in [0,1]$. The rule $R2$ is defined by equations [3.23]:

$$R2: b_i^d = \begin{cases} 1 \ if \ rand \ \leq \ p_i^d \\ 0 \ else \end{cases} \qquad [3.23]$$

This rule has been used in the bDA metaheuristics (Mafarja *et al.* 2018) and has provided very good results.

The rule $R3$ that we will see below is a variant of $R2$.

### 3.6.2.3. *1's complement rule R3*

The 1's complement rule $R3$ is similar to the standard rule $R2$. There are two differences:

– the rule $R3$ is used with V transfer functions while $R2$ is used with S transfer functions;

– $R3$ uses the 1's complement to calculate the value $b_i^d(t)$ of the binary vector $B_i = \left(b_i^1, ..., b_i^n\right)$.

The rule $R3$ is defined by equation [3.24]:

$$R3: b_i^d = \begin{cases} complement\,(b_i^d(t))\ if\ rand\ \leq\ p_i^d \\ b_i^d(t)\ else \end{cases} \qquad [3.24]$$

The rule $R3$ has been used in the bPSO metaheuristic (Collette and Siarry 2002) by demonstrating the performances of V transfer functions compared to S transfer functions.

The three rules $R1$, $R2$ and $R3$ provide a binary value $b_i^d$ from a logical condition. The statistic rule $R4$ will make it possible to make a choice between three binary values depending on the probability value $p_i^d$ and a real value $\theta$.

### 3.6.2.4. *Statistic rule R4*

As explained above, the statistical rule $R4$ uses the probability value $p_i^d$ and $\tau$ to generate three logical conditions. These three logical conditions form a stochastic crossover operation between the values $a_i^d$, $b_i^d$ and $c_i^d$. At the end of this operation, $p_i^d$ will take one of the values $a_i^d$, $b_i^d$ or $c_i^d$. The rule $R4$ is defined by equation [3.25]:

$$R4: b_i^d(t+1) \begin{cases} a_i^d(t)\ if\ p_i^d \leq \tau \\ b_i^d(t)\ if\ \tau < p_i^d \leq \frac{1}{2}(1+\tau) \\ c_i^d(t)\ if\ p_i^d \geq \frac{1}{2}(1+\tau) \end{cases} \qquad [3.25]$$

This rule will be used in the bGWO metaheuristic (Emary *et al.* 2016) below.

We now have all theoretical knowledge and mathematical tools to adapt the GWO to optimization in a binary research space. This adaptation will lead to the bGWO metaheuristic that will provide an acceptable solution in a reasonable time to the problem of feature selection.

## 3.7. Adaptation of the grey wolf algorithm to feature selection in a binary search space

In this section, we build on the work of Emary *et al.* on the grey wolf binary optimization approaches for feature selection (Emary *et al.* 2016). These works propose two binarization algorithms of the GWO algorithm.

The first algorithm will have the same steps as the continuous version GWO until the pack hierarchy update $\overrightarrow{X_\alpha}$, $\overrightarrow{X_\beta}$ and $\overrightarrow{X_\delta}$.

On the other hand, the stages of calculating the vectors $\vec{X}_1$, $\overrightarrow{X}_2$ and $\overrightarrow{X}_3$ will be binarized with the modules $M1$ and $M2$. And to get the next grey wolf bit position update $\vec{X}(t+1)$, a statistical logic rule will be used.

The second algorithm makes it possible to keep almost all steps of the continuous version GWO. Only the update operation of $\vec{X}(t+1)$ will be binarized with $M1$ and $M2$.

### 3.7.1. *First algorithm bGWO1*

In this approach, each bit $b_i^d(t)$ of the binary vectors $\vec{X}_1$, $\overrightarrow{X}_2$ and $\overrightarrow{X}_3$ is calculated respectively using equations [3.27]–[3.29], [3.30]–[3.32] and [3.33]–[3.35].

In this approach, the module $M1$ will use the following S transfer function [3.26]:

$$T(x) = \frac{1}{1+e^{-10(x-0.5)}} .$$ [3.26]

The module $M2$ uses the standard rule $R2$ and the statistical rule $R4$ to calculate the next bit position of the grey wolves.

In the following we will implement the modules $M1$ and $M2$ on the vector $\vec{X}_1$. The process is the same for vectors $\vec{X}_2$ and $\vec{X}_3$.

### 3.7.1.1. Module M1

In the continuous version GWO version $\vec{X_1} = \vec{X_\alpha} - \vec{A_1}.\vec{D_\alpha}$ with $\vec{D_\alpha} = |\vec{C_1}.\vec{X_\alpha} - \vec{X}|$.

The module $M1$ uses the value $A_1^d.D_\alpha^d$ to measure the remoteness from the position of the prey. Let $x = A_1^d.D_\alpha^d$ in the S transfer function [3.27]. The result $cstep_\alpha^d$ measures the probability of having the value 1 or 0.

$$cstep_\alpha^d = \frac{1}{1+e^{-10(A_1^d*D_\alpha^d-0.5)}} \qquad [3.27]$$

### 3.7.1.2. Module M2

The module $M2$ uses the standard rule [3.28] to obtain the binary value $bstep_\alpha^d$, and the logic rule [3.29] to obtain the binary value $X_1^d$ knowing that $X_\alpha^d$ is a binary value.

**Vector $\vec{X}_1$**

$$bstep_\alpha^d = \begin{cases} 1 \; if \; cstep_\alpha^d \geq rand \\ 0 \; else \end{cases} \qquad [3.28]$$

$$X_1^d = \begin{cases} 1 \; if \; (X_\alpha^d + bstep_\alpha^d) \geq 1 \\ 0 \; else \end{cases} \qquad [3.29]$$

Equations [3.30]–[3.32] and [3.33]–[3.35] apply the modules $M1$ and $M2$ in the same way in order to calculate the vectors $\vec{X}_2$ and $\vec{X}_3$.

**Vector $\vec{X}_2$**

$$cstep_\beta^d = \frac{1}{1+e^{-10(A_2^d*D_\beta^d-0.5)}} \qquad [3.30]$$

$$bstep_\beta^d = \begin{cases} 1 \; if \; cstep_\beta^d \geq rand \\ 0 \; else \end{cases} \qquad [3.31]$$

$$X_2^d = \begin{cases} 1 \; if \; (X_\beta^d + bstep_\beta^d) \geq 1 \\ 0 \; else \end{cases} \qquad [3.32]$$

**Vector $\vec{X}_3$**

$$cstep_\delta^d = \frac{1}{1+e^{-10(A_3^d * D_\delta^d - 0.5)}} \qquad [3.33]$$

$$bstep_\delta^d = \begin{cases} 1 \; if \; cstep_\delta^d \geq rand \\ 0 \; else \end{cases} \qquad [3.34]$$

$$X_3^d = \begin{cases} 1 \; if \; (X_\delta^d + bstep_\delta^d) \geq 1 \\ 0 \; else \end{cases} \qquad [3.35]$$

The module $M2$ ends by calculating the next binary position $X_i^d(t+1)$ with the statistical rule [3.36] by performing a stochastic crossing of $X_1^d$; $X_2^d$; $X_3^d$ with $\tau = \frac{1}{3}$.

$$X_i^d(t+1) \begin{cases} X_1^d(t) \; if \; rand \leq \frac{1}{3} \\ X_2^d(t) \; if \; \frac{1}{3} \leq rand < \frac{2}{3} \\ X_3^d(t) \; else \end{cases} \qquad [3.36]$$

The first algorithm bGWO1 makes it possible to search for the best binary position of a wolf agent to solve the optimization problem in a binary search space $\mathcal{B}^N$ with $N$ features. The quality of bGWO1 is that it retains the same optimization strategy as GWO while binarizing it thanks to modules $M1$ and $M2$. Indeed, these two modules are implemented to calculate the binary positions $\vec{X}_1$, $\vec{X}_2$ and $\vec{X}_3$ in the surrounding areas created by the hierarchy of the pack and then to calculate the new binary position of the wolf agents of the pack.

In the second algorithm, bGWO2 reduces the binarization phases. Only the calculation for updating the positions of wolf agents is binarized.

### 3.7.2. Second algorithm bGWO2

In this second approach, as in the first approach, the module $M1$ uses the transfer function [3.26] and the standard rule $R2$ in the module $M2$.

As we have just explained, in bGWO2, only the update phase of the bit positions is binarized. To do this, each component $X_i^d$ of $\vec{X}(t+1)$ will be calculated using the average of $X_1^d$, $X_2^d$ and $X_3^d$ from the positions $\vec{X}_1$, $\vec{X}_2$ and $\vec{X}_3$. Therefore, $x = \frac{(X_1^d(t)+X_2^d(t)+X_3^d(t))}{3}$ in function tranfers [3.26].

Thus, the module $M1$ calculates $cstep_i^d$ in [3.37] which makes it possible to evaluate the probability that $X_i^d(t+1)$ takes the value 1 or 0.

$$cstep_i^d = T\left(\frac{(X_1^d(t)+X_2^d(t)+X_3^d(t))}{3}\right)$$    [3.37]

The module $M2$ calculates the next value of $X_i^d(t+1)$ by using the standard rule $R2$ in [3.38].

$$X_i^d(t+1) = \begin{cases} 1 \; if \; cstep_i^d \geq rand \\ 0 \; else \end{cases}$$    [3.38]

The bGWO2 algorithm is more attractive than bGWO1 because only the step of updating the pack positions is binarized. Everything else in the bGWO2 algorithm is identical to GWO.

The pseudocodes of bGWO1 and bGWO2, respectively, provided by Algorithm 2 and Algorithm 3 allow them to be compared to the GWO algorithm and to confirm the consistency of the hunting strategy used in the GWO.

### 3.7.3. Algorithm 2: first approach of the binary GWO

**In**: Population size $N$, Number of iterations **ItMax**, fitness function **F**
**Out**: Binary vector $\vec{X_\alpha}$ and fitness value $F(\vec{X_\alpha})$

Initialization of the grey wolf binary population agents $\vec{X_i} \; i \in [\![1, N]\!]$
Initialize a, A, and C
Calculate the fitness $F(\vec{X_i})$ of each search agent $\vec{X_i}$
Define:
      $\vec{X_\alpha}$=the first best search agent
      $\vec{X_\beta}$=the second best search agent
      $\vec{X_\delta}$=the third best search agent

**While** (t < *ItMax*)

    **For** each search agent $\overrightarrow{X_i}$

    **For each** feature $d$

        Calculate $X_1^d, X_2^d, X_3^d$ with (28) to (35)

        Calculate $X_i^d(t+1)$ with (36)

        **End for**

    **End for**

    Update a, A, and C with equation (3) to (5)

    Calculate the fitness $F(\overrightarrow{X_i})$ of all binary agents $\overrightarrow{X_i}$

    Update $\overrightarrow{X_\alpha}, \overrightarrow{X_\beta}$ and $\overrightarrow{X_\delta}$

    t=t+1

**End while**

### 3.7.4. Algorithm 3: second approach of the binary GWO

**In**: Population size *N*, Number of iterations *ItMax*, fitness function *F*
**Out**: Binary vector $\overrightarrow{X_\alpha}$ and fitness value $F(\overrightarrow{X_\alpha})$

Initialization of the grey wolf binary population agents $\overrightarrow{X_i}$ $i \in [\![1, N]\!]$
Initialize a, A, and C
Calculate the fitness $F(\overrightarrow{X_i})$ of each search agent $\overrightarrow{X_i}$
Define:

    $\overrightarrow{X_\alpha}$=the best search agent

    $\overrightarrow{X_\beta}$=the second best search agent

    $\overrightarrow{X_\delta}$=the third best search agent

**While** (t < *ItMax*)

    **For** each search agent $\overrightarrow{X_i}$

    **For each** feature $d$

        Calculate $X_i^d(t+1)$ with (37) and (38)

        **End for**

    **End for**

    Update a, A, and C with equation (3) to (5)

    Calculate the fitness $F(\overrightarrow{X_i})$ of all binary agents $\overrightarrow{X_i}$

    Update $\overrightarrow{X_\alpha}, \overrightarrow{X_\beta}$ and $\overrightarrow{X_\delta}$

    t=t+1

**End while**

## 3.8. Experimental implementation of bGWO1 and bGWO2 and discussion

The wrapper feature selection method was used in Emary *et al.* (2016) to select the features of 18 datasets from the UCI reference system (Frank and Asuncion 2010). They are compared to known metaheuristics in the literature: genetic algorithm (GA) and PSO.

The wrapper consists of bGWO1 and bGWO2 metaheuristics and the KNN classification algorithm.

Each dataset is divided into three portions: training data, validation data and test data. Only training and validation data are used for feature selection. The test data will be used to test the final classifier with the selected features.

The objective function is composed of the error rate $\varepsilon$ provided by the validation phase and the number of features $D$ calculated by the sum of the bits equal to 1 in the binary vectors. $\theta$ is set at 0.99. Therefore, this is the minimization of the error rate $\varepsilon$ which is favored.

In order to confirm the repeatability of the experimental results and to test the stability and robustness of the metaheuristics, it is necessary to perform several runs of bGWO1 and bGWO2 on the datasets. $NE$ is the number of runs.

In Emary (2016), the parameters of the experiment are provided by Table 3.2.

| Parameters | Values |
|---|---|
| Number of wolf agents | 8 |
| Number of iterations | 70 |
| $NE$ | 20 |
| $\theta$ | 0.99 |
| K | 5 |

**Table 3.2.** *Wrapper parameters*

The complete experimental results are provided by Emary (2016). We described in Table 3.3 the main experimental performance metrics which make it possible to validate the feature selection of the 18 UCI datasets with the bGWO-KNN wrapper.

| Performance metrics | Description |
|---|---|
| The average error rate of the KNN classifier | Sum of error rates divided by $NE$. This is an indicator of the quality of the classifier on the selected data subset |
| Best solution found | This is the solution that provided the best results on $NE$ runs |
| Worst solution found | This is the solution that provided the worst results on $NE$ runs |
| The average of the solutions over the $NE$ runs of the algorithm | Sum of the solutions on the $NE$ executions divided by $NE$. It is a performance indicator of the algorithm. |
| Standard deviation of the solutions found on the $NE$ runs of the algorithm | Measures the average variation of the solutions found on the runs. This is an indicator of the stability and robustness of the algorithm |
| The average size rate of the selected features divided by the feature size $N$ of the data on the number $NE$ of runs of the algorithm | Sum of features selected $D$ divided by $N \times NE$ during $NE$ runs |
| The mean Fisher score of the selected data subset | The Fisher score measures the separability of data by measuring the inter-class and intra-class distances of the selected data subset. The inter-class distances must be as large as possible and the intra-class distances as small as possible |

**Table 3.3.** *Wrapper performance metrics*

By analyzing the results provided by Emary *et al.* (2016) we can see that globally the metaheuristics bGWO1 and bGWO2 are more competitive and efficient than GA and PSO.

## 3.9. Conclusion

This chapter has revealed another usefulness of population-based metaheuristics in data processing for the benefit of machine learning algorithms. Indeed, metaheuristics are able to solve with very good results the optimization problems of feature selection. Feature selection provides strategic advantages in the training of classifiers by increasing their performance while reducing their complexity.

In addition, we learned to adapt a continuous population-based metaheuristic to optimization in a binary search space. To this end, we have chosen a recent metaheuristic to explain the binarization methods: the grey wolf metaheuristics GWO.

The binarization methods are composed of two modules and they made it possible to create two new metaheuristics for feature selection: bGWO1 and bGWO2.

The experimental results, on 18 datasets from the UCI reference system, demonstrated the superiority of bGWO1 and bGWO2 compared to the bGA and bPSO algorithms.

The performance of bGWO has attracted the attention of several researchers and has led to improvements through hybridization techniques such as bPSOGWO (Al-Tashi *et al.* 2017). This shows that the room for maneuver for improvements in metaheuristic GWO is extensive.

## 3.10. References

Afshinmanesh, F., Marandi, A., Rahimi-Kian, A. (2005). A novel binary particle swarm optimization method using artificial immune system. *EUROCON 2005 – The International Conference on Computer as a Tool.* IEEE, Belgrade.

Al-Tashi, Q., Abdulkadir, S.J., Rais, H.M., Mirjalili, S., Alhussian, H. (2017). Binary optimization using hybrid grey wolf optimization for feature selection. *IEEE Access*, 7, 39496–39508.

Almomani, A., Alweshah, M., Al Khalayleh, S., Al-Refai, M., Qashi, R. (2019). Metaheuristic algorithms-based feature selection approach for intrusion detection. *Machine Learning for Computer and Cyber Security: Principles, Algorithms and Practices*, Gupta, B.B., Sheng, Q.Z. (eds). CRC Press, Boca Raton, FL.

Chandrashekar, G. and Sahin, F. (2014). A survey on feature selection methods. *Computers & Electrical Engineering*, 40(1), 16–28.

Collette, Y. and Siarry, P. (2002). *Optimisation Multiobjectif.* Eyrolles, Paris.

Crawford, B., Soto, R., Astorga, G., García, J., Castro, C., Paredes, F. (2017). Putting continuous metaheuristics to work in binary search spaces. *Hindawi*, 2017, 8404231.

Emary, E., Zawbaab, H.M., Hassanien, A.E. (2016). Binary grey wolf optimization approaches for feature selection. *Distributed Learning Algorithms for Swarm Robotics*, 172, 371–381.

Faris, H., Aljarah, I., Al-Betar, M.A., Mirjalili, S. (2017). Grey wolf optimizer: A review of recent variants and applications. *Neural Computing and Applications*, 30, 413–435.

Fong, S., Deb, S., Yang, X.S., Li, J. (2014). Feature selection in life science classification: Metaheuristic swarm search. *IEEE, IT Professional*, 16(4), 24–29.

Frank, A. and Asuncion, A. (2010). UCI Machine Learning Repository [Online]. Available at: http://archive.ics.uci.edu/ml/index.php.

Hodashinsky, I.A. and Sarin, K.S. (2019). Feature selection: Comparative analysis of binary metaheuristics and population based algorithm with adaptive memory. *Programming and Computer Software*, 45(5), 221–227.

Mafarja, M., Eleyan, D., Abdullah, S., Mirjalili, S. (2017). S-shaped vs. V-shaped transfer functions for ant lion optimization algorithm in feature selection problem. *Proceedings of the International Conference on Future Networks and Distributed Systems (ICFNDS '17)*. Association for Computing Machinery, New York.

Mafarja, M., Aljarah, I., Heidari, A.H., Faris, H., Fournier-Viger, P., Li, X., Mirjalili, S. (2018). Binary dragonfly optimization for feature selection using time-varying transfer functions. *Knowledge-Based Systems*, 161, 185–204.

Mirjalili, S. and Lewis, A. (2013). S-shaped versus V-shaped transfer functions for binary particle swarm optimization. *Swarm and Evolutionary Computation*, 9, 1–14.

Mirjalili, S., Mirjalili, S.M., Lewis, A. (2014). Grey wolf optimizer. *Advances in Engineering Software*, 69, 46–61.

Sakr, M.M., Tawfeeq, M.A., El-Sisi, A.B. (2019). Filter versus wrapper feature selection for network intrusion detection system. *Ninth International Conference on Intelligent Computing and Information Systems (ICICIS)*, IEEE, Cairo.

Schiezaro, M. and Pedrini, H. (2013). Data feature selection based on artificial bee colony algorithm. *Journal on Image and Video Processing*, 2013, 47.

Sharma, M. and Kaur, P. (2021). A comprehensive analysis of nature-inspired meta-heuristic techniques for feature selection problem. *Archives of Computational Methods in Engineering*, 28, 1103–1127.

Siarry, P. (2014). *Métaheuristiques*. Eyrolles, Paris.

Vale, Z.A., Ramos, C., Faria, P., Soares, J.P., Canizes, B., Teixeira, J., Khodr, H.M. (2010). Comparison between deterministic and metaheuristic methods applied to ancillary services dispatch. *International Conference on Industrial, Engineering and Other Applications of Applied Intelligent Systems*. Springer, Córdoba.

**4**

# Solving the Mixed-model Assembly Line Balancing Problem by using a Hybrid Reactive Greedy Randomized Adaptive Search Procedure

**Belkharroubi LAKHDAR and Khadidja YAHYAOUI**
*University of Mascara, Algeria*

In order to meet customer demand for different products at any one time, many industries use special mixed-model assembly lines where different product models are assembled in an inter-mixed sequence. In designing these types of lines, a critical problem – the mixed-model assembly line balancing problem – must be solved, in order to minimize the number of workstations (type-1) or the cycle time (type-2). This chapter addresses the type-2 mixed-model assembly line balancing problem with deterministic task times. To solve this problem, an enhancement of the greedy randomized adaptive search procedure (GRASP) is proposed; it is known as the reactive GRASP. This reactive version is based on the variation of the value of the restricted candidate list parameter alpha, in contrast to the basic version which is based on the fixed value. The variation of the value of the alpha helps the algorithm to find better solutions that cannot be found with a fixed value. Furthermore, the basic GRASP is limited by not drawing fully on previous iterations; using information from previous solutions can influence the construction phase. The proposed reactive GRASP is hybridized with the

*Optimization and Machine Learning,*
coordinated by Rachid CHELOUAH and Patrick SIARRY © ISTE Ltd 2022.

ranked positional weight heuristic to construct initial solutions; the neighborhood search procedure is then applied in the local search phase in order to improve constructed solutions. Results obtained by the proposed hybrid reactive GRASP are compared with those obtained by the basic GRASP, in order to demonstrate the effect of the learning mechanism in expanding the search space, thus increasing the chances of finding good solutions.

## 4.1. Introduction

An assembly line is a production system that contains several workstations arranged in a serial manner and related by a material handling system such as a conveyor. In each workstation, a set of tasks is performed by different operators such as humans, robots and machines. In 1913, the assembly line balancing problem (ALBP) was applied for the first time in the automotive industry by Henry Ford. Its aim was to find the best assignment of tasks, while respecting precedence relations, in order to optimize different measures (Zhang *et al.* 2019). In the literature, the ALBP is divided into two categories, as shown in Figure 4.1: the simple assembly line balancing problem (SALBP) and the generalized assembly line balancing problem (GALBP). The SALBP concerns traditional assembly lines on which a single product is assembled and it is classified into four types: SALBP-1, SALBP-2, SALBP-E and SALBP-F (Yadav *et al.* 2020). Table 4.1 shows the objective of each type. In the GALBP, different assumptions of the SALBP can be changed; for example, instead of producing a single model, different similar models can be assembled on the same assembly line. Workstations can be arranged in a U-shaped assembly line which can reduce the idle time, with the introduction of parallel lines, two-sided lines and robotic lines.

| Problem | Objective |
|---------|-----------|
| SALBP-1 | Minimize number of workstations |
| SALBP-2 | Minimize cycle time |
| SALBP-E | Maximize line efficiency |
| SALBP-F | Obtain feasible balance |

**Table 4.1.** *The classification of simple assembly line balancing problems with their objectives*

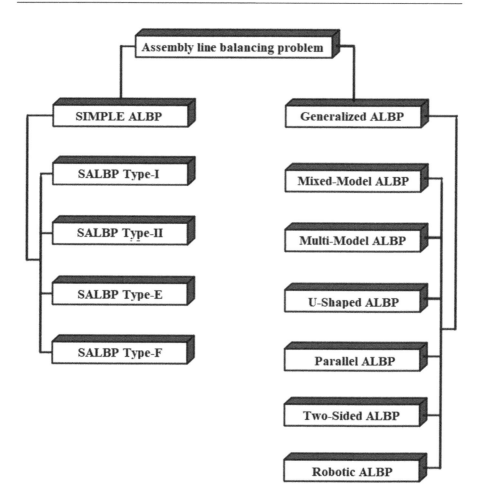

**Figure 4.1.** *Assembly line balancing problem categories*

The elimination of some SALBP assumptions creates new ALBPs that fall under the GALBP (Saif *et al*. 2014). With variation in customer demand for different models, industrial campaigns have been obliged to deal with this problem by applying new types of lines in their manufacturing systems. These are known as mixed-model assembly lines or multi-model assembly lines, as shown in Figure 4.2.

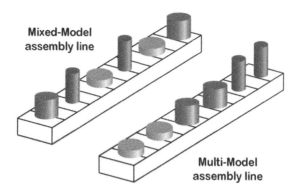

**Figure 4.2.** *Mixed- and multi-model assembly lines. For a color version of this figure, see www.iste.co.uk/chelouah/optimization.zip*

On mixed-model assembly lines, units of different models are produced in an arbitrary sequence, whereas on a multi-model assembly line, units are produced in batches (Becker and Scholl 2006). According to van Zante-de Fokkert and de Kok (1997), the mixed-model and multi-model lines differ in terms of lot size; mixed-model lines have a lot size of one, whereas multi-model lines have a lot size greater than one. Furthermore, the setup time needed between batches on multi-model lines is ignored on mixed-model lines. Balancing a mixed-model assembly line is also a critical problem that takes into consideration all the different models of products and is known as the mixed-model assembly line balancing problem (MiMALBP). It can be classified into two types: MiMALBP-1 and MiMALBP-2 (Zhang *et al.* 2019). Resolution of the MiMALBP involves targeted objectives, as in the SALBP. The classification of MiMALBPs with their objectives is shown in Table 4.2.

| Problem | Objective |
|---|---|
| MiMALBP-1 | Minimize number of workstations |
| MiMALBP-2 | Minimize cycle time |

**Table 4.2.** *The classification of mixed-model assembly line balancing problems with their objectives*

Unlike the SALBP, in the MiMALBP each model has its own precedence relations diagram. To balance the mixed-model line, the problem can be transformed into an SALBP by combining all the diagrams of models into one combined precedence diagram. All tasks are thus assigned to workstations based on the new diagram and tasks of different models that are similar are assigned to the same workstations. This reduces setup time to a minimal value where it can be ignored (Saif *et al.* 2014).

On assembly lines, task time can be deterministic, varying and stochastic or uncertain. Deterministic task time is assumed to be a fixed variable, and it is also assumed that it remains unchanged during the production process. In general, an assembly line with reliable operators who perform simple tasks reduces variation in task time; it is thus considered deterministic. Varying task time is generally considered in assembly lines where manual workers perform a set of tasks; thus, the task time changes based on different worker factors. These factors can relate to their level of skill in performing tasks, their experience, motivation and ability to communicate within the group. Machine breakdowns also cause variation in task time. Finally, stochastic or uncertain task time is considered an unknown variable and, in the literature, researchers have used different methods to represent uncertain variables, for example, fuzzy variables and independent normally distributed variables (Becker and Scholl 2006; Rekiek and Delchambre 2006).

In the literature, research has been conducted to solve both the type-1 MiMALBP and the type-2 MiMALBP. In this chapter, we address the type-2 MiMALBP, given its importance in increasing production rate. Therefore, the aim is to find the optimal average cycle time, for a given number of workstations, which satisfies the workloads of all similar products that must be assembled on the same line. In some cases, workloads of models in some workstations on mixed-model assembly lines can exceed the cycle time, resulting in work overload. In order to minimize the number of work overloads on the line during production, another problem must be solved: the mixed-model sequencing problem (MMSP) (Becker and Scholl 2006). Solving the MMSP involves finding the best sequence of models within which the number of work overloads is the minimum. The MMSP is not solved as part of this study.

## 4.2. Related works from the literature

Several works in the literature have dealt with the MiMALBP with the objective of minimizing the cycle time using different approaches. For example, a hybrid genetic algorithm (HGA) has been proposed by

Zhang *et al.* (2019) for a robust MiMALBP type-2 with interval task times, and results show that the proposed HGA is efficient to find solutions for large-sized problems. Aufy *et al.* (2020) have used a consecutive heuristic algorithm for balancing an MiMALBP type-2 using a worker-task assigned to a workstation heuristic model that has been developed for straight and U-shaped lines. An iterative procedure for solving MiMALBP type-2 using a genetic algorithm with parallel workstations has been proposed by Raj *et al.* (2016) in order to maximize the production rate of the assembly line for a predefined number of operators.

Rabbani *et al.* (2016) have proposed a multi-objective metaheuristic for solving a robotic MiMALBP type-2. These proposed metaheuristics have been developed for a U-shaped assembly line, the first is the non-dominating sorting genetic algorithm NSGA-2, and the second is multi-objective particle swarm optimization MOPSO. Results show that, generally, NSGA-2 is better than the MOPSO in terms of performance when solving problems with different sizes. Lalaoui and Afia (2019) have proposed a reactive generalized simulated annealing (GSA) using a fuzzy controller to solve the MiMALBP type-2. The fuzzy controller has been used to guide the algorithm to explore the entire search space in early iterations, and results show that this approach can obtain better quality solutions than its original approach counterpart. Çil *et al.* (2020) have formulated a mathematical model and implemented a bee algorithm for solving MiMALBP with physical human–robot collaboration to minimize the cycle times of models. The mathematical model has been used to solve small-sized problems and bee algorithms for large-sized problems, and results show that the proposed model and algorithms can help managers to solve the MiMALBP effectively.

Ramezanian and Ezzatpanah (2015) have developed a novel imperialist competitive algorithm to solve multi-objective mixed-model assembly line balancing and worker assignment problems. Minimizing the cycle time was the first objective and costs related to workers was the second objective to be minimized. The results obtained show that the proposed ICA is performant in finding near goal values. Aghajani *et al.* (2014) have presented a mixed-integer programming model for solving a robotic mixed-model two-sided assembly line with robot setup times type-2 in order to minimize the cycle time for a given number of mated stations, and simulated annealing metaheuristic has been used to avoid the large computational time in solving large-sized problems. To evaluate the SA performance, four problems have been solved with SA and a software named General Algebraic Modeling System and, by comparing the results, it is found that SA is more efficient in finding optimal solutions in less time than the GAMS software, and can be used to solve large-sized problems. Rabbani *et al.* (2012) have dealt with a mixed-model two-sided assembly lines balancing problem with multiple U-shaped layouts to minimize the cycle time and the number of workstations, they have developed a mixed integer programming problem formulation to model such a manufacturing system, and a heuristic algorithm based on the genetic algorithm to solve it due to its complexity. Results show that the proposed framework is better than previous methods in the literature in terms of flexibility and the utilization of manufacturing resources in order to accelerate the production rate. Çil *et al.* (2017) have developed an efficient heuristic algorithm based on beam search in order to solve the type-2 robotic MiMALBP by minimizing the sum of cycle times over all models. The proposed algorithm has been compared with mathematical models to prove its efficiency in solving different benchmark problems, and results show that it is a competitive tool. Tang *et al.* (2016) have proposed an HGA with logic strings for balancing a mixed-model assembly line with sequence dependent tasks in order to optimize the cycle time and workload variance. Three heuristics have been hybridized to improve the quality of the population of initial solutions. Results have shown that the proposed algorithm can solve problems to near-optimality and even optimality with less computational effort.

## 4.3. Problem description and mathematical formulation

### 4.3.1. *Problem description*

For a given number of workstations $K$, arranged in a serial manner, the optimal cycle time $C$ must be found. Different models of products $M$ with similar characteristics are assembled on the same line, and each model has its own precedence relations diagram $G$ which determines the priority of execution of tasks $T$. Task times are deterministic and may differ from model to model; tasks that are not needed for the assemblage of model $m$ are ignored by fixing their processing times at $0$. Each task $i$ is assigned to one workstation and must be performed before all of its successors $Si$. Thus, the index of the workstation to which task $i$ is assigned must be equal or lower than all indexes of workstations to which the successors of this task are assigned. The sum of task times of tasks assigned to the same workstation must not exceed the cycle time $C$. In order to balance the mixed-model assembly line based on this information, two methods are possible, balancing the line for each model based on its precedence relations diagram or by combining all diagrams of models to form a final diagram known as the combined precedence diagram. The second method is the most commonly used because it helps to find the average cycle time for all models and guarantees that common tasks between models are assigned to the same workstation.

The addressed MiMALBP-2 has the following assumptions:

– the assembly line is serial;

– the number of workstations is known and fixed;

– the task time of each model is deterministic;

– common tasks must be assigned to the same workstation;

– the combined precedence diagram is obtained by combining precedence diagrams for different models;

– the assignment of tasks is restricted by precedence constraints.

### 4.3.2. *Mathematical formulation*

| | |
|---|---|
| $T$ | number of tasks |
| $i$ | task $i$ where $i = 1, ..., T$ |
| $K$ | number of workstations |
| $k$ | workstation $k$ where $k = 1, ..., K$ |
| $t_i$ | processing time of task $i$ |
| $p_i$ | the set of predecessors of task $i$ |
| $X_{ik} = 1$ | if task $i$ is assigned to workstation $k$, otherwise $X_{ik} = 0$ |

The objective is to find the optimal average cycle time for all models using the combined precedence diagram, and this can be formulated as follows:

**min C** [4.1]

Subject to:

$$\sum_{k=1}^{K} X_{ik} = 1, \text{ for } i = 1,\ldots, T \tag{4.2}$$

$$\sum_{i=1}^{T} t_i * X_{ik} \leq C, \text{ for } k = 1,\ldots, K \tag{4.3}$$

$$\sum_{k=1}^{K} k * X_{hk} \leq \sum_{k=1}^{K} k * X_{ik}, \text{ where } h \in P_i \tag{4.4}$$

$$X_{ik} \in \{0, 1\} \tag{4.5}$$

Constraint [4.2] requires that the task *i* is assigned to one workstation. Constraint [4.3] ensures that the sum of the process times of all tasks assigned to the same workstation does not exceed the cycle time. Constraint [4.4] ensures that precedence relations between tasks are respected. Finally, constraint [4.5] relates to decision variables integrity.

## 4.4. Basic greedy randomized adaptive search procedure

The greedy randomized adaptive search procedure (GRASP) is a multi-start metaheuristic, it consists of two phases in each iteration: the construction phase and the local search phase. In the construction phase, a feasible solution is constructed using two lists, the candidate list (CL) and the restricted candidate list (RCL). The CL is formed by all elements that can be added to the partial solution without destroying its feasibility, then all elements are evaluated by a greedy function, and the best elements with the smallest incremental costs are chosen to form the RCL. The RCL is limited either by the number of elements (cardinality-based) or by the quality of elements (value-based). In the cardinality-based case, the RCL can contain $E$ elements with the best incremental costs where $E$ is a parameter. In the value-based case, the number of elements of the RCL is based on the $\alpha$ parameter where $\alpha \in [0, 1]$ and a threshold value $TC_{th} = T_{min} + \alpha$ $(T_{max} - T_{min})$ where $T_{min}$ and $T_{max}$ are the smallest and largest incremental costs, respectively. All elements in the CL with an incremental cost no greater than the threshold value are inserted into the RCL. From the RCL an element is chosen randomly to be added to the partial solution, once an element is selected, the CL is updated. The constructed solution is not necessarily the optimal one, thus it is passed to the local search phase. The local search algorithm replaces the current solution by a better solution that is in the neighborhood of the current solution, and it stops if no better neighbor solution is found. At the end of each iteration, the solution found by the local search phase is compared with the previous solution kept as the best solution, and if it has a better objective value it replaces the previous solution and becomes the best solution found (Glover and Kochenberger 2003; Marti *et al.* 2018).

## 4.5. Reactive greedy randomized adaptive search procedure

The big disadvantage of the basic GRASP is that it does not learn from the history of previous iterations by discarding all information about obtained solutions. Different enhancements that let the GRASP learn from the previous iterations have been proposed, which influence the construction phase: the reactive GRASP, memory and learning, cost perturbations, local search on partially constructed solutions and bias functions (Marti *et al.* 2018). The reactive GRASP is the first enhancement of the basic GRASP proposed for the first time by Prais and Ribeiro (2000) to find approximate solutions to the time slot assignment problem. This reactive version of GRASP integrates the concept of a learning mechanism in the construction phase. In each GRASP iteration, the value of $\alpha$ parameter is selected randomly from a discrete set of possible values $Alpha = \{\alpha_i,..., \alpha_n\}$ using probabilities $P_i$, $i=1,..., n$ where $n$ is the number of possible values of $\alpha$. The probabilities depend on previously obtained solutions. At the first GRASP iteration, all possible values of $\alpha$ have the same probability of selection $P_i=1/n$. At any subsequent iteration let $\hat{Z}$ be the best solution found, and let $A_i$ be the average value of all solutions found using $\alpha=\alpha_i$, $i=1,..., n$, the probabilities of selection are updated periodically using the following equation:

$$P_i = \frac{q_i}{\sum_{j=1}^{n} q_j} \qquad [4.6]$$

where $q_i = \hat{Z}/A_i$, $i=1,..., n$. The value of $q_i$ is increased if the values of $\alpha = \alpha_i$ lead to best solutions on average. The probabilities of appropriate values will then increase when they are updated (Glover and Kochenberger 2003).

## 4.6. Hybrid reactive greedy randomized adaptive search procedure for the mixed model assembly line balancing problem type-2

In order to solve the MiMALBP with the objective of minimizing the cycle time for the same line in which a set of models are assembled, we propose a hybridization between the reactive GRASP and a well-known heuristic that has been used to solve the assembly line balancing problem known as ranked positional weight (RPW). Using RPW, all tasks are ordered in a list based on their positional weights, the positional weight of task $i$ is the sum of its processing time and all processing times of its successors $S_i$. The task with the greatest weight is the priority, if all its predecessors are already assigned, to be assigned to the opened workstation. The RPW is used in the construction phase to construct a feasible solution that respects precedence relations, but this constructed solution may not be the optimal one, this means that another optimal cycle time can be found by searching for another solution, thus the local search phase is used to escape from the local optimal. Before entering the construction phase, the alpha takes a random value from a set of values based on the probability of selection, as shown in the pseudocode of the proposed hybrid reactive GRASP:

**hybrid_reactive_grasp** (tasks_list, alpha_values $\leftarrow$ {alpha$_1$,..., alpha$_m$}, max_iterations, period, max_search, n_workstations)

| | |
|---|---|
| 1 | optimal_value $\leftarrow \infty$; |
| 2 | $P_i \leftarrow 1/m$, i = 1, ..., m; |
| 3 | sum$_i \leftarrow 0$, i = 1, ..., m; |
| 4 | n$_i \leftarrow 0$, i = 1, ..., m; |
| 5 | **for** j in max_iterations **do** |
| 6 | alpha $\leftarrow$ select alpha$_i$ from alpha_values randomly using probabilities; |
| 7 | solution $\leftarrow$ **construction_phase** (alpha, tasks_list); |
| 8 | solution $\leftarrow$ **local_search_phase** (solution, max_search); |

```
9                     if (f(solution, n_workstations) < optimal_value)
10                            then do
11                                    best_solution ← solution;
12                                    optimal_value ← f(best_solution,
                                      n_workstations);
13                            end then;
14                    n_j ← n_j + 1;
15                    sum_j ← sum_j + f(solution, n_workstations);
16                    if (modulo (j, period) = 0)
17                            then do
18                                    A_i ← sum_i/n_i, i = 1, ..., m;
19                                    q_i ← optimal_value/A_i, i = 1, ..., m;
20                                    P_i ← q_i/∑_{j=1}^{m} q_j, i = 1, ..., m;
21                            end then;
22            end for;
23    return best_solution;
end hybrid_reactive_grasp;
```

The algorithm requires six inputs: the list of all available tasks that must be assigned, *list_tasks*, the set of possible values of $\alpha$ parameter, the maximum number of iterations of the hybrid reactive GRASP, *max_iterations*, the *period* parameter that defines the iterations in which probabilities must be updated, the *max_search* parameter that defines the maximum number of iterations of the local search phase and, finally, the number of workstations *n_workstations*.

### 4.6.1. *The proposed construction phase*

```
construction_phase (alpha, tasks_list)
1        s ← ∅;
2        Create the RPW_list by applying RPW on task_list based on
         precedence_relations;
3        Associate for each task in RPW_list a new weight nw, where nw ←
         1/positional weight;
4        while (RPW_list not empty)
5                Create CL by choosing assignable tasks from RPW_list;
```

6            Based on the **nw** of tasks in CL, calculate the threshold using
                    **TCth ← nwmin + alpha (nwmax + nwmin);**
7            RCL ← {task ∈ CL, **nw**(task) <= **TCth**};
8            x ← random_choice (RCL);
9            s ← s U x;
10           Delete selected task from RPW_list;
11       **end while;**
12       **return s;**
**end construction_phase;**

The construction phase of the proposed hybrid reactive GRASP requires two parameters: the selected **alpha** value and the **tasks_list**. In our approach, we use the RPW heuristic in the construction phase as a greedy function, in order to evaluate tasks based on their positional weights. To build a feasible solution, first, a list is created named **RPW_list** in which tasks are ordered based on their positional weight. We then associate each task in the **RPW_list** to a new value called **new_weight** (**nw**), where **nw** = *1/positional_weight*. By using the *new_weight* value (the inverse of the positional weight), we can exploit the value-based technique of the GRASP which is based on the threshold value. From the **RPW_list**, assignable tasks are chosen to form the CL; and based on new associated weights of tasks in the CL, the threshold value is calculated using the following equation:

$$TC_{th} = nw_{min} + \alpha\,(nw_{max} - nw_{min})$$    [4.7]

where $nw_{min}$ is the smallest new weight (greatest positional weight in reality) and $nw_{max}$ is the greatest new weight (smallest positional weight in reality). All tasks with a **new_weight** smaller than or equal to the threshold value are selected to form the RCL. From the RCL a task is chosen randomly to build the partial solution. The aim of using the inverse of the positional weight in this hybrid reactive GRASP is to use the value-based technique in the right way, this means if $\alpha = 0$ the selection of a task from the RCL becomes pure greedy, otherwise, if $\alpha = 1$ the selection becomes totally random. The selected task is then deleted from the CL and the **RPW_list**, and the CL is updated by adding all assignable tasks from the **RPW_list** to continue the construction process.

To illustrate how the proposed construction phase works, we assume that we have the following SALBP type-2:

– Six tasks must be assigned.

– Each task has a fixed processing time *t*.

– The number of workstations is fixed **wr** = 3.

– The precedence relations are given in Figure 4.3.

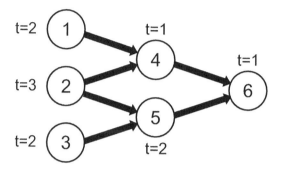

**Figure 4.3.** *Precedence relations*

The **RPW_list**, as shown in Table 4.3, is generated by the application of RPW to the problem. Tasks are ordered based on their positional weights and the **new_weight** is calculated for each task. We suppose that in three different iterations, x, y and z, the *α* parameter takes values 1, 0.5 and 0.8, respectively. The execution of the construction phase for each iteration (x, y, z) is shown in Tables 4.4, 4.5 and 4.6, respectively.

| Task | Positional weight | new_weight |
|------|-------------------|------------|
| 2 | 7 | 1/7 = 0.14 |
| 3 | 5 | 1/5 = 0.2 |
| 1 | 4 | 1/4 = 0.25 |
| 5 | 3 | 1/3 = 0.33 |
| 4 | 2 | 1/2 = 0.5 |
| 6 | 1 | 1/1 = 1 |

**Table 4.3.** *Ranked positional weight list (RPW_list)*

| RPW_list | CL | Threshold | RCL | Solution |
|---|---|---|---|---|
| 1, 2, 3, 4, 5, 6 | 1, 2, 3 | 0.25 | 1, 2, 3 | 1 (random selection) |
| 2, 3, 4, 5, 6 | 2, 3 | 0.2 | 2, 3 | 1, 2 (random selection) |
| 3, 4, 5, 6 | 3, 4 | 0.5 | 3, 4 | 1, 2, 4 (random selection) |
| 3, 5, 6 | 3 | 0.2 | 3 | 1, 2, 4, 3 |
| 5, 6 | 5 | 0.33 | 5 | 1, 2, 4, 3, 5 |
| 6 | 6 | 1 | 6 | 1, 2, 4, 3, 5, 6 |

**Table 4.4.** *Iteration x (α = 1)*

| RPW_list | CL | Threshold | RCL | Solution |
|---|---|---|---|---|
| 1, 2, 3, 4, 5, 6 | 1, 2, 3 | 0.195 | 2 | 2 |
| 1, 3, 4, 5, 6 | 1, 3 | 0.225 | 3 | 2, 3 |
| 1, 4, 5, 6 | 1, 5 | 0.29 | 1 | 2, 3, 1 |
| 4, 5, 6 | 4, 5 | 0.415 | 5 | 2, 3, 1, 5 |
| 4, 6 | 4 | 0.5 | 4 | 2, 3, 1, 5, 4 |
| 6 | 6 | 1 | 6 | 2, 3, 1, 5, 4, 6 |

**Table 4.5.** *Iteration y (α = 0.5)*

| RPW_list | CL | Threshold | RCL | Solution |
|---|---|---|---|---|
| 1, 2, 3, 4, 5, 6 | 1, 2, 3 | 0.228 | 2, 3 | 3 (random selection) |
| 1, 2, 4, 5, 6 | 1, 2 | 0.228 | 2 | 3, 2 |
| 1, 4, 5, 6 | 1, 5 | 0.314 | 1 | 3, 2, 1 |
| 4, 5, 6 | 4, 5 | 0.47 | 5 | 3, 2, 1, 5 |
| 4, 6 | 4 | 0.5 | 4 | 3, 2, 1, 5, 4 |
| 6 | 6 | 1 | 6 | 3, 2, 1, 5, 4, 6 |

**Table 4.6.** *Iteration z (α = 0.8)*

The solutions found are compared in Table 4.7.

| Iteration | Solution | Assignment of tasks | Cycle time |
|-----------|----------|---------------------|------------|
| $x\,(\alpha = 1)$ | 1, 2, 4, 3, 5, 6 | Wr 01: 1, 2<br>Wr 02: 4, 3, 5<br>Wr 03: 6 | 5 |
| $y\,(\alpha = 0.5)$ | 2, 3, 1, 5, 4, 6 | Wr 01: 2<br>Wr 02: 3, 1<br>Wr 03: 5, 4, 6 | 4 |
| $z\,(\alpha = 0.8)$ | 3, 2, 1, 5, 4, 6 | Wr 01: 3, 2<br>Wr 02: 1, 5, 4<br>Wr 03: 6 | 5 |

**Table 4.7.** *Comparison of solutions*

### 4.6.2. *The local search phase*

**Local_search_phase** (solution, max_search)
1       neighbor_solution ← ∞;
2       best_solution ← solution;
3       **for** j in max_search **do**
4               neighbor_solution ← random_swap (best_solution);
5               **if** (f(neighbor_solution, n_workstations) < f(best_solution,
                n_workstations))
6                       **then do**
7                               best_solution ← neighbor_solution;
8                       **end then;**
9       **end for;**
10      **return** best_solution;
**end local_search_phase;**

As inputs, the proposed local search function needs the *solution* found by the construction phase and the maximum number of searches, *max_search*, as a stopping criterion. The GRASP algorithm uses the local search phase in order to enhance constructed solutions in the construction phase. In our proposed hybrid reactive GRASP, a simple local search procedure is used. This procedure searches for the best neighbor solution that has a better objective value in comparison with the solution found in the construction phase, and, to find a neighbor solution, the swap operation is applied on two different tasks chosen randomly in the original solution. The swap operation must not affect the feasibility of the solution. As shown in Figure 4.4, the assignment of tasks according to the constructed solution has a possible optimal cycle time of C = 6, with an idle time of id = 3. Applying the neighborhood search on the constructed solution, by swapping tasks 3 and 4, a better optimal cycle time is found (C = 5), with an idle time of id = 1.

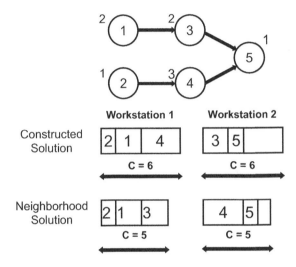

**Figure 4.4.** *Neighborhood search procedure for the ALBP*

## 4.7. Experimental examples

The developed algorithms were implemented using Python 3.7 on a PC with an Intel Core i3 1.70 GHz CPU. They were tested on three problems (small-sized problem, medium-sized problem and large-sized problem) which represent different mixed-model assembly lines. As shown in the following tables, if model *j* requires task *i* during assemblage, the column takes 1 as the value and 0 otherwise. The task time is calculated after all precedence graphs of models have been combined in one graph.

Problem 01: taken from Grzechca (2011).

| Task | Model 1 (usage) | Model 2 (usage) | Task time | Immediate successors | Number of workstations |
|------|------|------|------|------|------|
| 1 | 1 | 1 | 4.5 | 3, 4, 2, 8 | |
| 2 | 1 | 0 | 4.0 | 7 | |
| 3 | 1 | 1 | 3.0 | 7 | |
| 4 | 0 | 1 | 6.0 | 5 | |
| 5 | 0 | 1 | 7.0 | 6 | |
| 6 | 0 | 1 | 3.0 | 7 | |
| 7 | 1 | 1 | 7.0 | 11 | 4 |
| 8 | 1 | 1 | 3.0 | 9 | |
| 9 | 1 | 0 | 3.0 | 10 | |
| 10 | 0 | 1 | 7.0 | 11 | |
| 11 | 1 | 1 | 4.5 | 12 | |
| 12 | 1 | 1 | 2.0 | - | |

**Table 4.8.** *Small-sized problem*

Problem 02: taken from a website "https://assembly-line-balancing.de".

| Task | Model 1 | Model 2 | Model 3 | Task time | Immediate successors | Number of workstations |
|------|------|------|------|------|------|------|
| 1 | 1 | 0 | 1 | 0.3 | 6, 7 | |
| 2 | 1 | 1 | 1 | 0.8 | 7, 8, 9 | |
| 3 | 0 | 1 | 1 | 0.3 | 9, 10, 16 | |
| 4 | 1 | 0 | 0 | 0.4 | 11 | |
| 5 | 1 | 1 | 1 | 0.2 | 11 | |
| 6 | 1 | 0 | 0 | 0.2 | 20 | |
| 7 | 1 | 1 | 1 | 0.5 | 12 | |
| 8 | 0 | 1 | 1 | 0.5 | 12 | |
| 9 | 1 | 1 | 1 | 0.3 | 15 | |
| 10 | 0 | 0 | 1 | 0.2 | 20 | |
| 11 | 1 | 1 | 1 | 0.3 | 13, 14, 16 | 5 |
| 12 | 1 | 1 | 1 | 0.3 | 15 | |
| 13 | 1 | 0 | 1 | 0.67 | 17 | |
| 14 | 1 | 1 | 1 | 0.2 | 18, 19 | |
| 15 | 1 | 1 | 1 | 0.77 | 20 | |
| 16 | 0 | 1 | 0 | 0.1 | 20 | |
| 17 | 1 | 1 | 0 | 0.5 | 19 | |
| 18 | 1 | 1 | 1 | 0.37 | 20 | |
| 19 | 1 | 1 | 0 | 0.35 | 20 | |
| 20 | 1 | 1 | 1 | 0.1 | - | |

**Table 4.9.** *Medium-sized problem*

Problem 03: taken from Thomopoulos (2014).

| Task | Model 1 | Model 2 | Model 3 | Model 4 | Task time | Immediate successors | Number of workstations |
|------|---------|---------|---------|---------|-----------|----------------------|------------------------|
| 1 | 1 | 1 | 1 | 1 | 2.4 | 3 | |
| 2 | 1 | 0 | 1 | 1 | 3.2 | 9, 8 | |
| 3 | 1 | 1 | 1 | 0 | 1.9 | 9 | |
| 4 | 1 | 0 | 1 | 1 | 0.7 | 7 | |
| 5 | 0 | 1 | 1 | 1 | 1.9 | 6 | |
| 6 | 1 | 0 | 0 | 1 | 0.8 | 10, 11 | |
| 7 | 1 | 0 | 1 | 0 | 1.5 | 8 | |
| 8 | 0 | 1 | 1 | 1 | 2.2 | 12, 13 | |
| 9 | 1 | 0 | 1 | 1 | 0.4 | 19, 20 | |
| 10 | 1 | 1 | 1 | 1 | 0.9 | 13 | |
| 11 | 1 | 0 | 1 | 0 | 1.4 | 15, 18 | |
| 12 | 0 | 1 | 0 | 1 | 2 | - | |
| 13 | 1 | 0 | 1 | 0 | 1.3 | 14 | 6 |
| 14 | 1 | 0 | 0 | 0 | 0.9 | - | |
| 15 | 0 | 1 | 0 | 0 | 3.3 | 16, 17 | |
| 16 | 0 | 0 | 0 | 1 | 1.6 | 24 | |
| 17 | 0 | 0 | 1 | 0 | 1.3 | 23 | |
| 18 | 1 | 1 | 0 | 0 | 1.5 | 23 | |
| 19 | 0 | 1 | 1 | 0 | 3.8 | - | |
| 20 | 0 | 0 | 1 | 1 | 1.6 | 21 | |
| 21 | 1 | 1 | 0 | 1 | 1.2 | 22 | |
| 22 | 0 | 1 | 1 | 1 | 2.5 | - | |
| 23 | 1 | 1 | 1 | 1 | 2.5 | 25 | |
| 24 | 0 | 1 | 1 | 1 | 2.4 | 25 | |
| 25 | 0 | 0 | 1 | 0 | 2.2 | - | |

**Table 4.10.** *Large-sized problem*

Each problem has been solved using the following parameters:

| Problem 01 (small-size) | | | | |
|---|---|---|---|---|
| **Parameters** | **Hybrid Reactive GRASP** | | | **Basic GRASP** |
| Number of iterations | 2000 | | | 2000 |
| Max search | 15 | | | 15 |
| Stopping criterion (local search) | 10 iterations | | | 10 iterations |
| Alpha values | 0 | 0.5 | 1 | 0.5 (fixed) |
| Update period | 100 | | | - |
| Initial cycle time | Maximum task time | | | Maximum task time |
| **Problem 02 (medium-size)** | | | | |
| **Parameters** | **Hybrid Reactive GRASP** | | | **Basic GRASP** |
| Number of iterations | 2000 | | | 2000 |
| Max search | 25 | | | 25 |
| Stopping criterion (local search) | 20 iterations | | | 20 iterations |
| Alpha values | 0.1 | 0.6 | 1 | 0 |
| Update period | 100 | | | 100 |
| Initial cycle time | Maximum task time | | | Maximum task time |
| **Problem 03 (large-size)** | | | | |
| **Parameters** | **Hybrid Reactive GRASP** | | | **Basic GRASP** |
| Number of iterations | 2000 | | | 2000 |
| Max search | 35 | | | 35 |
| Stopping criterion (local search) | 30 iterations | | | 30 iterations |
| Alpha values | 0 | 0.4 | 0.9 | 0 |
| Update period | 100 | | | 100 |
| Initial cycle time | Maximum task time | | | Maximum task time |

**Table 4.11.** *Parameters used in solving proposed problems*

## 4.7.1. *Results and discussion*

Table 4.12 presents a comparison between results obtained by the proposed hybrid GRASP and the basic GRASP in solving the small-sized problem. The optimal cycle time found by the hybrid reactive GRASP is $c = 14.1$ and is the same as that obtained by the basic GRASP. The hybrid reactive GRASP requires more calculations than the basic GRASP and, for this reason, we can see that the execution time taken by the hybrid reactive GRASP is longer than the time taken by the basic GRASP. By taking the highest number of solutions obtained by different alpha values, the total number of solutions found by the hybrid reactive GRASP is 362 whereas in the basic GRASP, 33 solutions are obtained by a fixed alpha value. In the hybrid reactive GRASP, the average cycle time (14.584, 14.408, 14.448) obtained by different alpha values are almost the same. Optimal solutions obtained using the hybrid reactive GRASP and the basic GRASP are very similar, differing only in the order of tasks 7 and 10. Figure 4.5 shows the variation of probabilities of selection during execution. From the first to the final period, alpha $= 0.5$ had the highest probability of being selected compared to the other alpha values. From period 1 to period 8, alpha $= 0.8$ had higher probabilities of selection than alpha $= 1$, but from period 10 to the final period, alpha $= 1$ became the second alpha value to have the highest probability of selection.

Results for problem 01:

| | Hybrid reactive GRASP | | | Basic GRASP | |
|---|---|---|---|---|---|
| **Execution time (min)** | 09:21.622616 | | | 07:54.325025 | |
| **Number of solutions found** | $\alpha = 0$ | $\alpha = 0.5$ | $\alpha = 1$ | $\alpha = 0.2$ (fixed) | |
| | 32 | 26 | 362 | 33 | |
| **Average cycle time** | $\alpha = 0$ | $\alpha = 0.5$ | $\alpha = 1$ | - | |
| | 14.584 | 14.408 | 14.448 | | |
| **Optimal cycle time/(found by alpha)** | 14.1/(0.5) | | | 14.1 | |
| | **Workstations** | **Tasks** | | **Workstations** | **Tasks** |
| **Task assignment** | 1 | 1, 4, 8 | | 1 | 1, 4, 8 |
| | 2 | 5, 2, 3 | | 2 | 5, 2, 3 |
| | 3 | 6, 9, 7 | | 3 | 6, 9, 10 |
| | 4 | 10, 11, 12 | | 4 | 7, 11, 12 |

**Table 4.12.** *Results obtained by hybrid reactive GRASP and hybrid basic GRASP after solving problem 01*

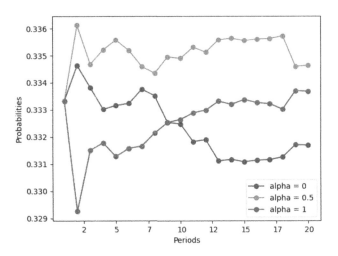

**Figure 4.5.** *Variation of probabilities during solving problem 01. For a color version of this figure, see www.iste.co.uk/chelouah/optimization.zip*

Results for problem 02:

| | Hybrid reactive GRASP | | | Basic GRASP | |
|---|---|---|---|---|---|
| Execution time (min.) | 06:20.682177 | | | 04:50.059025 | |
| Number of solutions found | $\alpha = 0$ | $\alpha = 0.6$ | $\alpha = 1$ | $\alpha = 0$ (fixed) | |
| | 47 | 683 | 671 | 47 | |
| Average cycle time | $\alpha = 0$ | $\alpha = 0.6$ | $\alpha = 1$ | - | |
| | 1.606 | 1.616 | 1.626 | | |
| Optimal cycle time/ (found by alpha) | 1.5/(0.6) | | | 1.6 | |
| | Workstations | Tasks | | Workstations | Tasks |
| Task assignment | 1 | 1, 4, 3, 5, 11 | | 1 | 2, 4, 5 |
| | 2 | 13, 2 | | 2 | 11, 1, 3, 8 |
| | 3 | 8, 14, 9, 7 | | 3 | 7, 13, 9 |
| | 4 | 17, 19, 18, 10 | | 4 | 12, 14, 17, 10, 18 |
| | 5 | 12, 15, 6, 16, 20 | | 5 | 19, 15, 6, 16, 20 |

**Table 4.13.** *Results obtained by hybrid reactive GRASP and hybrid basic GRASP after solving problem 02*

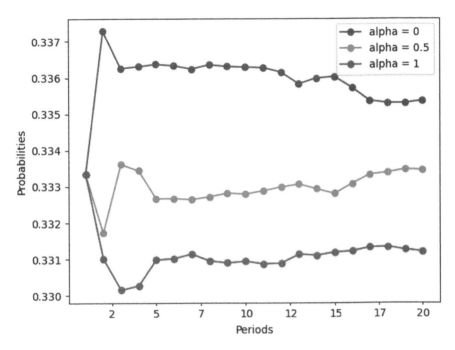

**Figure 4.6.** *Variation of probabilities during solving problem 02. For a color version of this figure, see www.iste.co.uk/chelouah/optimization.zip*

From the results in Table 4.13, obtained after solving the medium-sized problem, the optimal cycle time found by the hybrid reactive GRASP is c = 1.5, better than that found by the basic GRASP c = 1.6. The hybrid reactive GRASP took more time to solve the problem compared to the basic GRASP. The number of solutions obtained by the hybrid reactive GRASP is higher than that obtained by the basic GRASP, which is based on a fixed alpha value: 683 > 47. In the hybrid reactive GRASP, the number of solutions obtained by alpha = 0.6 and alpha = 1 are close. We can observe that the number of solutions obtained by the hybrid GRASP and the basic GRASP when alpha takes the value of 0 is the same, that is, 47. Solutions obtained by both algorithms are very different in terms of task order. Figure 4.6 shows that there was no change in the ranking of the probabilities of selection from period 1 to period 20.

Results for problem 03:

| | Hybrid reactive GRASP | | | Basic GRASP | |
|---|---|---|---|---|---|
| Execution time (min.) | 40:01.294147 | | | 35:23.330624 | |
| Number of solutions found | $\alpha = 0$ | $\alpha = 0.4$ | $\alpha = 0.9$ | $\alpha = 0$ (fixed) | |
| | 16 | 665 | 671 | 23 | |
| Average cycle time | $\alpha = 0$ | $\alpha = 0.4$ | $\alpha = 0.9$ | - | |
| | 8 | 8.340 | 8.233 | | |
| Optimal cycle time/ (found by alpha) | 7.7/(0.9) | | | 8 | |
| | Workstations | Tasks | | Workstations | Tasks |
| | 1 | 2, 1, 5 | | 1 | 5, 6, 2, 11 |
| | 2 | 3, 9, 4, 6, 19 | | 2 | 1, 15, 3, 9 |
| Task assignment | 3 | 7, 8, 11, 20, 10 | | 3 | 4, 7, 8, 16, 18 |
| | 4 | 18, 15, 21, 16 | | 4 | 17, 20, 23, 24 |
| | 5 | 22, 24, 13, 17 | | 5 | 12, 21, 10, 22, 13 |
| | 6 | 23, 12, 25, 14 | | 6 | 25, 19, 14 |

**Table 4.14.** *Results obtained by hybrid reactive GRASP and basic GRASP after solving problem 03*

The results in Table 4.14, regardless of the execution time, show that the hybrid reactive GRASP had an advantage in solving the large-sized problem by finding an optimal cycle time of c = 7.7, compared to that found by the basic GRASP: c = 8. The total number of solutions obtained by the hybrid reactive GRASP is also higher than the number obtained by the basic GRASP, that is, 671 > 16. The average cycle time, calculated using different alpha values, is not the same but is not very different. The assignment of tasks found by each algorithm is very unique in terms of task order. From Figure 4.7, we can see that the selection probabilities were stable during execution of the hybrid reactive GRASP from period 1 to period 20.

As a general comparison, the hybrid reactive GRASP is more efficient than the basic GRASP in finding optimal solutions for problems that differ in size (except for the small-sized problem) and this appears to be the result of using a set of alpha values instead of using a fixed value. In the hybrid reactive GRASP, when the alpha parameter takes a greater value, the chance of finding more solutions increases, thus increasing the chance of finding optimal solutions. Table 4.15 shows a general comparison between the hybrid reactive GRASP and the basic GRASP.

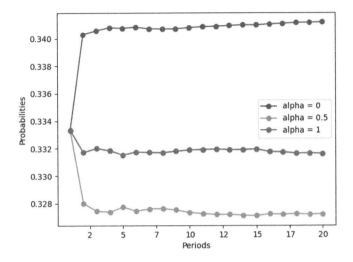

**Figure 4.7.** *Variation of probabilities during solving problem 03. For a color version of this figure, see www.iste.co.uk/chelouah/optimization.zip*

|  | Hybrid reactive GRASP | Basic GRASP |
|---|---|---|
| Execution time | Higher | Lower |
| Cycle time found in general | Good | Bad |
| Number of solutions found | Higher | Lower |
| Task assignment | Better | Worse |
| Chance of obtaining good results | Better | Worse |
| Algorithm complexity | More complex | Less complex |
| Learning from obtained solutions | Yes | No |

**Table 4.15.** *General comparison between the hybrid reactive GRASP and the basic GRASP*

## 4.8. Conclusion

The type-2 MiMALBP is an NP-hard combinatorial problem aimed at finding an optimal cycle time in order to increase the production rate of different models with similar characteristics. In this chapter, a hybrid reactive GRASP has been proposed for solving the MiMALBP-2. To build feasible solutions, a well-known heuristic referred to as RPW – used in several assembly line balancing problems – is hybridized with the reactive GRASP in the construction phase as a greedy function. Furthermore, a neighborhood search method is used in the local search phase to improve constructed solutions at each iteration. To test the proposed hybrid reactive GRASP, different size problems have been used, and the results obtained have been compared with those obtained by the basic GRASP. The comparison shows that the hybrid reactive GRASP achieves good solutions which cannot be found by the basic GRASP. This confirms that using a set of alpha values and the mechanism of learning from information obtained from previous solutions enable the algorithm to expand the search space. In addition, the comparison shows that although the hybrid reactive GRASP is more complex than the basic GRASP, the times taken for execution are close. In future research, the proposed method can be improved by proposing new hybridizations with other heuristics or metaheuristics, or by using the proposed GRASP enhancement to solve the following: mixed or simple robotic assembly line balancing problems, assembly line balancing problems with zoning constraints, two-sided assembly line balancing problems, and U-shaped and parallel assembly line balancing problems.

## 4.9. References

Aghajani, M., Ghodsi, R., Javadi, B. (2014). Balancing of robotic mixed-model two-sided assembly line with robot setup times. *The International Journal of Advanced Manufacturing Technology*, 74(5–8), 1005–1016.

Aufy, S.A. and Kassam, A.H. (2020). A consecutive heuristic algorithm for balancing a mixed-model assembly line type II using a (W-TAWH) model developed for straight and U-shaped layouts. *IOP Conference Series: Materials Science and Engineering*, 671, 012147.

Becker, C. and Scholl, A. (2006). A survey on problems and methods in generalized assembly line balancing. *European Journal of Operational Research*, 168(3), 694–715.

Çil, Z.A., Mete, S., Ağpak, K. (2017). Analysis of the type II robotic mixed-model assembly line balancing problem. *Engineering Optimization*, 49(6), 990–1009.

Çil, Z.A., Li, Z., Mete, S., Özceylan, E. (2020). Mathematical model and bee algorithms for mixed-model assembly line balancing problem with physical human–robot collaboration. *Applied Soft Computing*, 93, 106394.

Glover, F. and Kochenberger, G.A. (eds) (2003). *Handbook of Metaheuristics*. Kluwer Academic Publishers, Boston.

Grzechca, W. (ed.) (2011). *Assembly Line: Theory and Practice*. InTechOpen [Online]. Available at: http://www.intechopen.com/books/assembly-line-theory-and-practice [Accessed 28 February 2021].

Lalaoui, M. and Afia, A.E. (2019). A versatile generalized simulated annealing using type-2 fuzzy controller for the mixed-model assembly line balancing problem. *IFAC-PapersOnLine*, 52(13), 2804–2809.

Martí, R., Pardalos, P.M., Resende, M.G.C. (eds) (2018). *Handbook of Heuristics*. Springer International Publishing, Cham [Online]. Available at: http://link.springer.com/10.1007/978-3-319-07124-4 [Accessed 27 February 2021].

Prais, M. and Ribeiro, C.C. (2000). Reactive GRASP: An application to a matrix decomposition problem in TDMA traffic assignment. *INFORMS Journal on Computing*, 12(3), 164–176.

Rabbani, M., Moghaddam, M., Manavizadeh, N. (2012). Balancing of mixed-model two-sided assembly lines with multiple U-shaped layout. *The International Journal of Advanced Manufacturing Technology*, 59(9–12), 1191–1210.

Rabbani, M., Mousavi, Z., Farrokhi-Asl, H. (2016). Multi-objective metaheuristics for solving a type II robotic mixed-model assembly line balancing problem. *Journal of Industrial and Production Engineering*, 33(7), 472–484.

Raj, A.S.V., Mathew, J., Jose, P., Sivan, G. (2016). Optimization of cycle time in an assembly line balancing problem. *Procedia Technology*, 25, 1146–1153.

Ramezanian, R. and Ezzatpanah, A. (2015). Modeling and solving multi-objective mixed-model assembly line balancing and worker assignment problem. *Computers & Industrial Engineering*, 87, 74–80.

Rekiek, B. and Delchambre, A. (2006). *Assembly Line Design: The Balancing of Mixed-Model Hybrid Assembly Lines with Genetic Algorithms*. Springer, London.

Saif, U., Guan, Z., Wang, B., Mirza, J., Huang, S. (2014). A survey on assembly lines and its types. *Frontiers of Mechanical Engineering*, 9(2), 95–105.

Tang, Q., Liang, Y., Zhang, L., Floudas, C.A., Cao, X. (2016). Balancing mixed-model assembly lines with sequence-dependent tasks via hybrid genetic algorithm. *Journal of Global Optimization*, 65(1), 83–107.

Thomopoulos, N.T. (2014). *Assembly Line Planning and Control.* Springer International Publishing, Cham [Online]. Available at: http://link.springer.com/10.1007/978-3-319-01399-2 [Accessed 28 February 2021].

Yadav, A., Verma, P., Agrawal, S. (2020). Mixed model two-sided assembly line balancing problem: An exact solution approach. *International Journal of System Assurance Engineering and Management*, 11(S2), 335–348.

van Zante-de Fokkert, J.I. and de Kok, T.G. (1997). The mixed and multi model line balancing problem: A comparison. *European Journal of Operational Research*, 100(3), 399–412.

Zhang, J.-H., Li, A.-P., Liu, X.-M. (2019). Hybrid genetic algorithm for a type-II robust mixed-model assembly line balancing problem with interval task times. *Advances in Manufacturing*, 7(2), 117–132.

# PART 2

# Machine Learning

# 5

# An Interactive Attention Network with Stacked Ensemble Machine Learning Models for Recommendations

Ahlem DRIF[1], SaadEddine SELMANI[1] and Hocine CHERIFI[2]

[1] *Computer Sciences Department, Ferhat Abbas University Setif 1, Algeria*
[2] *LIB, University of Burgundy Franche-Comté, Dijon, France*

Recommender systems are broadly used to suggest goods (e.g. products, news services) that best match user needs and preferences. The main challenge comes from modeling the dependence between the various entities incorporating multifaceted information, such as user preferences, item attributes and users' mutual influence, resulting in more complex features. To deal with this issue, we design a recommender system incorporating a collaborative filtering (CF) module and a stacking recommender module. We introduce an interactive attention mechanism to model the mutual influence relationship between aspect users and items. It allows the mapping of the original data to higher order feature interactions. In addition, the stacked recommender, composed of a set of regression models and a meta-learner, optimizes the weak learners' performance with a strong learner. The developed stacking recommender considers the content for recommendation to create a profile model for each user. Experiments on

For a color version of all the figures in this chapter, see: www.iste.co.uk/chelouah/optimization.zip

real-world datasets demonstrate that the proposed algorithm can achieve more accurate predictions and higher recommendation efficiency.

## 5.1. Introduction

Recommender systems have become an integral part of e-commerce sites and other platforms, such as social networking and movie/music rendering websites. They have a massive impact on the revenue earned by these businesses and also benefit users by reducing the cognitive load of searching and sifting through an excessive amount of data. Research around recommender systems falls into three main categories: collaborative filtering (CF) approaches, content-based approaches and hybrid approaches that combine the two techniques. CF recommender systems imput the unspecified ratings because observed ratings are often highly correlated across various users and items. Content-based recommender systems use the descriptive attributes of items that are labeled with ratings as training data to create a user-specific classification or regression modeling. Hybrid recommenders provide many opportunities. Indeed, various aspects originating from different systems are combined to achieve the best of both worlds. Many researchers deploy deep learning algorithms into recommendation systems to increase accuracy and solve the cold start problem. Furthermore, deep learning has shown its effectiveness in capturing the nonlinearity of user-item interconnections. He *et al.* (2017) propose a neural architecture with the potential to learn better representations, extract features and generate users-item interaction history. In the works (Musto *et al.* 2016; Tan *et al.* 2016; Okura *et al.* 2017), the authors develop recommender systems based on recurrent neural networks (RNNs) to model the temporal dynamics and sequential evolution of content information. Tang *et al.* (2018) propose a sequential recommendation with convolutional neural networks (CNNs). Sequential patterns are learned as local features of images using convolutional filters. In addition, autoencoders prove their effectiveness in representing user-item interactions for easy and accurate collaborative filtering. Liang *et al.* (2018) propose variational autoencoders for collaborative filtering (MultiVAE).

The authors define a generative model with a multinomial likelihood representation. They use Bayesian inference for parameter estimation. Drif *et al.* (2020) propose an ensemble variational autoencoder framework for recommendations (EnsVAE). This architecture allows the transformation of the sub-recommenders' predicted utility matrix into interest probabilities based on a variational autoencoder.

Various entities drive the recommendation process, including item features, user preferences and user-item history interactions. In general, item profiles may be available in the form of descriptions of products. Similarly, users may have created profiles explicitly describing their interests. Numerous works propose modeling the context-dependence between these different entities. However, there is less work exploring users' mutual influence on the item. In this chapter, we introduce a novel framework that models higher order user-item features, as well as interactions between users and items in latent spaces to tackle these limitations. Our main contributions are summarized as follows:

– The proposed Interactive Personalized Recommender (IPRec) learns the weight of interactions between user actions and various features, such as user-item profile information and side information; the pieces of side information are the attributes. For example, users might be associated with a demographic, such as their name, address, age, gender or profession. An item, such as a movie, might have side information associated with it, such as the title, actors, directors and so on. Attributes are not only associated with the user and item dimensions, but also with the contextual dimensions. Providing additional side information improves rating prediction accuracy. The two components developed are (1) an interactive neural attention network-based collaborative filtering recommender; and (2) a stacked content-based recommender. Integrating these components optimizes the recommendation task. Approximating the results of this mixture model can be attempted using a weighted average of the predictions of the two different models.

– The interactive neural attention network-based collaborative filtering recommender exploits the encoding ability of the interactive attention between users and items. It learns the most relevant weights representing users' mutual influence on the item. Therefore, it boosts the accuracy of recommender systems by indicating which higher order feature interactions are informative for the prediction.

– The stacked content-based recommender is composed of a stack of machine learning (ML) models. Combining the predictive power of its constituents leads to improved predictive accuracy. This recommender creates a profile model for each user and extracts valuable features from the item-based side information.

– The empirical evaluation demonstrates that the proposed framework of "IPRec" significantly outperforms state-of-the-art baselines on several real-world datasets.

The remainder of the chapter is organized as follows. Related literature is described in section 5.2. Section 5.3 presents the proposed architecture. Experimental settings are presented in Section 5.4. Experimental results are reported and discussed in section 5.5. Section 5.6 summarizes the conclusions.

## 5.2. Related work

### 5.2.1. *Attention network mechanism in recommender systems*

Although several deep learning models provide a satisfactory solution to recommendation systems, they are less effective when new items do not accumulate enough data. The attention mechanism (Vaswani *et al.* 2017) has attracted interest from researchers as a solution to this cold start problem in recommendation systems. The attention mechanism enables the model to impose different weights on inputs, depending on the context. Tay *et al.* (2018) propose a multi-pointer learning scheme that learns to combine multiple views of user-item interactions based on the pointer networks. They apply a co-attention mechanism to select the most informative review from the review bank of each user and item, respectively. Liu *et al.* (2021) have developed a sequential neural recommendation to model users' long- and short-term preferences through aspect-level reviews. The model embeds user-related and item-related reviews into a continuous low-dimensional dense vector space using aspect-aware convolution and self-attention. Ying *et al.* (2018) introduce a memory attention-aware recommender system based on a memory component and an attentional mechanism to learn deep adaptive user representations.

Kang *et al.* (2018) propose a self-attention-based sequential model that allows long-term semantics to be captured, but makes its predictions based on relatively few actions. At each time step, the model seeks to identify which items are relevant from a user's action history and use them to predict the next item. Zhou *et al.* (2018) developed a Deep Interest Network (DIN) by designing a local activation unit to adaptively learn the representation of user interests from historical behaviors concerning a particular ad. The algorithm learns to aggregate the sequence of users' history to form a user embedding. User embedding is regarded as the weighted sum of item embeddings, and an attention network obtains the weight of each item embedding. In Yakhchi *et al.* (2020), the authors propose a Deep Attention-based Sequential (DAS) model. It deals with the representation of false dependencies between items when modeling a user's long-term preferences by attention mechanism.

The recommender engine learns to aggregate the users' history sequence to compute the attention weighted sum of item embeddings in previous work. By contrast, the proposed framework does not only learn the interaction between user interests and item embeddings, but it also adds a new component to learn the mutual influence generated by the contributions of items that carry collaborative signals on user decisions, helping to account for complex user-item interactions.

## 5.2.2. Stacked machine learning for optimization

Ensemble machine learning algorithms enhance the predictions of simple and understandable models. They require a more sophisticated technique to prepare the model and more computational resources to train the model. They are wrappers for a set of smaller, concrete pre-trained models. The wrapper then follows a well-defined strategy to aggregate their predictions into a final one. Several ensemble approaches have been proposed, such as voting classifiers, bagging and pasting, boosting and stacking (Pavlyshenko *et al.* 2018). Stacking is a rather simple idea that can leverage one of the most powerful ensemble models possible. Instead of using a trivial aggregation function such as "mode" and "mean", stacking uses a meta-learner model that learns the mapping from lower predictions to the label. A stacked generalization ensemble can use the set of predictions as a context and conditionally decide to weigh the input predictions differently, potentially resulting in better performance (Wolpert *et al.* 1992).

Numerous approaches combining multiple classifiers based on meta-learning have been proposed. Reid and Grudic (2009) apply regularization to linear stack generalization at the combiner level to avoid the over-fitting problem and improve performance. Jurek *et al.* (2014) propose a meta-learning-based approach incorporating an unsupervised learning method at the meta-level. All of the base classifiers initially classify each instance from the validation set (Jurek *et al.* 2014). Outputs of the classification process are considered later as new attributes. The K-Means clustering technique divides all instances from the validation set into clusters according to the new attributes. The collection of clusters is considered as a final meta-model, where each cluster represented one class. Deng *et al.* (2012b) propose a kernel deep convex networks (K-DCN) architecture composed of a variable number of modules stacked together to form the deep architecture. The deep stacking network (DSN) enabling parallel training on very large-scale datasets is proposed in Deng *et al.* (2012a).

For recommendation, Otunba *et al.* (2019) stack an ensemble of a generalized matrix factorization (GMF) and multi-layer perceptron (MLP) that propagates the prediction from constituent models through other constituent models to final output. Bao *et al.* (2009) combine predictions from multiple recommendation engines to generate a single prediction. They first define each component recommendation engine as a level-1 predictor. Then they learn a level-2 predictor, using a meta-learning algorithm, with predictions of the component engines as meta-features. The level-2 predictor can be either a linear function or a nonlinear function based on the meta-learning algorithm employed. They define a new meta-feature which represents properties of the input users/items as additional meta-features. It allows the combination of component recommendation engines at runtime based on user/item characteristics. In Da *et al.* (2016), the authors develop three ensemble approaches based on multimodal interactions. Different types of users feedback processed individually by traditional recommendation algorithms are combined in order to optimize the modeling of users' profiles. Unlike previous works with stacked recommenders, the stacking content-based recommender considers the content for recommendation to create a profile model for each user. Its main advantage is the ability of the embedding representation to integrate the side information in the hybrid architecture.

## 5.3. Interactive personalized recommender

The proposed framework is a mixture of a collaborative interactive attention network recommender and a deep-stacked recommendation component. It gives more capacity to model the interaction characteristic. We build a joint user and item interactive attention maps to predict a distribution over the items. The main idea behind this attention network model is to learn the most relevant weights that represent the users' mutual influence on the item. Figure 5.1 illustrates the mutual interactions between users and items. For example, both user 1 and user 3 rate the same item. User 2 and user 3 rate item 4. Therefore, we deduce that item 4 can be interesting for user 1. This is a kind of a first-order interaction. In the same way, we can observe the interaction between user 1 and user 2 regarding item 6. Moreover, we deduce a mutual influence that can be defined as entities dependencies of more than one order interaction level. For example, user 3 is influenced by the interest of user 2 (a similar user to user 1) generating an interest toward item 6. This component aims at modeling the context-dependence between the different entities by integrating the user-item interaction and the users' mutual influence on items.

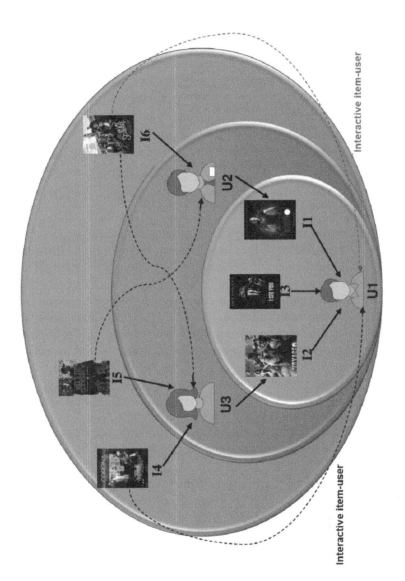

**Figure 5.1.** *The Interactive Personalized Recommender framework models the mutual influence between the different entities*

### 5.3.1. *Notation*

A robust way to formulate a recommendation task is to approach it as a prediction problem. Thus, the interactions between users and items are represented in the form of a utility matrix R. For each user $u \in U$, the recommender system attempts to predict all of the unspecified ratings $\hat{r}_u$. Let $U = u_1, u_2, ..., u_n$ and $I = i_1, i_2, ..., i_m$ be the sets of users and items, respectively, where $n$ is the number of users, and $m$ is the number of items. The matrix factorization algorithm decomposes a matrix $M_{(n \times m)}$ into two matrices $P \in \mathbb{IR}^{N \times K}$ and $Q \in \mathbb{IR}^{M \times K}$. A user's interaction on an item is modeled as the inner product (interaction function) of their latent vectors. Let $ui$ be the ground truth rating assigned by the user $u$ on the item $i$. The utility matrix is defined as:

$$\widehat{R_{ui}} = P\,Q^T = \sum_{k=1}^{K} p_{uk} q_{ki} \tag{5.1}$$

where $K$ denotes the dimension of the latent space. Latent factor models are a state-of-the-art methodology for model-based collaborative filtering. Matrix factorization techniques are a class of widely successful latent factor models that attempt to characterize items and users using vectors of factors inferred from item rating patterns. High correspondence between item and user factors leads to a recommendation. The matrix factorization performs remarkably well on dyadic data prediction tasks. However, it fails to capture the heterogeneous nature of objects and their interactions, as well as failing to model the context in which a rating is given. In fact, latent factor models are inherently linear, which limits their modeling capacity for recommendation. Recently, a growing body of work adding crafted nonlinear features into the linear latent factor models has been introduced, powered by neural networks. In this chapter, we use the GloVe embedding with 50 dimensions in order to represent the latent space.

A training set T is consisted of N tuples. Each tuple $(u, i, \hat{r}ui)$ denotes a rating by user $u$ for item $i$. For a given predicted rating matrix, the normalization is done on a user-basis. For each user $\in U$, the minimal rating min = min ($r^s(ui)$) and the maximal rating max = max ($r^s(ui)$) are extracted. Then, the min/max scaling function is applied to $\hat{R}$ as follows:

$$minmax(x) = \frac{x - min}{max - min} \quad \forall x \in \hat{r}(ui) \tag{5.2}$$

The normalization step can be performed before, during or after the generation of the rating matrix. Moreover, one can easily adjust neural-based recommenders for this purpose. Sigmoid is used as the activation function for the output layer, ultimately skipping the use of the Min/Max scaler. In the remainder of this chapter, we use the notations given in Table 5.1.

| Symbol | Definitions and descriptions |
|---|---|
| $r_{ui}$ | The rating value of item $i$ by user $u$ |
| $P \in \mathrm{IR}^{N \times K}$ | The latent factors for user $u$ |
| $Q \in \mathrm{IR}^{M \times K}$ | The latent factors for item $i$ |
| $g_1(), g_2()$ | The LSTM models applied to users and items, respectively |
| $e_u$ | The user embedding layer |
| $e_i$ | The item embedding layer |
| $a^*u$ | Attention network of user $u$ |
| $a^*i$ | Attention network of item $i$ |
| $a_u$ | The final attention weights of user $u$ |
| $a_i$ | The final attention weights of item $i$ |
| $\wp$ | Each possible combination of the prediction set |
| $C$ | The number of observed ratings |
| $\oplus$ | The concatenation operator |
| $r'_{ij}$ | A scalar referring to the rating of an item $i$ as specified by user $u$ |
| $W, b$ | The weight and bias in the interactive attention neural network. |

**Table 5.1.** *Notations*

## 5.3.2. *The interactive attention network recommender*

The first component of the proposed framework is an interactive attention network recommender. Its role is to discover latent features that exhibit mutual influence between users and items. The attention mechanism has proved to be effective in various machine learning tasks such as image/video captioning (Rital *et al.* 2002, 2005; Xu *et al.* 2015) and machine translation (Bahdanau *et al.* 2014). It allows different parts to contribute when compressing them to a single representation. The attention mechanism is a process that mimics the actions of the human brain to selectively concentrate on a few relevant things, while ignoring others in deep neural networks. The attention mechanism emerged naturally from problems that deal with time-varying data. The core idea is that we can look at all of the different words at the same time and learn to pay attention to the correct ones depending on the task at hand.

The attention mechanism, which is simply a notion of memory, gained from attending at multiple inputs through time, emerged from problems that deal with time-varying data.

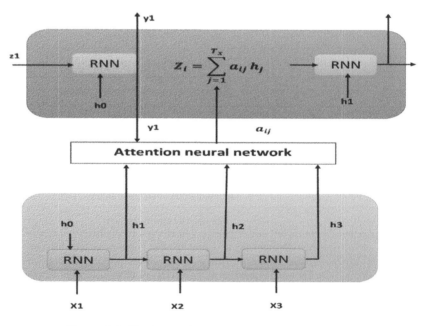

**Figure 5.2.** *The Interactive Personalized Recommender*
*framework models the mutual influence between the different entities*

The attention network is based on the encoder and decoder which are stacked RNN layers. The encoder processes the input and produces one compact representation, called z, from all of the input time steps. It can be regarded as a compressed format of the input. The attention ensures a direct connection with each timestamp, in which the context vector z should have access to all parts of the input sequence instead of just the last one (see Figure 5.2). Thus, applying a co-attention mechanism in the context of collaborative filtering recommendation allows the discrimination of the items that are interesting for users, even those with no previous interaction, through higher attention weights.

The attention network-CF approach is inspired by the paper by Chen *et al.* (2017). Previous works put more emphasis on only learning the complex relationship between the target users (or items) and their neighbors by attention network. Here, we aim to exploit the encoding ability of the interactive attention between the users and the items to learn the most relevant weights that represent the users' mutual influence on the item. The underlying idea is that some correlation between users and items with particular characteristics can reveal the possibility that an item is interesting for similar users (see Figure 5.3).

First, the list of users $U$ and the list of items $I$ are fed into two different embedding layers: $e_u$ and $e_i$, respectively. It makes it possible to capture some useful latent properties of users $p_u$ and items $q_i$. Each of these embedding layers is chained with a long short-term memory (LSTM) layer. The LSTM (Sherstinsky *et al.* 2020) is a variety of RNNs that can learn long sequences with long time lags. The advantage of this architecture is that LSTM units are recurrent modules, which enable long-range learning. Each LSTM state has two inputs, the current feature vector and the output vector of the previous state, $h_{t-1}$, and one output vector $h_t$. The LSTM based representation learning can be denoted as follows:

$$h_{tu} = g_1(p) \qquad\qquad [5.3]$$

$$h_{ti} = g_2(q) \qquad\qquad [5.4]$$

The learned representation can be denoted as $H$ and $H$, respectively. The respective dimensions of $H$ and $H$ are $d \times n$ and $d \times m$ (d-dimensional vectors of LSTM).

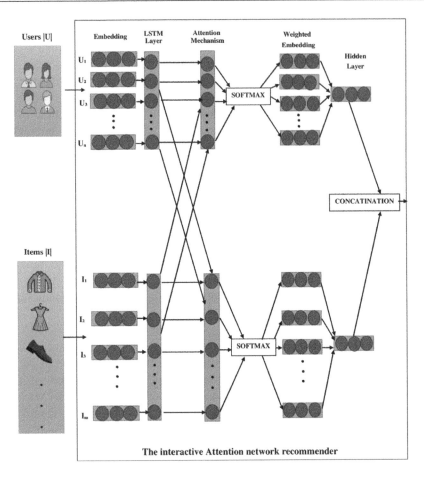

**Figure 5.3.** *The interactive attention network recommender*

The attention mechanism is used to project the users and items embedding inputs into a common representation space. The proposed neural attention framework can model the high-order nonlinear relationship between users and items and mutual influence. Indeed, interactive attention on both the users and items is applied. The final rating prediction is based on all the interactive users and items features. This mechanism is explored as follows: joint user and item interactive attention maps are built and combined recursively to predict a distribution over the items. First, a matrix $L \in \mathrm{IR}^{n \times m}$ as $L = tanh\left(H_p^\top W_{pq} H_q\right)$ is computed, where $W_{pq}$ is a $d \times d$

matrix of learnable parameters. The feature interaction attention map is given by:

$$\alpha_p^* = tanh\left(W_p H_p + \left(W_q H_q\right)L^T\right) \tag{5.5}$$

$$\alpha_q^* = tanh\left(W_q H_q + \left(W_p H_p\right)L\right) \tag{5.6}$$

Therefore, the interactive attention models the mutual interactions between the user latent factors and item latent factors by applying a tangent function (tanh). Subsequently, an attention distribution is calculated as a probability distribution over the embedding space. The attention weights are generated through the softmax function:

$$\alpha_i = Softmax\left(f\left(a_p^*\right)\right) \tag{5.7}$$

$$\alpha_i = Softmax\left(f\left(\alpha_q^*\right)\right) \tag{5.8}$$

The function $f$ is a multi-layer neural network (MLP). Besides, the attention vectors of high-order interaction features can be generated by a weighted sum using the derived attention weights or a *sigmoid* function, given by $\beta_p$ and $\beta$. These latent spaces of users and items are then concatenated as follows:

In order to form the predicted score $R_{ui}$, the concatenation spaces are fed into a dense layer with a sigmoid activation function as follows:

$$f_1 = [\beta_u \oplus \beta_i] \tag{5.9}$$

$$\hat{R}_{ui} = f(f_1) \tag{5.10}$$

During the training phase, a grid-search method is used to learn the model parameters and set the cost function as defined below:

$$L\left(R_{ui}, \widehat{R_{ui}}\right) = \frac{1}{|C|}\Sigma_{(u,i)\in C}\left(R_{ui} - \widehat{R_{ui}}\right) \tag{5.11}$$

The model predicts interest probabilities for each possible combination of the prediction set $\wp$, as shown in Algorithm 1.

---

**Algorithm 1:** The Interactive Attention network recommender.

---

**Input**   : $U$: list of user ids : size $n$
  $I$: list of item ids: size $m$
  $R$: list of groundtruth ratings per couple $(u, i)$: size $s \leq n \times m$
  $embU$ : user's embedding
  $embI$ : item's embedding
  $lstmU$ : LSTM of user
  $lstmI$ : LSTM of item
  $attU$ : iteractif user-user
  $attI$ : iteractif item-item
  $coatt$: iteractif user-item
  $InteractiveAttention$: Neural Network of Attention mechanism
  $\Theta_f$: the model parameters.
**Output:** $\hat{R}$: predicted utility matrix: size $(n \times m)$
**begin**

> // Preparing data to be passed to the network
> **foreach** $u \in U$ **do** $R_i = \text{minmax}(R_i)$ ;
> $\wp = U \times I$ ;                          /* cartesian product */
> $D = \emptyset$ ;                             /* training set */
> **foreach** $(u, i) \in D$ **do** $D \leftarrow (u, i, R_{ui})$ **if** $R_{ui} \neq null$ **else** $(u, i, 0)$ ;
> // Creating User  Item embedding $U_i$
> $embU = \text{Embedding}(D)$ ;
> $embI = \text{Embedding}(I)$ ;
> // Following LSTM layer to the User  Item embedding
> $lstmU = \text{LSTM}(embU)$ ;
> $lstmI = \text{LSTM}(embU)$ ;
> // Applying Attention mechanism
> $attU = \text{Attention}(lstmU)$ ;
> $attI = \text{Attention}(lstmU)$ ;
> // CoAttention-Class()
> $coatt = \text{CoAttention}(lstmU, lstmI)$ ;
> // Concatenating The outputs of User embedding and Item
>    embedding after applying CoAttention Mechanism to have a
>    single output of the component which is user-item space
> $A = attU, attI, coatt$ ;
> $InteractiveAttention = \text{BuildModel}(A, \Theta)$ ;
> $InteractiveAttention.\text{trainModel}(D)$;
> **return** $\hat{R}_{ui} = InteractiveAttention.\text{predict}(\wp)$

**end**

---

### 5.3.3. *The stacked content-based filtering recommender*

The content-based recommender system injects item attributes as a deciding factor for recommendations. The stacked recommender generates a user profile for each user in the form of a learned model. First, the recommender extracts "tags" from item descriptions or reviews and uses them to calculate each item's embedding vector with the help of Stanford's pre-trained GloVe vectors (Pennington *et al.* 2014). Afterward, the recommender employs the stacking ensemble learning technique to learn the profile for each user, as shown in Figure 5.4.

Let $L = \{L_1, L_2, ..., L_l\}$ be different regression models, and $x_{train}$ be the training dataset. $U$ and $emb$ are independent variables. The base regression models' hyperparameters are $\forall l \in L$ $\theta_l$. The number and the type of regression algorithms are tunable.

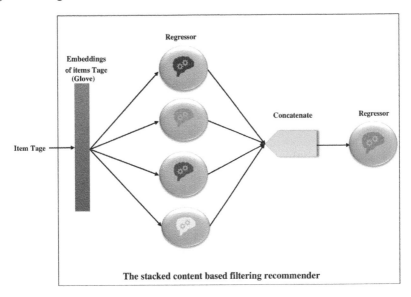

**Figure 5.4.** *The stacked content-based filtering recommender*

Each $l \in L$ is trained separately with the same training dataset. Each model provides predictions for the outcomes (R), which are then cast into a meta-learner (blender). In other words, the $L$ predictions of each regressor become features for the blender. The latter can be any model, such as linear regression, SVR or Decision Tree,...etc., as expressed in [5.11].

$$f_{featu\,e}(x) = f_{S\,K}(L_1(x), L_2(x), ..., L_l(x)) \qquad [5.12]$$

where the weight vector $w$ is learned by a meta-learner.

A blender model can then be defined and tuned with its hyperparameters $O_{blende}$. It is then trained on the outputs of the stack $L$. It learns the mapping between the outcome of the stacked predictors and the final ground-truth ratings. The expression of the final prediction is as follows:

$$\widehat{R_{BL}} = \phi\left(f_{blender}(x), f_{STK}(L_1(x), L_2(x), ..., L_l(x))\right) \qquad [5.13]$$

In order to train the two recommenders needed for the task at hand, one applies an aggregation function to merge their outputs into a single utility matrix. The IPRec framework uses the simple unweighted average aggregation function followed by encoder layers. The final predicted utility matrix $ui$ is as follows.

$$\widehat{r_{ui}} = f_{agg}\left(\widehat{R_{ui}}, \widehat{R_{BL}}\right) \qquad [5.14]$$

## 5.4. Experimental settings

This section briefly reviews the datasets, evaluation measures and alternative techniques used in the experiments.

### 5.4.1. *The datasets*

*MovieLens dataset*: It presents real, timestamped 5-star ratings, as given by users of the MovieLens Website on different films. Furthermore, GroupLens supplied movies with their genomic tags to describe them in a machine-friendly manner. The dataset has several versions, depicted by the total number of ratings packaged in the files (Harper *et al*. 2015). They are:

– *MovieLens 25M*: this huge dataset offers 25 million ratings, applied to 62,000 movies by 162,000 users. It was released in December 2019.

– *MovieLens 20M*: the predecessor of the previous version offers 20 million ratings given by 138,000 users over 27,000 movies. It was first released in April 2015 and last updated in October 2016. Its support has been discontinued ever since.

– *MovieLens 10M*: it is a rather old dataset, dated February 2009. It provides 10 million ratings applied to 10,000 movies by 72,000 users.

– *MovieLens 1M*: this is the most popular MovieLens Dataset version. It is widely used for research and benchmarking recommender systems. It contains 1 million ratings from 6,000 users over 4,000 movies. Its exact specifications are in Table 5.2.

– *MovieLens Small*: a small subset of the latest MovieLens Dataset version (currently MovieLens 25M), which usually contains 100,000 ratings applied to 9,000 movies over 600 users. It is generally used for educational purposes only, such as learning recommender systems.

| # of Users | 6,040 |
|---|---|
| # of Movies | 3,883 |
| # of Ratings | 1,000,209 |
| Sparsity % | 95.5% |
| Item Description | Genomic Tags |
| User Description | Demographics |

**Table 5.2.** *MovieLens 1M specifications*

### 5.4.2. *Evaluation metrics*

Two influential metrics are adopted to evaluate the predictive accuracy of the recommendation framework: the mean average precision and the normalized discounted cumulative gain.

The mean average precision (*MAP*) is a popular metric in measuring the accuracy of information retrieval, and object detection systems (Lasfar *et al.* 2000; Labatut *et al.* 2012). For a set of queries $Q$, MAP calculates the mean of the average precision scores for each query $q \in Q$, The result is always a value between 0 and 1, where the higher the score, the better the accuracy.

$$Pr = \frac{TP}{TP+FP} \qquad [5.15]$$

$$MAP = \frac{\sum_{q=1}^{Qavg}(Pr_q)}{Q} \qquad [5.16]$$

where:

– *TP*: True Positives: positive items that are detected by the system as positive;

– *FP*: False Positives: negative items that are detected by the system as positive;

– Pr: the precision value considering only q-first items.

In recommender systems, we usually trim the results to return the top-k elements, where $1 <k<=q$. The number of elements k depends on use: a system may show the top three trending items or the best 10 items that match the taste of the current user, etc. Therefore, a more flexible variant of *MAP*, referred to by *MAP* @, is used. The latter performs the same calculation procedure but over the smaller set of top-k elements:

$$MAP@k = \frac{\sum_{q=1}^{kavg}(Pr_q)}{K}$$                           [5.17]

The rank in which recommendations are shown has an impact on the performance of a recommender system. The normalized discounted cumulative gain (*NDCG*) is a ranking quality evaluation metric that is also used in information retrieval systems (Demirkesen *et al.* 2008; Balakrishnan *et al.* 2012). NDCG measures the *normalized* usefulness of items based on their positions in the resulting list by calculating the ratio between discounted cumulative gain (DCG) of the recommended items over the DCG of their ideal ranking. The result $\in$ [0 −1] indicates the gain of the recommender. Hence, the higher this value, the better.

$$NDCG = \frac{DCG}{iDCG}$$                           [5.18]

$$DCG = \sum_{q=1}^{Q} \frac{2^{Pos(q)-1}}{\log_2(i+1)}$$                           [5.19]

$$iDCG = \sum_{q=1}^{Q} \frac{2^{iPos(q)-1}}{\log_2(i+1)}$$                           [5.20]

where:

– *DCG*: the discounted cumulative gain of the predicted item set ranked by the recommender system;

– *i DCG*: the discounted cumulative gain of the ideal ranking of predicted items;

– Pos(q): the position of q, as predicted by the recommender system;

– iPos(q): the ideal position of q.

*NDCG@k* is used to evaluate the ranking quality of the top-k recommended items.

### 5.4.3. *Baselines*

The personalized recommender system is compared with the following recommender systems:

– *Interactive attention network recommender*: it is a novel collaborative filtering recommender system. This state-of-the-art technique is based on the co-attention mechanism. It takes its power from discriminating the importance of different feature interactions between all of the entities (user-user, item-item and users-item).

– *The stacked content-based filtering recommender*: this content-based recommender system is proposed in Drif *et al.* (2020). The stacked ensemble exploits the strengths of embedding representation and the stacking ensemble learning for modeling the content. Here, we adopt a Random forest (Chollet *et al.* 2021) model as a meta-learner because it improves the predictive accuracy by fitting several decision tree classifiers on various sub-samples of the dataset.

– *Neural Collaborative Filtering (NCF)* (He *et al.* 2017): this recommender system applies the MLP to learn the user-item interaction function.

– *Variational Autoencoders for Collaborative Filtering* (MultiVAE) (Liang *et al.* 2018): this technique models the collaborative information in a multinomial distribution to sample prediction for items on the long tail.

– *EnsVAE:Ensemble Variational Autoencoders for Recommendations* (Drif *et al.* 2020): the EnsVAE-compliant recommender system provides simple guidelines to build hybrids for a plethora of use cases. It is adjusted to output interest probabilities by learning the distribution of each item's ratings and attempts to provide various novel items pertinent to users.

## 5.5. Experiments and discussion

### 5.5.1. *Hyperparameter analysis*

This section depicts the hyperparameters analysis step performed separately on each recommender. The proposed implementation method is based on Keras (Chollet *et al.* 2021). In addition, the latter runs over Tensorflow (Abadi *et al.* 2016), which ensures the ability to reproduce the same results by replicating the same developing and evaluating environment. The machine used throughout the whole development and evaluation phases is a MacBook Pro (16 GB 1600 MHz DDR3, GPU 2.2GHz 6-core Intel Core i7).

The stacked content-based recommender is composed of a set of regression models and a meta-learner. The idea behind stacking is to enhance weak learners with a strong learner. Therefore, a small group of weak learners that exhibit different errors would perform the same as a large set of powerful learners with similar errors (Géron *et al.* 2019). Consequently, we perform the analysis on  stacks 1–5 and focus on the learning algorithms used by each learner, alongside the meta-learner's hyperparameters.

The first step is to find the combination of regression models that compose the best stack. A grid search is performed over six algorithms: *polynomial-kernel support vector machines* (SVM$_{poly}$) (Singh *et al.* 2016), *RBF-kernel support vector machines* (SVM$_{rbf}$), *decision trees* (DT), *automatic relevance detection regression* (ARD), the simple *linear regression* (LR) and the Random Forest. Table 5.3 reports the results of the top 5 stacks for k= 10, 30 and 50.

| Stack | Mean Average Precision | | | Normalized DCG | | |
|---|---|---|---|---|---|---|
| | MAP@10 | MAP@30 | MAP@50 | NDCG@10 | NDCG@30 | NDCG@50 |
| Stack 1 | 0.75 | 0.72 | 0.7 | 0.62 | 0.71 | 0.74 |
| Stack 2 | 0.79 | 0.75 | 0.73 | 0.65 | 0.72 | 0.76 |
| Stack 3 | 0.80 | 0.77 | 0.76 | 0.66 | 0.73 | 0.76 |
| Stack 4 | 0.82 | 0.78 | 0.77 | 0.66 | 0.75 | 0.77 |
| Stack 5 | 0.8 | 0.78 | 0.76 | 0.65 | 0.73 | 0.76 |

**Table 5.3.** *The best scoring stacked content-based filtering recommenders*

Stack 4 exhibits the higher score compared to the other stacks. The structure of each stack is as follows:

- *Stack 1*: DT – LR – SVM$_{rbf}$ | ARD

- *Stack 2*: LR – DT – ARD | SVM$_{poly}$

- *Stack 3*: DT – LR – SVR$_{poly}$ | ARD

- *Stack 4*: LR – SVR$_{poly}$ – ARD | Random Forest

- *Stack 5*: LR – SVR$_{poly}$ – Random Forest| ARD

The second step is to fine-tune the stack's learners and the meta-learners hyperparameters. Here, we present the results of fine-tuning the Stack base Random Forest meta-learner. A grid search algorithm over Random Forest hyperparameters, namely: $n_{estimators}$ *(the number of trees in the forest)*, $max_{depth}$ *(the maximum number of levels in each decision tree)*, $max_{features}$ *(the maximum number of features considered for splitting a node)*, $min_{sample\ Leaf}$ *(min number of data points allowed in a leaf node)*, $min_{sample\ Split}$ *(the minimum number of data points placed in a node before the node is split)*, is performed. The evaluation metric used is the normalized discounted cumulative gain (NDCG) at k = 10. Figure 5.5 shows the changes in NDCG scores while tweaking these hyperparameters.

The final meta-learner hyperparameters for the stacked recommender are as follows: $n_{estimators} = 300$, $max_{depth} = 40$,

$$max_{feature} = 2, min_{sample\ Leaf} = 4, min_{sample\ Split} = 2.$$

We developed an interactive attention network recommender that learns the interaction between the users and items and the mutual influence between the items and user interaction. The predicted utility matrix is generated based on the learned embeddings. Figure 5.6 illustrates the hyperparameters analysis.

For each hyperparameter, a range of values is explored to find the best set of hyperparameters. They are: the dimensions of the embedding $a \in [30, 100]$, the number of dense layers after $o \in [2, 20]$, the number of neurons per dense layer $r \in [30, 150]$, the activation function used in the dense layers $<Y \in \{ selu, elu, relu\}$ and the optimizer $Jc \in \{ sgd, adam, adagrad\}$. Results

show that the best performance is achieved for the following settings: $a = 50$, $o = 03$, $r = 100$, $<Y = elu$, $Jc = Adam$.

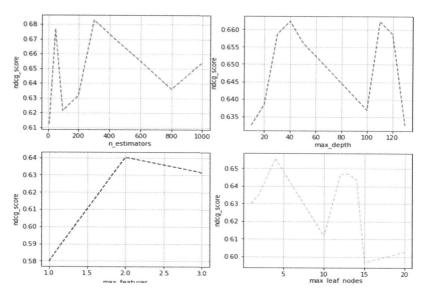

**Figure 5.5.** *Hyperparameter searching for the stack-based random forest*

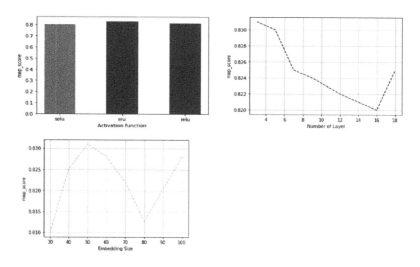

**Figure 5.6.** *Hyperparameters analysis for interactive attention network recommender*

## 5.5.2. *Performance comparison with the baselines*

To provide a better insight into the interactive attention network recommender results, we visualize a sample of the interactive co-attention weights for 10 items and four users. Figure 5.7 shows that this recommender constructs a user-item co-attention map for the final rating prediction. It identifies the most relevant weights that represent users' mutual influence on the item. This is due to its ability to capture complementary information from each user contribution and combine them to predict the utility matrix. Indeed, the co-attention module emphasizes the dependencies between the different entities.

Table 5.4 presents the recommendation performance of all methods on MovieLens. The proposed framework outperforms all baselines according to the mean average precision. The most likely reason is that the IPRec can model the higher order feature interactions. Figure 5.8 represents the MAP@k performance versus k-top items. IPRec generates a personalized recommendation, as the MAP measure represents the fraction of relevant items in the top k recommendations averaged over all of the users.

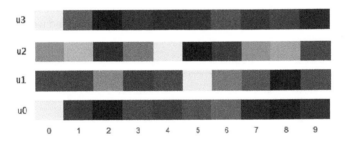

**Figure 5.7.** *Visualization of the interactive co-attention weights for 10 items and four users, dark colors refer to low attention weights*

To put it differently, IPRec can recall the relevant items for the user better than the other models. It acquires the user-item interaction and creates a user personalized task recommendation justifying its high recorded scores. In addition, both the interactive attention recommender and EnsVAE recommender produce competitive empirical results. For example, the IPRec, EnsVAE and Inter-active attention recommenders achieve MAP@10=0.89, MAP@10=0.87 and MAP@10=0.86, respectively, which are higher than the baselines. The MultiVAE models the collaborative information in the form of a multinomial distribution to sample the likelihood of presenting certain items to certain users. However, it scores weak MAP values because it does not model a rich semantic representation of data. The neural collaborative filtering (NCF) method  gives a good score with k=10, MAP@10=0.74 due to the modeling of the interaction between user and item features.

| Recommender Systems | Mean Average Precision | | | Normalized DCG | | |
|---|---|---|---|---|---|---|
| | MAP@10 | MAP@30 | MAP@50 | NDCG@10 | NDCG@30 | NDCG@50 |
| Interactive attention recommender | 0.86 | 0.84 | 0.83 | **0.72** | **0.78** | **0.8** |
| Stacked recommender | 0.82 | 0.78 | 0.77 | 0.67 | 0.74 | 0.77 |
| IPRec | **0.89** | **0.87** | **0.86** | 0.55 | 0.65 | 0.69 |
| EnsVAE | 0.87 | 0.84 | 0.82 | 0.7 | 0.75 | 0.77 |
| MultiVAE | 0.62 | 0.58 | 0.54 | 0.57 | 0.62 | 0.65 |
| NCF | 0.74 | 0.68 | 0.65 | 0.68 | 0.73 | 0.76 |

**Table 5.4.** *Recommendation accuracy scores (%) of compared methods conducted on MovieLens 1M dataset. We generate Top 10, 30 and 50 items for each user. The best performance of MAP@k and NDCG@k are highlighted with a bold font*

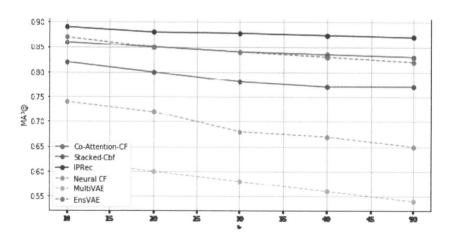

**Figure 5.8.** *Results of the comparison on MovieLens dataset. Evaluation of the performance of top-K recommended lists, in terms of MAP. The ranking position K ranges from 1 to 50*

As shown in Figure 5.9, we observe that the interactive attention recommender (Co-attention-CF) records a high NDCG score on the MovieLens dataset. In other words, the rank of an item in its top-k recommendation list is close to the one observed in the ground-truth list. Applying the attention mechanism enhances the modeling of user-item interaction. Indeed, the more positive the users toward an item, the more likely it is recommended by users with similar preferences. Note that the EnsVAE recommender and the stacked recommender still exhibit good NDCG scores. The stacked recommender is effective in obtaining the user's overall interest built by the stack's learners. It captures the side-information to create a profile model for each user, while optimizing the stack's learners' objective function.

The IPRec scores are lower compared to the above models. Due to the average aggregation of the two recommenders, it reduces the rating probabilities of some items. Given that NDCG is a ranking metric, this reduction may cause items to be misplaced on the query, reducing the NDCG score. Nevertheless, the high MAP values indicate that the top-k items are still relevant to the user, although ranked differently. In general, many opportunities exist for the hybridization of recommender systems. The ultimate goal is to use all of the knowledge available in different data sources and the algorithmic power of these various recommender systems to make robust inferences. The content-based recommender tends to integrate the various data sources more tightly (side information). In addition, the collaborative recommender is more effective when a lot of data is available. Here, we combine the scores of the two recommender systems into a single unified score by computing the weighted aggregates (average aggregation) of the scores from individual ensemble components. Using different combinations of features for building the entire recommendation system is challenging because we consider two aspects: tailoring the recommender system and improving performance. Therefore, it is a complex task to find a tradeoff between these two aspects. The main advantage of the proposed approach is that we simulate the different configurations in some recommender systems where user behavior is tightly related to the content information available in the items. Leveraging a combination of recommendation techniques boosts the recommendation system performance. Hence, the IPRec framework outperforms other baselines with a significant margin in terms of the mean average precision.

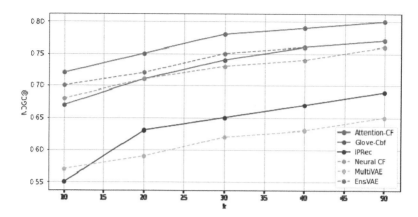

**Figure 5.9.** *Results of the comparison on MovieLens dataset. Evaluation of the performance of top-K recommended lists, in terms of NDCG. The ranking position K ranges from 1 to 50*

## 5.6. Conclusion

In this chapter, we have proposed and investigated a hybrid recommender system where the recommended content is accurate and personalized for each user. The IPRec model incorporates two models: the first exploits the collaborative interactions between users and items in latent spaces, and infers the mutual interactions as a result of a co-attention mechanism; the second model consists of a stacked ensemble recommender that combines several base estimator predictions with a given machine learning algorithm, in order to maximize the predictive performance. The empirical study on real-world datasets proves that IPRec significantly outperforms state-of-the-art methods in recommendation performance. In future work, we plan to extend this novel framework to other recommendation tasks that provide contextual data.

## 5.7. References

Abadi, M., Barham, P., Chen, J., Chen, Z., Davis, A., Dean, J., Devin, M., Ghemawat, S., Irving, G., Isard, M., Kudlur, M., Levenberg, J., Monga, R., Moore, S., Murray, D., Steiner, B., Tucker, P., Vasudevan, V., Warden, P., Wicke, M., Yu, Y., Zheng, X. (2016). Tensorflow: A system for large-scale machine learning. *Proceedings of the 12th Symposium on Operating Systems Design and Implementation*, 265–283.

Bahdanau, D., Cho, K., Bengio, Y. (2014). Neural machine translation by jointly learning to align and translate. *ACM International Conference on Web Search and Data Mining*, arXiv preprint: 1409.0473.

Balakrishnan, S. and Chopra, S. (2012). Collaborative ranking. *Proceedings of the 5th ACM International Conference on Web Search and Data Mining*, 143–152.

Bao, X., Bergman, L., Thompson, R. (2009). Stacking recommendation engines with additional meta-features. *Proceedings of the 3rd ACM Conference on Recommender Systems*, 109–116.

Chen, J., Zhang, H., He, X., Nie, L., Liu, W., Chua, T.S. (2017). Attentive collaborative filtering: Multimedia recommendation with item and component-level attention. *Proceedings of the 40th International ACM SIGIR Conference on Research and Development in Information Retrieval*, 335–344.

Chollet, F. (2021). *Keras: The Python Deep Learning Library*. Astrophysics Source Code Library, ascl: 1806.022.

Da Costa, A.F. and Manzato, M.G. (2016). Exploiting multimodal interactions in recommender systems with ensemble algorithms. *Information Systems*, 56, 120–132.

Demirkesen, C. and Cherifi, H. (2008). A comparison of multiclass SVM methods for real world natural scenes. *Proceedings of the International Conference on Advanced Concepts for Intelligent Vision Systems*, 752–763.

Deng, L., Yu, D., Platt, J. (2012a). Scalable stacking and learning for building deep architectures. *Proceedings of the IEEE International Conference on Acoustics, Speech and Signal Processing (ICASSP)*, 2133–2136.

Deng, L., Tur, G., He, X., Hakkani-Tur, D. (2012b). Use of kernel deep convex networks and end-to-end learning for spoken language understanding. *Proceedings of the IEEE Spoken Language Technology Workshop (SLT)*, 210–215.

Drif, A., Zerrad, H.E., Cherifi, H. (2020). EnsVAE: Ensemble Variational Autoencoders for Recommendations. *IEEE Access*, 8, 188335–188351.

Géron, A. (2019). *Hands-On Machine Learning with Scikit-Learn, Keras, and TensorFlow: Concepts, Tools, and Techniques to Build Intelligent Systems*. O'Reilly Media, Sebastopol.

Harper, F.M. and Konstan, J.A. (2015). The MovieLens datasets: History and context. *ACM Transactions on Interactive Intelligent Systems (TIIS)*, 5(4), 1–19.

He, X., Liao, L., Zhang, H., Nie, L., Hu, X., Chua, T.S. (2017). Neural collaborative filtering. *Proceedings of the 26th International Conference on World Wide Web*, 173–182.

Jurek, A., Bi, Y., Wu, S., Nugent, C. (2014). A survey of commonly used ensemble-based classification techniques. *The Knowledge Engineering Review*, 29(5), 551–581.

Kang, W.C. and McAuley, J. (2018). Self-attentive sequential recommendation. *Proceedings of the IEEE International Conference on Data Mining (ICDM)*, 197–206.

Labatut, V. and Cherifi, H. (2012). Accuracy measures for the comparison of classifiers. arXiv preprint: 1207.3790.

Lasfar, A., Mouline, S., Aboutajdine, D., Cherifi, H. (2000). Content-based retrieval in fractal coded image databases. *Proceedings of the 15th International Conference on Pattern Recognition. ICPR-2000*, 1, 1031–1034.

Liang, D., Krishnan, R.G., Hoffman, M.D., Jebara, T. (2018). Variational autoencoders for collaborative filtering. *Proceedings of the World Wide Web Conference*, 689–698.

Liu, Y., Wang, Y., Zhang, J. (2012). New machine learning algorithm: Random forest. *Proceedings of the International on Information Computing and Applications*, 246–252.

Liu, Y., Zhang, Y., Zhang, X. (2021). An end-to-end review-based aspect-level neural model for sequential recommendation. *Discrete Dynamics in Nature and Society*, 2021, 6693730, Hindawi, London.

Musto, C., Greco, C., Suglia, A., Semeraro, G. (2016). Ask me any rating: A content-based recommender system based on recurrent neural networks. *Proceedings of the 7th Italian Information Retrieval Workshop*, 1–4.

Okura, S., Tagami, Y., Ono, S., Tajima, A. (2017). Embedding-based news recommendation for millions of users. *Proceedings of the 23rd ACM SIGKDD International Conference on Knowledge Discovery and Data Mining*, 1933–1942.

Otunba, R., Rufai, R.A., Lin, J. (2019). Deep stacked ensemble recommender. *Proceedings of the 31st International Conference on Scientific and Statistical Database Management*, 197–201.

Pavlyshenko, B. (2018). Using stacking approaches for machine learning models. *Proceedings of the 2nd International Conference on Data Stream Mining & Processing (DSMP)*, 255–258.

Pennington, J., Socher, R., Manning, C.D. (2014). Glove: Global vectors for word representation. *Proceedings of the 2014 Conference on Empirical Methods in Natural Language Processing (EMNLP)*, 1532–1543.

Reid, S. and Grudic, G. (2009). Regularized linear models in stacked generalization. *International Workshop on Multiple Classifier Systems*, 112–121.

Rital, S., Bretto, A., Cherifi, H., Aboutajdine, D. (2002). A combinatorial edge detection algorithm on noisy images. *Proceedings of the International Symposium on VIPromCom Video/Image Processing and Multimedia Communications*, 351–355.

Rital, S., Cherifi, H., Miguet, S. (2005). Weighted adaptive neighborhood hypergraph partitioning for image segmentation. *Proceedings of the International Conference on Pattern Recognition and Image Analysis*, 522–531.

Robertson, S. (2009). Evaluation in information retrieval. *Proceedings of the 18th Annual International ACM SIGIR Conference on Research and Development in Information Retrieval*, 81–92.

Sherstinsky, A. (2020). Fundamentals of recurrent neural network (RNN) and long short-term memory (LSTM) network. *Physica D: Nonlinear Phenomena*, 404, 132306.

Tan, J., Wan, X., Xiao, J. (2016). A neural network approach to quote recommendation in writings. *Proceedings of the 25th ACM International on Conference on Information and Knowledge Management*, 65–74.

Tang, J. and Wang, K. (2018). Personalized top-N sequential recommendation via convolutional sequence embedding. *Proceedings of the 11th ACM International Conference on Web Search and Data Mining*, 565–573.

Tay, Y., Luu, A.T., Hui, S.C. (2018). Multi-pointer co-attention networks for recommendation. *Proceedings of the 24th ACM SIGKDD International Conference on Knowledge Discovery & Data Mining*, 2309–2318.

Vaswani, A., Shazeer, N., Parmar, N., Uszkoreit, J., Jones, L., Gomez, A.N., Kaise, L., Polosukhin, I. (2017). Attention is all you need. *Advances in Neural Information Processing Systems*, 5998–6008, arXiv: 1706.03762.

Wolpert, D.H. (1992). Stacked generalization. *Neural Networks*, 5(2), 241–259.

Xu, K., Ba, J., Kiros, R., Cho, K., Courville, A., Salakhudinov, R., Zemel, R., Bengio, Y. (2015). Show, attend and tell: Neural image caption generation with visual attention. *Proceedings of the International Conference on Machine Learning*, 2048–2057.

Yakhchi, S., Beheshti, A., Ghafari, S.M., Orgun, M.A., Liu, G. (2020). Towards a deep attention-based sequential recommender system. *IEEE Access*, 8, 178073–178084.

Ying, H., Zhuang, F., Zhang, F., Liu, Y., Xu, G., Xie, X., Xiong, H., Wu, J. (2018). Sequential recommender system based on hierarchical attention network. *Proceedings of the IJCAI International Joint Conference on Artificial Intelligence*, July, 3926–3932.

Zhou, G., Zhu, X., Song, C., Fan, Y., Zhu, H., Ma, X., Yan, Y., Jin, J., Li, H., Gai, K. (2018). Deep interest network for click-through rate prediction. *Proceedings of the 24th ACM SIGKDD International Conference on Knowledge Discovery & Data Mining*, 1059–1068.

# 6

# A Comparison of Machine Learning and Deep Learning Models with Advanced Word Embeddings: The Case of Internal Audit Reports

Gustavo FLEURY SOARES[1] and Induraj PUDHUPATTU RAMAMURTHY[2]

[1] *Brazilian Office of the Comptroller General (CGU), Brazil*
[2] *CYTech, Cergy, France, and University of India, India*

When conducting an audit, the ability to make use of all the available information relating to the audit universe or subject could improve the quality of results. Classifying text documents in the audit (unstructured data) could enable the use of additional information to improve existing structured data, leading to better knowledge to support the audit process. To provide better automated support for knowledge discovery, natural language processing (NLP) could be applied. This chapter compares the results of classical machine learning and deep learning algorithms, combined with advanced word embeddings in order to classify the findings of internal audit reports.

## 6.1. Introduction

Internal Audits, as defined by the IIA (2012), are "an independent, objective assurance and consulting activity designed to add value and improve an organization's operations". To achieve this, the internal auditor endeavors to collect all available information relating to the organization – internal or external. This can be in the form of either structured or unstructured data, which the auditor analyzes in order to provide useful insights. Considering the volume of data created nowadays, it is crucial for data tools to be used efficiently.

Data science is widely used in the areas of finance and accounting, evidenced by various related articles and research work. Typically, a number of different financial parameters are used for fraud detection. However, over the last decade, research has been conducted using NLP by making use of textual information. Auditing, however, is behind in making use of these methods, compared to other lines of research (Gepp *et al.* 2018).

Deep learning (DL), undoubtedly the driving force behind artificial intelligence, has accelerated the quality of automated systems, employing deep hierarchical neural networks within which complex and abstract features – mostly unidentifiable by classic machine learning (ML) algorithms – are easily detectable. Use of textual analytics that leverage the power of DL is continuing to grow within the field of auditing, in particular for the automation of fraud detection. The auditing profession has recognized the need for textual big data analysis in order to enhance the quality and relevance of audits (EY_Reporting 2015). Deloitte, one of the Big Four audit firms, uses DL within its "document review" platform which it has developed in-house. Similarly, EY (formerly Ernst & Young) uses applied artificial intelligence (AI) for the analysis of lease contracts. It is important to note that EY's fraud detection system has 97% accuracy according to a Forbes report. Furthermore, Deloitte's "Kira" platform is used within its audit business, under the name D-ICE. In view of the novel methods used by fraudsters, 84% of financial statement preparers, 76% of audit committees and 70% of financial statement users who participated in Deloitte's Audit of the Future Survey 2016 expressed the need for advanced technologies (EY_Reporting 2015).

As auditing becomes more prevalent, and an increasing number of financial fraud instances is being exposed, the techniques used for committing this type of fraud are becoming more advanced and more prolific. The most common technique, used to deceive stakeholders and other associated entities, was impression management (Jaafar *et al.* 2018). However, since most firms tend to engage in impression management (as a means of enhancing and engaging in retrospective sensemaking regardless of financial position), tracking fraudulent firms by using their impression management techniques is difficult.

In general, a mass of documents in the real word are not labeled or only a small portion have been classified. The need to apply unsupervised or semi-supervised algorithms to these documents – to automatically classify them as fraudulent or non-fraudulent – is therefore mandatory. However, the complexity of grouping these documents and the risk of misclassification remain.

A number of works in ML, DL and textual data have been suggested to identify fraudulent firms using standard financial ratios. However, writing styles, assessment techniques, analysis techniques and reporting procedures all vary. Therefore, in the case of internal auditing, only focusing on financial aspects in an attempt to isolate areas that require further investigation – addressing discrepancies and implementing corrective action – is not possible.

Consequently, in this chapter, we only use textual information in combination with state-of-the-art techniques that have been developed in recent years. We present an extensive comparison of different combinations of machine learning algorithms with advanced word embeddings. This comparison brings to light the fastest and most effective techniques for automating the process of identifying risky and non-risky sections within a document, or within a multitude of documents.

The automated classification of whole documents or content within documents as "risky" or "non-risky" will be an effective tool for auditors to create a risk ranking for documents or audit objects that require further manual analysis.

Our primary focus is comparing the performance of ML and DL models using classical word embedding techniques, for example bigram and TF-IDF. We also test performance using advanced state-of-the-art word embeddings such as Word2Vec, Word2Vec-Avg, FastText and GloVe. We demonstrate our experiments using classical ML classification algorithms and DL models, namely, CNN (convolutional neural network), LSTM (long short-term memory) and BERT (Bidirectional Encoder Representations from Transformers).

This chapter is organized as follows. Section 6.2 discusses related works and briefly elaborates on word embeddings, classical ML and DL model architecture, indicating the most common algorithms and recent related research. Section 6.3 outlines the experiments and provides an evaluation. Results, conclusions and future work are addressed in section 6.4.

## 6.2. Related work

To process textual information using computer technology, several different NLP approaches can be used, the simplest being the one where the textual input is represented by a vector of weighted word counts (Manning and Schütze 1999). Feature representation based on the Bag of Words (BoW) model or exquisitely designed patterns are typically extracted as features; nevertheless these feature representation methods ignore word order, and thus, contextual information as well. Considering the curse of dimensionality posed by the BoW model, TF-IDF and Word2Vec is a better choice for forming a word vector matrix. Word embeddings are efficient in capturing context similarity, that is, analogies, and have generated state-of-the-art results in a wide range of NLP tasks (Turney and Pantel 2010; Lilleberg *et al.* 2015; Cambria *et al.* 2017). Using Word2Vec yields more satisfactory results compared to TF-IDF in the random forest classifier when compared to logistic regression (Waykole and Thakare 2018). Furthermore, these authors suggest experimentation using the GloVe word embedding, which we include in our research.

Classical ML techniques like the artificial neural network (ANN) and the decision tree (DT) were used by Albashrawi (2016), along with auditor opinions and other financial variables; these included the company's liquidity ratio and its operating efficiency, which were subjected to Kolmogorov–Smirnov, Shapiro–Wilk and Mann–Whitney tests. Another research experiment using DT, NN and the Bayesian belief network was conducted on a dataset comprising 76 Greek manufacturing firms, 38 of which were classified as fraudulent by the auditors. The neural classifier had 100% accuracy (Desai and Deshmukh 2013).

Another study used data mining techniques such as the multilayer feed forward (MLFF) neural network, support vector machines (SVM), genetic programming (GP), group method of data handling (GMDH), logistic regression (LR) and the probabilistic neural network (PNN) on 202 Chinese firms with and without feature selection (Ravisankar *et al.* 2011). Similarly, Yim (2011) took account of the financial ratios of 100 Turkish firms and used classifiers such as the decision tree and NN.

Yim (2011) adapted a new approach to labeling which involves fraud scoring. Fraud scoring assignments conducted on 72 firms were used to label them as either fraudulent or non-fraudulent. With nine financial properties, methods such as linear regression, NN, KNN, SVM, Decision Stump, M5P Tree and the Decision Table were tested. Random forest was found to be the best performing model (Yim 2011).

Abulaish and Sah (2019) propose a data augmentation approach with n-grams, the Latent Dirichlet Allocation (LDA) technique and the DL technique of a CNN to identify class specific phrases for enrichment of the underlying corpus to increase classifier performance; this approach enriches the corpus based on class labels.

Certain research (Mahmoud Hussein 2016) has suggested that the non-stemmed corpus achieved 87.79% and 88.54% accuracy with SVM and Naive Bayes, respectively. In contrast, the stemmed corpus achieved lower accuracy of 84.49% and 86.35%. Hence, we try traditional machine learning algorithms with stemmed and non-stemmed corpuses in order to verify their performance in the case of internal audit document classification.

The DL models prove to be more suitable than the classical ML for text classification (Yin *et al.* 2017; Young *et al.* 2017; Menger *et al.* 2018) and compares NN, NB, SVM, DT with Recurrent Neural Network (RNN) and CNN using bigram, TF-IDF, word embedding and document embedding. RNN was found to outperform other techniques, and the same holds true for other researchers (Yin *et al.* 2017). Fair comparison of Word2Vec, CNN, Gated Recurrent Unit (GRU) and long short-term memory (LSTM) in sentiment analysis of Russian tweets was conducted (Arkhipenko *et al.* 2016) and it was found that GRU outperforms LSTM and CNN, while Chung (2014) and Jozefowicz and Zaremba (2015) state that there is no clear winner between GRU and LSTM.

The bias problem posed by RNN can be alleviated by using an unbiased CNN model (Lai *et al.* 2015). The RNN captures text semantics via a tree structure but it is difficult to represent the relationship between two sentences using this structure. Although RNN can capture semantics of long text, later words are more dominant than earlier words, thus pose limitations during the capture of semantics of whole documents.

Data augmentations like synonym replacement, random insertion, random swap and random deletion are performed for smaller datasets and the performances of CNN and LSTM are compared (Wei and Zou 2019). However, our dataset is bigger and the maximum length of certain individual corpora approximates to 1 million characters.

Various metrics such as accuracy, precision, recall and F1 score are used by many researchers, depending on the problem addressed by modeling. Interestingly we find that accuracy is not a preferred performance measure for imbalanced datasets (Anand *et al.* 2010), because the classifier will result in high predictive accuracy. Hence, we consider other metrics such as precision, recall and F1 score, as well as accuracy, for evaluating the goodness of the classifier.

The two significant problems of data quality and data governance have to be taken into account (Claudiu *et al.* 2018); the use of data augmentation for text (Wei and Zou 2019) could lead to some improvement in quality, even for less intensive ML methods. In our dataset, we have highly imbalanced data, which needed oversampling before the ML classifier and DL models were trained.

Inspired by these research works, we experimented using classical ML algorithms such as Naive Bayes (NB), Logistic Regression (LR), NN, SVM and Random Forest; we also incorporated DL models such as CNN, LSTM and BERT. We tested these different algorithms with respect to different classical word feature extraction techniques, such as TF-IDF, Word2Vec, Word2Vec-Avg, as well as advanced word embedding techniques, namely, FastText and GloVe. The results of the training of machine learning models and deep learning models with different word embeddings are detailed in section 6.3.

### 6.2.1. *Word embedding*

As well as testing our algorithms with classical feature representations like Bag of Words (BoW) and TF-IDF, we test them using advanced word embedding like Word2Vec, Word2Vec-Avg, FastText and GloVe.

Word2vec focuses on increasing the quality of word representation while using the neural network language model with a linear projection layer and nonlinear hidden layers. Distributed representation of words learned by neural networks preserves linear regularities among words and is found to be better than Latent Semantic Analysis (LSA) and LDA (Mikolov *et al.* 2013). Word2Vec with a weighted average is a variation to try to improve the model. It is possible to use the TF-IDF parameter to measure the importance of the word in the context (Djaballah *et al.* 2019).

On the other hand, unlike Word2Vector, FastText is provided as a black box to the end user. However, Bojanowski *et al.* (2017) and Joulin *et al.* (2016a, 2016b) fairly depict their working principles. FastText is faster than any word embedding. It is possible to train it on more than one billion words in less than 10 minutes using a standard multicore CPU, and to classify half a million sentences into 312k classes in less than a minute (Joulin *et al.* 2016b).

The most recent word embedding method is known as GloVe (Global Vectors for Word Representation). Developed by Stanford (Pennington *et al.* 2014), it is an unsupervised learning algorithm for obtaining vector representations for words. It takes a corpus of text and intuitively transforms it into a matrix, formulated by considering the context in which the word appears. GloVe takes advantage of the global matrix factorization method (i.e. the LSA) and the local context window method (i.e. skip-gram).

### 6.2.2. *Deep learning models*

#### 6.2.2.1. *CNN architecture*

A CNN is a multilayer neural network architecture, developed specifically for image classification by accepting two-dimensional (2D) input representing pixel and color channels of images. We adapt the CNN architecture for text classification where the input is a 1D sequence of features. We compute index mapping words to known embedding by parsing the data dump of pre-trained embeddings. This embedding index and word index are used further to compute the embedding matrix.

We built our five-layer CNN architecture with output filters set to 200 and the kernel size of each layer incrementing from two to six; each layer is followed by a pooling layer. The nonlinear function ReLu (rectified linear unit) is applied in all layers for faster convergence and for backpropagation. Finally, we used a flatten layer to flatten the outputs and feed them to a dense layer. The output layer is employed with the softmax function.

### 6.2.2.2. BERT architecture

Implementation of the BERT architecture is performed in two stages: pre-training and fine-tuning. At the pre-training stage, masked language modeling (MLM) and next sentence prediction (NSP) are used (Devlin *et al.* 2018). BERT is a bidirectional deep neural network model that is based on the Transformer architecture. A transformer only makes use of an attention mechanism and replaces the recurrent layers commonly used in encoder–decoder implementations (Vaswani *et al.* 2017). Transformers function in parallel and require fewer computing resources compared to RNN solutions. Our BERT implementation involved text preprocessing to add necessary tokens [CLS] and [SEP] for each text followed by BERT layer and pooling layer. The output layer has been implemented to make use of the sigmoid activation function.

### 6.2.2.3. LSTM architecture

Recurrent neural networks look at the current input $x_t$ as well as the previous output $h_{t-1}$ at each time step, but they struggle to learn long-term dependencies; this has led to the development of the LSTM architecture. LSTM consists of a recurrent network with the main blocks of input and output, as well as three gates: the input gate, the output gate and the forget gate.

The block input receives the signal from the last recurrent block. The input gate is the new value from data, and the output gate is a filtered version of the block output. The forget gate applies a function to "forget" some elements. We used an embedding layer with an embedding size of 32, an embedding dimension of 300 with bidirectional LSTM layer and a flattening layer, followed by an output layer with a softmax activation function. For each case of word embeddings like GloVe and FastText, we extract the appropriate embedding weights and feed them into our architecture.

## 6.3. Experiments and evaluation

The internal audit reports of the Brazilian government are public and are available on the Internet as PDF files. Similarly, there is a significant amount of information relating to the various sub-entities of the government which could add value.

In order to locate this information, we created a model defining the type and the limits of all of the data under consideration. Since the Brazilian Government Internal Audit Reports (CGU)[1] uses JavaScript, it was not possible to simply use the "wget" tool to retrieve a list of links in order to download the documents. To download this data (typically PDF files, as mentioned) we used the Selenium Automation Framework, which comes with the headless web browser, PhantomJS. The next step was to parse the PDF files in order to retrieve the information needed. There are several different libraries and tools for converting PDFs to plain text files. We achieved the best results, in terms of performance and quality, with the Tika Parser from the Apache Software Foundation. As the reports were text in the PDFs, it was not necessary to perform the OCR process.

Each audit report contained one or more findings which were initially classified as "*informação*" (information), "*constatação*" (finding) and "*conclusão*" (conclusion). We parsed a total of 89k documents and compiled structured data by extracting the necessary segments from the documents with regex (regular expressions).

Due to the unavailability of a Brazilian Portuguese lemmatizer, we used stemming; identifying parts of speech for semantic processing was therefore not possible. Stemming leads to words in a sentence losing their contextual meaning and therefore, in this research, we consider both the stemmed and non-stemmed version of the corpora to verify the results in both cases.

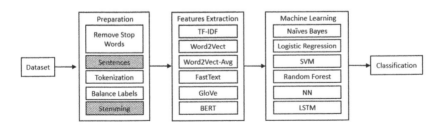

**Figure 6.1.** *Text classification steps and methods tested*

---

1 http://www.eaud.cgu.gov.br/relatorios.

We segmented our dataset of 89,000 documents by year, selecting 2016–2019 so as to work with the latest corpora and apply our tests to modern day scenarios.

As in fraud detection datasets, labels in audit report datasets are very imbalanced. The percentage of high risk findings is only 3% (approximately). When we use imbalanced datasets to train the standard ML algorithms, the data corresponding to the dominant class will influence the result and the result is not an accurate and representative of the whole dataset.

After oversampling the train dataset, we extracted features using the bag of words model, TF-IDF, Word2Vec and Word2Vec-Avg; we trained our ML models using techniques such as Naive Bayes, logistic regression, SVM, random forest and neural networks. As well as experimenting with classical feature extraction techniques, we also used popular word embeddings, namely, FastText and GloVe. The train and test sets were partitioned in the ratio of 70:30 and all of our ML models were trained and tested. To experiment with DL models, based on CNN and LSTM architectures discussed in the previous section, we again used FastText and GloVe word embeddings with the same dimensions. In addition, we also conducted tests using BERT by applying it to our scenario.

In the following paragraphs, we discuss experiments using classical ML techniques with classical word embeddings. At first glance, it could appear that random forest and neural network techniques are better, yet the results are in fact not good, as detailed below.

The random forest method achieved accuracy, precision, recall and an F1 score of 100% in the training set, which is better than any other algorithm. The test set had 78% accuracy and an F1 score of 6%. Such high accuracy alongside a very low F1 score can be explained by the fact that the dataset is very much imbalanced with more "low" risk labels than "high", resulting in most of the test sets being correctly labeled "low" thus resulting in high accuracy; in reality, this is not a good result. The same is also true for other algorithms. The accuracy of logistic regression and SVM seems better than naive Bayes, but they also suffer from the same problem of model overfitting.

| Extracted Features | | Naive Bayes (NB) | | Logistic Regression (LR) | | Support Vector Machines (SVM) | |
|---|---|---|---|---|---|---|---|
| | | Acc | F1 | Acc | F1 | Acc | F1 |
| TF-IDF | Train | 0.51 | 0.51 | 0.51 | 0.53 | 0.61 | 0.67 |
| | Test | 0.48 | 0.06 | 0.51 | 0.06 | 0.44 | 0.06 |
| Word2Vector | Train | 0.66 | 0.63 | 0.94 | 0.94 | 0.94 | 0.95 |
| | Test | 0.70 | 0.11 | 0.88 | 0.21 | 0.88 | 0.21 |
| Word2Vector-Avg | Train | 0.66 | 0.63 | 0.93 | 0.93 | 0.93 | 0.93 |
| | Test | 0.70 | 0.11 | 0.87 | 0.20 | 0.86 | 0.19 |

**Table 6.1.** Results for composition Extract Features and ML algorithms – Simple Extraction Features on NB, LR and SVM

| Extracted Features | | Random Forest (RF) | | Neural Network (NN) | | Long Short-Term Memory (LSTM) | |
|---|---|---|---|---|---|---|---|
| | | Acc | F1 | Acc | F1 | Acc | F1 |
| TF-IDF | Train | 1.00 | 1.00 | 0.99 | 0.99 | 1.00 | 1.00 |
| | Test | 0.78 | 0.06 | 0.80 | 0.06 | 0.80 | 0.06 |
| Word2Vector | Train | 1.00 | 1.00 | 0.99 | 0.99 | 0.86 | 0.85 |
| | Test | 0.97 | 0.18 | 0.94 | 0.27 | 0.88 | 0.09 |
| Word2Vector-Avg | Train | 0.99 | 0.99 | 0.99 | 0.99 | 0.86 | 0.85 |
| | Test | 0.96 | 0.18 | 0.93 | 0.24 | 0.88 | 0.08 |

**Table 6.2.** Results for composition Extract Features and ML algorithms – Simple Extraction Features on RF, NN and LSTM

| Extracted Features | | Naive Bayes | | Logistic Regression | | SVM | |
|---|---|---|---|---|---|---|---|
| | | Acc | F1 | Acc | F1 | Acc | F1 |
| FastText | Train | 0.71 | 0.10 | 0.80 | 0.57 | 0.82 | 0.61 |
| | Test | 0.97 | 0.30 | 0.93 | 0.21 | 0.94 | 0.24 |
| GloVe | Train | 0.70 | 0.03 | 0.80 | 0.59 | 0.82 | 0.63 |
| | Test | 0.97 | 0.06 | 0.92 | 0.21 | 0.92 | 0.20 |

**Table 6.3.** Results for composition Extract Features and ML algorithms – FastText and GloVe Extraction Features on NB, LR and SVM

| Extracted Features | | RF | | NN | | LSTM | |
|---|---|---|---|---|---|---|---|
| | | Acc | F1 | Acc | F1 | Acc | F1 |
| FastText | Train | 1.00 | 1.00 | 0.97 | 0.98 | 0.70 | 0.82 |
| | Test | 0.97 | 0.20 | 0.96 | 0.98 | 0.96 | 0.98 |
| GloVe | Train | 1.00 | 1.00 | 0.96 | 0.97 | 0.99 | 0.99 |
| | Test | 0.97 | 0.20 | 0.89 | 0.94 | 0.96 | 0.98 |

**Table 6.4.** *Results for composition Extract Features and ML algorithms – FastText and GloVe Extraction Features on RF, NN and LSTM*

| Extracted Features | | BERT NN | |
|---|---|---|---|
| | | Acc | F1 |
| BERT | Train | 0.70 | 0.82 |
| | Test | 0.96 | 0.98 |

**Table 6.5.** *Results for composition Extract Features and ML algorithms – BERT*

The following confusion matrix exemplifies this result. From a total of 6,084, the predictions for "low risk" are 5,888 (97%) and just 196 for "high risk". Hence, the accuracy of any given algorithm tends to be very high and yet other metrics come out very low.

| Assigned Category | | True Category | |
|---|---|---|---|
| | | Low Risk | High Risk |
| | Low Risk | TP = 4714 | FP = 1174 |
| | High Risk | FN = 145 | TN = 51 |

**Table 6.6.** *Confusion matrix*

The major difference presented by the metrics of the training and test datasets exposes the overfitting of classical ML algorithms. The random forest technique presents a "perfect" classification for TF-IDF (accuracy, precision, recall and F1 score all are 100%). When applied to the test dataset, however, similarly good metrics are not produced. To prevent this overfitting, modifications could be made to the parameters of the algorithm or a different testing approach could be used.

We have shown that classical ML models, combined with different classical word embeddings, are not the best choice for automating the process of identifying particular sections within internal audit documents that may pose potential risks. However, significant improvements were observed when using advanced word embeddings with DL models. Training DL models such as CNN, LSTM and BERT with the advanced word embeddings FastText and GloVe produced better results without the problem of overfitting. We obtained better results in the training set and very similar results in the test sets without having to account for bias and variance. It is evident that CNN and LSTM both perform extraordinarily well compared to BERT and other algorithms. The choice of whether to use CNN or LSTM comes down to the speed of the algorithm. In our experiments, we found LSTM to be noticeably faster than CNN, but this does largely depend on the architecture of the deep learning model constructed. For the architecture presented in this chapter, we found LSTM to be better. It is important to note, however, that the training speed of both CNN and LSTM was quite a bit faster when using FastText as the word embedding.

## 6.4. Conclusion and future work

The results show that it is possible to use machine learning algorithms to discern the level of risk posed by audit findings. The best model can be used to automate classification of external reports to support ongoing audits or the selection of audit objects in annual planning.

The DL models prove to be more suitable than the classical ML techniques for this type of text classification. These results are corroborated by similar research work conducted by Young *et al.* (2017) and Yin *et al.* (2017). We have proved, however, that the accuracy of the model, as well as the F1 score, are significantly better when using recently released, advanced word embeddings such as GloVe and FastText. Furthermore, the classical ML approaches used are unable to create a good classifier model. Conversely, the DL models produced impressive metrics. The difference between CNN and LSTM is not statistically relevant. Therefore, in real-world applications, deciding which of the discussed DL methods to use depends largely on requirements relating to response time and available resources.

To train our models, we used a dataset spanning from 2016 to 2019, with approximately 17,000 occurrences. This dataset is in fact relatively small for training DL models. Our decision to use this filtered dataset was based on limited availability of computational resources. Training DL algorithms using larger datasets would likely result in the model producing an even better generalization.

The speed of the training model and the performance metrics are very important parameters that need to be considered in any research of this kind. In our research, we found that FastText with LSTM and CNN was faster when training the model – while also producing excellent performance metrics – whereas BERT took many hours of fine-tuning to achieve the text classification for our particular case, with equivalent performance metrics.

For this project, we used two strategies. In the first strategy, all the text was within a single audit finding as an individual training sample. In the second strategy, we divided each of the sentences within each audit finding into individual samples and labeled each one according to the category they fell under. However, initial comparison tests showed that the model trained using data prepared using the second strategy performed the worst. Further research could help in understanding the reason for these results.

In order to deal with label imbalance, we worked with oversampling which produced reasonably good results. Further study on the impact of other sampling methodologies to solve this type of imbalance could be interesting. The use of data augmentation for text, such as synonym insertion or evolutionary algorithms (Wei and Zou 2019), could lead to some improvement in quality, primarily for less intensive ML methods.

Other advanced ensemble algorithms could also be tried. Furthermore, fine-tuning the hyperparameters of the DL models would provide better performance. An important aspect would be to verify if the quality of model improves while keeping the time and computational cost justifiable.

As an extension to our research, hybrid DL architectures like CNN-BILSTM and LSTM-CNN can be used with model parameter tuning. Some research also suggests using a 2D max pooling layer with LSTM whereas we used 1D max pooling layers. Once lemmatizers for Portuguese become available, tokenizing the sentences with POS and using fine-tuned versions of text as inputs could provide newer dimensions to the results obtained.

## 6.5. References

Abulaish, M. and Sah, A.K. (2019). A text data augmentation approach for improving the performance of CNN. *11th International Conference on Communication Systems & Networks (COMSNETS)*, 625–630.

Albashrawi, M. (2016). Detecting financial fraud using data mining techniques: A decade review from 2004 to 2015. *Journal of Data Science*, 14, 553–570.

Anand, A., Pugalenthi, G., Fogel, G.B., Suganthan, P.N. (2010). An approach for classification of highly imbalanced data using weighting and undersampling. *Amino Acids*, 39, 1385–1391.

Arkhipenko, K., Kozlov, I., Trofimovich, J., Skorniakov, K., Gomzin, A., Turdakov, D. (2016). Comparison of neural network architectures for sentiment analysis of Russian tweets. *Proceedings of the International Conference on Computational Linguistics and Intellectual Technologies*, 50–58.

Bojanowski, P., Grave, E., Joulin, A., Mikolov, T. (2017). Enriching word vectors with subword information. *Transactions of the Association for Computational Linguistics*, 5, 135–146.

Cambria, E., Poria, S., Gelbukh, A., Thelwall, M. (2017). Sentiment analysis is a big suitcase. *IEEE Intelligent Systems*, 32(6), 74–80.

Chung, J., Gulcehre, C., Cho, K., Bengio, Y. (2014). Empirical evaluation of gated recurrent neural networks on sequence modeling. *NIPS 2014 Deep Learning and Representation Learning Workshop* [Online]. Available at: https://nips.cc/ Conferences/2014/Schedule?type=Workshop.

Claudiu, B., Muntean, M., Didraga, O. (2018). Intelligent decision support in auditing: Big Data and machine learning approach. *17th International Conference on INFORMATICS in ECONOMY (IE 2018)*, Education, Research & Business Technologies, 425–430.

Desai, A.B. and Deshmukh, R. (2013). Data mining techniques for fraud detection. *International Journal of Computer Science and Information Technologies*, 4, 1–4.

Devlin, J., Chang, M.-W., Lee, K., Toutanova, K. (2018). BERT: Pre-training of Deep Bidirectional Transformers for Language Understanding. *2019 Annual Conference of the North American Chapter of the Association for Computational Linguistics (NAACL)*, 1, 4171–4186.

Djaballah, K.A., Boukhalfa, K., Boussaid, O. (2019). Sentiment analysis of Twitter messages using Word2vec by weighted average. *Sixth International Conference on Social Networks Analysis, Management and Security (SNAMS)*, 223–228.

EY_Reporting (2015). How big data and analytics are transforming the audit [Online]. Available at: https://www.ey.com/en_gl/assurance/how-big-data-and-analytics-are-transforming-the-audit.

Gepp, A., Linnenluecke, M.K., O'Neill, T.J., Smith, T. (2018). Big Data techniques in auditing research and practice: Current trends and future opportunities. *Research Methods & Methodology in Accounting eJournal*, 40, 102–115.

IIA (2012). *International Standards for the Professional Practice of Internal Auditing*. Institute of Internal Auditors, Altamonte Springs, FL.

Jaafar, H., Halim, H.A., Ismail, R., Ahmad, A.S. (2018). Fraudulent financial reporting and impression management: An examination of corporate accounting narratives. *International Journal of Academic Research in Business and Social Sciences*, 8, 824–837.

Joulin, A., Grave, E., Bojanowski, P., Douze, M., Jégou, H., Mikolov, T. (2016a). *FastText.zip: Compressing Text Classification Models*. ICLR 2017, arXiv:1612.03651v1.

Joulin, A., Grave, E., Bojanowski, P., Mikolov, T. (2016b). Bag of tricks for efficient text classification. *Proceedings of the 15th Conference of the European Chapter of the Association for Computational Linguistics*, 427–431.

Jozefowicz, R. and Zaremba, W. (2015). An empirical exploration of recurrent network architectures. *ICML'15: Proceedings of the 32nd International Conference on Machine Learning*, 37, 2342–2350.

Lai, S., Xu, L., Liu, K., Zhao, J. (2015). Recurrent convolutional neural networks for text classification. *Proceedings of the 29th AAAI Conference on Artificial Intelligence*, 29(1), 2267–2273.

Lilleberg, J., Zhu, Y., Zhang, Y. (2015). Support vector machines and Word2vec for text classification with semantic features. *Proceedings of the 14th International Conference on Cognitive Informatics and Cognitive Computing*, IEEE, Beijing.

Manning, C. and Schütze, H. (1999). *Foundations of Statistical Natural Language Processing*, 1st edition. MIT Press, Cambridge, MA.

Menger, V., Scheepers, F., Spruit, M. (2018). Comparing deep learning and classical machine learning approaches for predicting inpatient violence incidents from clinical text. *Applied Sciences*, 8(6), 981.

Mikolov, T., Chen, K., Corrado, G., Dean, J. (2013). Efficient estimation of word representations in vector space. *1st International Conference on Learning Representations*, arXiv:1301.3781.

Pennington, J., Socher, R., Manning, C. (2014). GloVe: Global vectors for word representation. *Proceedings of the 2014 Conference on Empirical Methods in Natural Language Processing (EMNLP)*, 1532–1543.

Ravisankar, P., Ravi, V., Rao, G., Bose, I. (2011). Detection of financial statement fraud and feature selection using data mining techniques. *Decision Support Systems*, 50, 491–500.

Stanton, G. (2012). Detecting fraud-utilizing new technology to advance the audit profession. Thesis, Univeristy of New Hampshire, Durham [Online]. Available at: https://scholars.unh.edu/honors/18.

Turney, P.D. and Pantel, P. (2010). From frequency to meaning: Vector space models of semantics. *Journal of Artificial Intelligence Research*, 141–188.

Vaswani, A., Shazeer, N., Parmar, N., Uszkoreit, J. (2017). Attention is all you need. *NIPS'17: Proceedings of the 31st International Conference on Neural Information Processing Systems*, 6000–6010.

Wahbeh, A., Al-Kabi, M., Al-Radaideh, Q., Al-shawakfa, E., Alsmadi, I. (2011). The effect of stemming on Arabic text classification: An empirical study. *International Journal of Information Retrieval Research (IJIRR)*, 1(3), 54–70.

Waykole, R.N. and Thakare, A.D. (2018). A review of feature extraction methods for text classification. *International Journal of Advance Engineering and Research Development*, 5(4), 351–354.

Wei, J. and Zou, K. (2019). EDA: Easy Data Augmentation techniques for boosting performance on text classification tasks. *Proceedings of the 2019 Conference on Empirical Methods in Natural Language Processing and the 9th International Joint Conference on Natural Language Processing (EMNLP-IJCNLP)*, 6382–6388.

Yim, A. (2011). Fraud detection and financial reporting and audit delay. Paper, Munich Personal RePEc Archive, Munich.

Yin, W., Kann, K., Yu, M., Schütze, H. (2017). Comparative study of CNN and RNN for natural language processing. arXiv:1702.01923v1.

Young, T., Hazarika, D., Poria, S., Cambria, E. (2017). Recent trends in deep learning based natural language processing. *IEEE Computational Intelligence Magazine*, 13, 55–75.

# 7

# Hybrid Approach based on Multi-agent System and Fuzzy Logic for Mobile Robot Autonomous Navigation

**Khadidja** YAHYAOUI
*University of Mascara, Algeria*

The design of a control architecture is a central problem in a project to realize an autonomous mobile robot. In the absence of a generic solution that overshadows all others, it is essential to come up with a new approach detailing the design process that will reach this goal. In this context, this chapter proposes to use the multi-agent paradigm and inference mechanism based on fuzzy logic in the design of the control architecture for the autonomous navigation of the mobile robot.

The architecture developed must take into account imposed constraints (obstacle avoidance, no collisions with the walls of the environment, unknown environment, optimal path, reaching the goal), actor-based system multi-agents and distributed non-hierarchical architecture built around several agents (databases knowledge), cognitive and reactive, that cooperate with each other to solve the problem of autonomous navigation of the mobile robot.

The method used allowed us to have an intelligent system capable of solving various problems produced during navigation.

*Optimization and Machine Learning,*
coordinated by Rachid CHELOUAH and Patrick SIARRY © ISTE Ltd 2022.

## 7.1. Introduction

The industry mainly uses poorly autonomous robots to perform repetitive tasks with the aim of reducing production costs. Robots can be used in tasks that are dangerous for humans, such as those carried out in underground mines, chemical or nuclear installations, the underwater world and planetary exploration. Thus, environments hostile to humans are at the origin of the growing interest in the development of robots capable of assisting humans and tending to an increasingly strong autonomy.

Navigating the robot to approach the target while avoiding any obstacle in a constrained environment, is one of the most complex problems, and the majority of robotics specialists have directed their research toward this axis.

This chapter presents two artificial intelligence tools: multi-agent systems (MAS) and fuzzy logic to design and implement the control architecture for autonomous navigation of a mobile robot, taking into account the changing nature of the environment.

We opted for a hybridization between MAS and fuzzy logic for several reasons:

– The principle of adjustment and control by fuzzy logic approaches the human approach in the sense that the variables processed are not logical variables (in the sense of binary logic, for example), but linguistic variables, close to human language. In addition, these linguistic variables are treated using rules which refer to knowledge about the behavior of the system to be controlled (Buhler 1994).

– MAS are ideally designed and implemented as a set of interacting agents, most often in modes of cooperation, competition or coexistence (Chaib-draa 1994; Ferber 1995; Moulin and Chaib-draa 1996; Chaib-draa *et al.* 2001). The control architecture of a mobile robot is an organization allowing the construction of a complex system from elementary bricks, which are the multiple modules that are each attached to the resolution of a sub-problem (Ahmadzadeh and Masehian 2015). In this context, the development of this control architecture based MAS allows the coordination of perception, decision and action functions.

– The remainder of the chapter is organized as follows: section 7.2 provides the key methods used for mobile robot navigation as related works.

Section 7.3 introduces the problem position. In section 7.4, we describe the control architecture based agent. The adopted method is explained in section 7.5. Section 7.6 provides a discussion on the methods for evaluating an agent system, and finally, section 7.7 concludes the chapter.

## 7.2. Related works

Mobile and autonomous robotics is one of the research areas for which the arrival of a new approach in artificial intelligence (AI) will have had an interesting impact. The transition from a classical approach (mathematical and algorithmic) to a behavioral approach (based on notions such as cognition, learning, emergence and corporeality) is not easy, because it involves radical changes of mentality and major changes in the designing of robotic control architectures. The main challenge for these architectures is to generate so-called "intelligent" behaviors when subjected to complex and dynamic environments, such as autonomy, learning, adaptation, deliberation, intentions and many others (Holzmann *et al.* 2005). Thus, navigation methods for mobile robots have two classes: classical approaches and advanced approaches. The nature of the environment determines the approach to navigation. For a known or partially known environment, we opt for conventional approaches and, on the other hand, if the environment is unknown then the current approaches are presented in Figure 7.1. In this case, there is no way to make a trajectory planning for the robot beforehand.

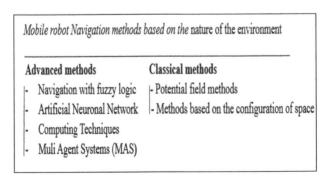

**Figure 7.1.** *Mobile robot navigation approaches*

## 7.2.1. *Classical approaches*

These approaches have the environment in common, which is totally or partially known, that is to say, a static and straightforward environment. Therefore, the mobile robot can plan a continuous trajectory, free of obstacles. These methods are based on the configuration of space and so-called potential field methods.

### 7.2.1.1. *Methods based on the configuration of space*

This is one of the techniques based on the cell decomposition process, using a discrete representation of the robot's environment. Exact decomposition gives a set of polygons dividing the space of free configurations from this representation; we create a graph connecting the various adjacent components of the environment. Next, the cells in which the initial configuration and the target configuration are located are identified. The planning problem then consists of a search problem in a graph. For this, we choose a route algorithm (A *, depth-first, breadth-first) to optimize the distance traveled, or any other criterion. Finally, the cells of the solution graph must be connected by a path without collisions. Several works have used these methods, including Lozano-Pérez (1983), Schwartz and Yap (1987) and Pan and Dinesh Manocha (2015).

### 7.2.1.2. *Potential field methods*

The potential method was initially introduced by Khatib (1986) to manipulate robots. It differs significantly from the other methods mentioned above, because it does not result from purely geometric reasoning. The principle of the method is as follows. The mobile robot is immersed in a field of potential which results from the superposition of an attractive potential, linked to the configuration to be reached, and a sum of repulsive potentials linked to obstacles. Several works have used these methods. In Matoui *et al.* (2017), the authors used the potential field method to plan the path of a group of robots in decentralized architecture. The fractional potential fields approach was applied for the navigation of autonomous vehicles in Moreau *et al.* (2017). Farhad *et al.* (2018) applied the electrostatic potential field approach for the navigation of mobile robots.

## 7.2.2. Advanced methods

The classical methods are methods used in the case where the displacement space is simple (without obstacles), but their limitations are revealed when the complexity of the environment increases. This is proven by the results obtained, for example, by the application of these conventional methods. Such methods generally suffer from the disadvantage of the presence of local minima (the robot is in a situation where it does not move when it has not reached its goal) (Reignier 1994). Several AI techniques are used for mobile robot navigation systems, such as Fuzzy logic systems, neural network (NN), multi-agent systems (MAS). The computing techniques such as the genetic algorithm (GA), Bee colony optimization (BCO) technique, simulated annealing (SA) and particle swarm optimization (PSO) are also applied. Some research works are presented in the following sections.

### 7.2.2.1. Navigation with fuzzy logic

Faisal *et al.* (2013) created a control architecture based on the Agent fuzzy controller for mobile robot autonomous navigation. Gul *et al.* (2019) steered the mobile robot to goal point and avoided obstacles. Benbouabdallah and Qi-dan (2013) created a fuzzy logic controller for searching target and path planning together with obstacle avoidance. Gul *et al.* (2019) gave a comprehensive study for robot navigation techniques. They cited several research works which applied fuzzy logic as a mobile robot navigation technique.

### 7.2.2.2. Artificial Neuronal Network

For many years, the Artificial Neuronal Network has been used as a tool for mobile robot navigation. Nguyen and Widrow (1989) gave an example of self-learning in neural networks. Engedy and Horváth (2009) described a dynamic artificial neural network based mobile robot motion and path planning system. The method made it possible to navigate a robot car on a flat surface among static and moving obstacles. Faisal *et al.* (2013) used the fuzzy logic for navigation and obstacle avoidance for a mobile robot in an unknown dynamic environment. Adv (2018) applied fuzzy logic as an efficient tool for the navigation of a mobile robot in an unknown dynamic environment. A performance comparison of fuzzy logic and neural network design for mobile robot navigation is given in Gul *et al.* (2019).

### 7.2.2.3. *Metaheuristic*

The Bee Algorithm was applied in Darwish and Joukhadar (2018). Qiongbing and Lixin (2016) used a new crossover mechanism for genetic algorithms with variable-length chromosomes for path optimization problems. The genetic algorithms were used by Alajlan *et al.* (2013). The Tabu search was applied as an approach for the autonomous navigation for a mobile robot in Chaaria *et al.* (2014). The particle swarm optimization (PSO) was used in Ahmad and Ghanavati (2012). Different nature-inspired techniques applied for motion planning of wheeled robots were used in Pandey (2018). In Capi *et al.* (2015), the authors used an evolutionary algorithm hybridized with the neural network for the mobile robot navigation.

### 7.2.2.4. *Multi-agent systems*

MAS have received tremendous attention from scholars in different disciplines, especially in mobile robotics. Using agents for robotics has been studied for over two decades, with the first article published in 1996 outlining the pros and cons of agents in robotics (Jenkin *et al.* 1996). The control architecture based on MAS was modelized for the autonomous navigation of a mobile robot. Iñigo-Blasco *et al.* (2012) presented a framework for multi-agent robotic systems development. Elfakharany *et al.* (2020) presented a method that combines both steps: Multi Robot Task Allocation (MRTA) and Multi Robot Path Planning (MRPP) by using a deep reinforcement learning model. A hybrid body sensor network architecture based on multi-sensor fusion (HBMF) was designed to support the most advanced smart medical services, which combine various sensor, communication, robot and data processing technologies. This study is realized in Lin *et al.* (2020).

## 7.3. Problem position

Figure 7.2 represents the global architecture of a mobile robot; it is a synthesis of robot architectures described in the literature.

The essential parts of this architecture are the perception module, the decision module and the locomotion module.

– *Perception module*: the notion of perception in mobile robotics relates to the capacity of the system to collect, process and format information useful to the robot, in order to act and react in the world around it. While for handling tasks we can consider the robot environment to be relatively structured, this is no longer the case when it comes to navigating autonomously in partially known places. In addition, to extract the information useful for the accomplishment of its task, the robot must have many sensors that measure both its internal state and the environment in which it operates. The choice of sensors obviously depends on the intended application. To focus on the navigation problem, in this chapter we will discuss the sensors that are useful for this task.

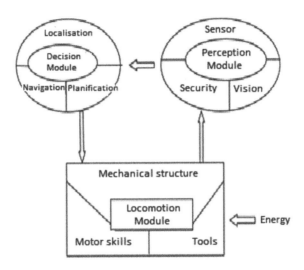

**Figure 7.2.** *Structure of robot architecture*

– *Decision module*: the information coming from various sensors must be interpreted as elements that are useful in making a decision on the action to be taken, the goal being to deliver the correct orders to the actuators, gripper arms or wheel motors. It is during this phase of the design of a robot that it is necessary to give it a form of intelligence, by giving it a choice on the action to be taken. This decision-making is often arbitrary at the beginning, but it helps to develop a form of learning that takes the results of previous decisions into account.

– *Locomotion module*: the locomotion module then comprises the mechanical structure, motricity and the energy used in the movement of the mobile robot. Mobile robots are indeed most often referred to by their type of locomotion, whether they are wheeled, walking, submarine or aerial. So far, different research laboratories have contributed to the construction of different mobile robots depending on the type of locomotion.

However, we note an architectural evolution of hierarchical architectures toward the "intelligent", which has been accompanied by a "tendency" toward more "autonomous" structures that locally manage their properties (organization, decision, action, information, communication, security, etc.) and use them to achieve the same purpose and goal (Lin *et al.* 2020).

Our problem is how to model and build a system that would have the main behavioral character, not to solve a well-posed problem, but to represent its environment in order to deploy it as best as possible, and to adapt to all changes that may occur during execution.

## 7.4. Developed control architecture

A robot is a complex system that must meet varied and sometimes contradictory requirements. A typical example for a mobile robot is the trade-off that must be made between the most precise execution of a pre-established plan to reach a goal and the unforeseen elements that should be taken into account, such as mobile obstacles. These arbitrations, whether in terms of the use of sensors, effectors or computing resources, are regulated by a software package called robot control architecture. This architecture therefore makes it possible to organize the relationships between the three main functions of perception, decision and action. In this context, a robot will be considered as a MAS and each of its components will be considered as an agent. The realization of the movement will then be the result of the coordination of a set of agents. Figure 7.3 shows the description of a mobile robot control architecture based agent.

An autonomous robot perceives the world through its sensors and acts on it via its effectors (perception-action loop). We want to have a relationship between sensors and motors to obtain the desired behavior. The global architecture developed is a fully distributed hybrid architecture and does not involve any supervisor. Agents can communicate with them directly through messages (mailboxes) or data (representations) available to the community of agents.

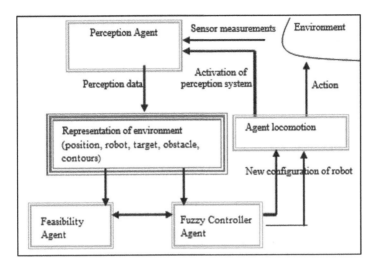

**Figure 7.3.** *Mobile robot control architecture based agent. For a color version of this figure, see www.iste.co.uk/chelouah/optimization.zip*

The system is designed around four agents (perception, locomotion, fuzzy controller and feasibility). They are classified into two groups. The first group contains the perception agent and the locomotion agent which have access and act on the environment. The other two, the fuzzy controller agent and the feasibility agent, are more cognitive and are strictly prohibited from having direct access to the environment. Each of these agents try to independently contribute to the system during navigation. The description of the agent system is given as follows:

## 7.4.1. *Agents description*

### 7.4.1.1. *Perception agent*

The perception agent creates representations of the environment from measurements provided by infrared sensors. For each intermediate situation, these representations are made available to other agents.

*Competences*:

– Give the current configuration of the robot.

– Determine the position of the target relative to the robot (distance and orientation).

– Determine the position of the obstacles relative to the robot for each new situation.

– Calculate the distances and orientations of the walls of the environment. Figure 7.4 illustrates the calculation of these measurements.

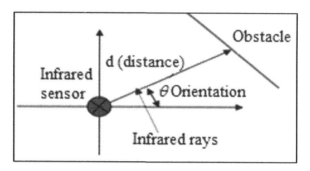

**Figure 7.4.** *Measurements provided by infrared sensors (information of perception agent and provided to all agents). For a color version of this figure, see www.iste.co.uk/chelouah/optimization.zip*

### 7.4.1.2. *Locomotion agent*

It is also called the agent of action. It establishes control laws intended for controlling the robot. These commands are made from a representation established by the fuzzy controller agent. In addition, the locomotion agent activates the perception agent when the robot is parked to start a new navigation. *This agent calculates the speed setpoints for the left and right wheel in order to reach the intermediate or final configuration.*

*Competences*:

– The procedure for calculating the values of the left and right speeds: $S_l, S_r$, as shown in Figure 7.5

with:

$T$: sampling time to be fixed.

The procedure for calculating is as follows:

$$\theta = \frac{S_l - S_r}{l} * T$$

If $\Delta S > 0$ then the robot must turn right

$$
\begin{bmatrix}
S_l = S \\
S_r = S - \dfrac{\Delta\theta * l}{T}
\end{bmatrix}
$$

If $\Delta S < 0$ then the robot must turn left

$$
\begin{bmatrix}
S_r = S \\
S_l = S - \dfrac{\Delta\theta * l}{T}
\end{bmatrix}
$$

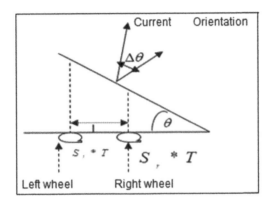

**Figure 7.5.** *Method for calculating speeds of the right and left wheels of the robot*

*Control plan*:

– Update its knowledge base.

– Support for a fuzzy controller message (the intermediate configuration to be achieved).

– Support for a deactivation or parking message in the event that the target is reached or in the event of a blocking situation.

– Sending an activation message (to launch a new navigation) or deactivation (target reached, blocking) to the collection agent.

*Action plan*:

It is described by the sequence of the following actions, according to the following diagram presented in Figure 7.6.

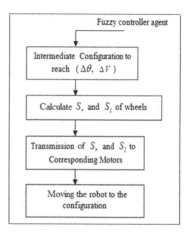

**Figure 7.6.** *Process of locomotion agent*

### 7.4.1.3. *Feasibility agent*

Its role consists of studying the feasibility of the robot's next action to avoid the risk of collision with a possible obstacle or the walls of the environment (selection of a new behavior). The primary role of the feasibility agent reflects the aspect of MAS in optimizing the navigation function.

*Competences*:

– Optimization of an objective function presented by the distance separating the intermediate configuration and the final configuration of the robot (the configuration of the target to be reached).

– From the set of intermediate configurations, select the most suitable to have an optimal path (to quickly reach the target) and not collide with the walls of the environment.

*Control*:

– Update its knowledge base (modification of the robot's intermediate configurations).

– Support for the message sent by the fuzzy controller agent (the list of intermediate robot configurations).

*Action plan*:

Figure 7.7 illustrates the feasibility agent diagram. This diagram shows the set of actions taken by the feasibility agent.

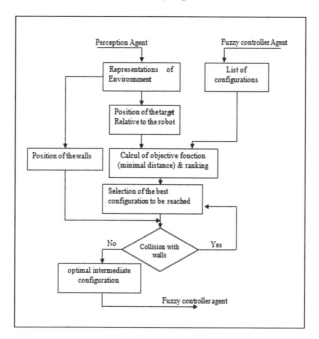

**Figure 7.7.** *Feasibility agent general process*

## 7.4.1.4. *Fuzzy controller agent*

Based on fuzzy reasoning and perception data, this agent tries to find possible openings in front of the robot to exit a given situation and continue on its way to the target. It gives the navigation information necessary for the locomotion of the robot to the locomotion agent, it also sends a deactivation order if the robot reaches the target or is in a blocking situation.

*Competences*:

– Establishment of inference rules linking inputs to outputs.

– Determine the possible outcomes in front of the robot.

– Stop the navigation process if the target is reached or if there is a blockage situation.

– Define the blocking situation.

*Control*:

– Take charge of the feasibility agent's message (the intermediate configuration to be reached selected).

– Update the knowledge base (updating local representations of the environment, adding and removing openings in front of the robot, the selected intermediate state becomes the current state).

*Action plan*:

The agent's action plan is presented by the following organigram:

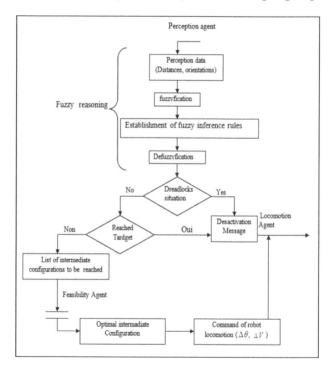

**Figure 7.8.** *Fuzzy controller agent general process*

The principle of navigation by fuzzy logic will be presented in the next section.

*Communication between agents*:

Communication between agents in this architecture takes place by sending and receiving asynchronous messages.

The inter agent communication is shown in Figure 7.9. It supports the transmission of messages between systems.

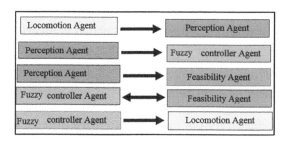

**Figure 7.9.** *Agent interaction and communication. For a color version of this figure, see www.iste.co.uk/chelouah/optimization.zip*

The messages are of following types: activation/deactivation message, request and message of results of execution of a task.

When a message is received from another agent, the decision to be made depends on the nature of the message:

– if the message is information from another agent → that agent is used to update the knowledge base of the receiving agent;

– if the message is a request → it is translated into a pending goal;

– if the message is an activation or deactivation order → it will be taken into account.

## 7.5. Navigation principle by fuzzy logic

### 7.5.1. *Fuzzy logic overview*

Fuzzy logic is a branch of mathematics and, as such, a whole series of fundamental concepts are developed in it. These concepts make it possible to justify and demonstrate certain basic principles. In the following, we will only retain the elements essential for understanding the principle of control by fuzzy logic. These are:

– fuzzy variables;

– inference rules.

In general, a fuzzy logic control system consists of three important modules: fuzzyfication module, which allows the passage from the digital domain to the symbolic domain; inference module, which establishes the rules linking the inputs to the outputs, and the defuzzyfication module, which makes the transformation fuzzy information in precise physical values (Pelletier 2000).

### 7.5.2. Description of simulated robot

The platform chosen for our mobile robot is the differential configuration comprising:

– two drive wheels controlled independently;

– two idler balancing wheels, which are added to the front of the robot to ensure its stability;

– three infrared sensors. One of these sensors is frontal and the other two are lateral to ensure the perception system of the mobile robot. This platform is very simple to control, since it suffices to specify the speeds of the two wheels, and in addition allows the robot to turn on the spot. This architecture is fairly standard and offers multiple areas of application.

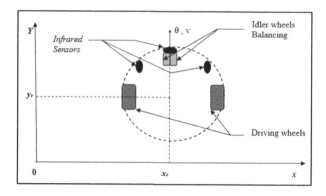

**Figure 7.10.** *Presentation of the robot*

The robot configuration can be described by its position at a given time presented by the following kinematic equations:

$$X(t) = X(t-1) + V(t)*\cos(\theta(t)) \tag{7.1}$$

$$Y(t) = Y(t-1) + V(t)*\sin(\theta(t)) \tag{7.2}$$

$$\theta(t) = \theta(t-1) + \Delta\theta(t) \tag{7.3}$$

$$S(t) = S(t-1) + \Delta S(t) \tag{7.4}$$

### 7.5.3. Strategy of navigation

The reflex action of the robot is deduced from the data analysis according to the three sides of the robot (dL, dF, dR: distances from obstacles) and the polar coordinates of the point of arrival in the robot's coordinate system (the orientation of the target noted γ, and the distance from the target noted d), as shown in Figure 7.11.

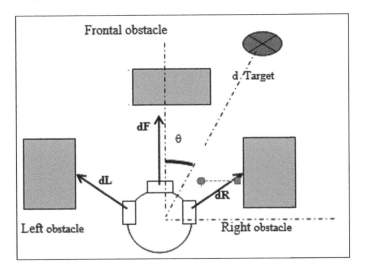

**Figure 7.11.** *Robot and obstacles information*

### 7.5.4. *Fuzzy controller agent*

Figure 7.12 shows the interaction and communication between the fuzzy logic agent and the others agents of the MAS.

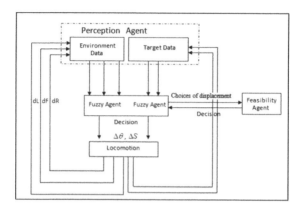

**Figure 7.12.** *Fuzzy controller agent interaction with navigation system agent*

*– Input Fuzzyfication*

The distances dL, DF, dR and d are evaluated with respect to the two fuzzy subsets N and F, which correspond respectively to Near and Far, as shown in Figure 7.13.

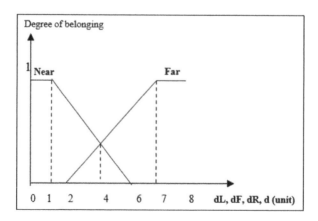

**Figure 7.13.** *Representation of fuzzy subsets of the distance*

The orientation angle of the target relative to the robot $\gamma$ is represented by five fuzzy intervals: ML (left large), LL (left small), Z (zero), LR (right small) and MR (right large) covering the frontal half space of the robot, as shown in Figure 7.14.

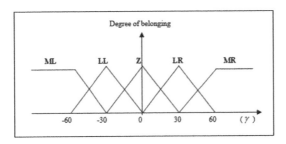

**Figure 7.14.** *Representation of fuzzy subsets of the* $\gamma$

*– Output Fuzzyfication*

These are the output variables $\Delta\theta$ and $\Delta v$.

– The robot's orientation angle $\Delta\theta$ (output variable) is represented by the five fuzzy subsets: $\theta$LM (theta left most), $\theta$LL (theta left little), $\theta$Z (theta zero), $\theta$RL (theta right little), $\theta$RM (theta right most). Figure 7.15 describes these fuzzy subsets.

– Speed variation $\Delta v$ is described by three subsets: Decspe (decrease speed), Zspe (no speed change) and Insp (increase speed). The description of these subsets is shown in Figure 7.16.

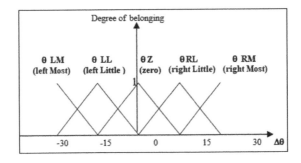

**Figures 7.15.** *Representation of output fuzzy subsets* $\Delta\theta$

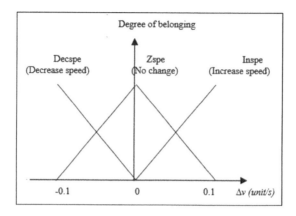

**Figure 7.16.** *Representation of output fuzzy subsets Δv*

*– Inference mechanism*

Navigation toward a goal can be broken down into a set of elementary behaviors (set of rules), each possessing a particular skill. For each obstacle avoidance situation, the robot has one or more choices to make and it is the role of the feasibility agent to select the best choice. For each perspective situation, the fuzzy controller agent provides the corresponding behavior based on the description of the feasibility agent. The answer is unique and only one behavior is active at a time and will have control of the robot at any time. At all times, the robot is in all situations but with different degrees of belonging.

The different behaviors we have implemented are based on:

– the distance separating the robot from an obstacle described using two linguistic data: near, far;

– the three input variables attached to the infrared sensors (left obstacle, right obstacle, front obstacle).

The overall behavior of the robot during its navigation is identified in two essential procedures:

1) Obstacle avoidance: The robot uses this procedure when it is faced with an obstacle, that is to say when it comes to situation 1, situation 7.

2) Approaching the goal: There are no obstacles. This is situation 8. These behaviors are presented in Figure 7.17.

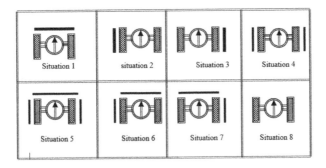

**Figure 7.17.** *Representation of the eight different situations listed*

**Situation 1:** "Avoid near in front of"

We stop the translational movement of the robot and ask for either:

– a right rotation;

– a left rotation;

– a half-turn rotation.

**Situation 2:** "Avoid near left"

No setpoint for the travel speed and either:

– a rotation to the right;

– a half-turn rotation;

– no change of direction.

**Situation 3:** "Avoid near right"

No setpoint for the travel speed and either:

– a rotation to the left;

– a half-turn rotation;

– no change of direction.

**Situation 4:** "Corridor"

No setpoint for angular speed and we ask for either:

– a half-turn rotation;

– no change in speed or rotation to stay in line with the lane.

**Situation 5**: "Blocking"

We stop the translational movement of the robot and ask the robot to do a turn around.

**Situation 6**: "Left corner"

We stop the movement and ask for either:

– a right rotation;

– a half-turn rotation.

**Situation 7**: "Right corner"

We stop the movement and ask for either:

– a left rotation;

– a half-turn rotation.

**Situation 8**: In this case, the "approaching the goal" procedure is used.

*– Inference rules*

The set of rules used in the eight situations that the robot can face is shown in Figures 7.18-7.25 below.

| | | dL | | dF | | dR | | d | | $\Delta\theta$ | $\Delta V$ |
|---|---|---|---|---|---|---|---|---|---|---|---|
| | | F | | N | | F | | F | | $\theta$LL | Decsped |
| | | F | | N | | F | | F | | $\theta$GL | Decsped |
| | | F | | N | | F | | F | | $\theta$LL | Decsped |
| If | | F | ∧ | N | ∧ | F | | N | Then | $\theta$LL | Decsped |
| | | | | | | | ∧ | | | | |
| | | F | | N | | F | | N | | $\theta$GL | Decsped |
| | | L | | P | | L | | P | | $\theta$ | Decsped |

**Figure 7.18.** *Situation 1 (avoid near in front of)*

|  | dG | | dF | | dD | d | | θΔ | ΔV |
|---|---|---|---|---|---|---|---|---|---|
| | | | F | | F | F | | θZ | Insped |
| | | | F | | F | F | | θLR | Zsped |
| | | | F | | F | F | | θMR | Zsped |
| IF | N | ∧ | F | ∧ | F | N | Then | θZ | Decsped |
| | | | F | | F | N | | θMRG | Decsped |
| | | | F | | F | N | | θML | Decsped |

Figure 7.19. *Situation 2 (avoid near left)*

| 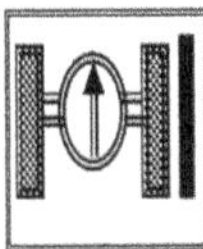 | dL | | dF | | dR | | d | | Δθ | ΔV |
|---|---|---|---|---|---|---|---|---|---|---|
| | F | | N | | N | | F | | θZ | Inspe |
| | F | | N | | N | | F | | θLL | Zsped |
| | F | | N | | N | | F | | θML | Zsped |
| If | F | ∧ | N | ∧ | N | ∧ | N | Then | θZ | Decsped |
| | F | | N | | N | | N | | θLL | Desped |
| | F | | N | | N | | N | | θML | Decsped |

Figure 7.20. *Situation 3 (avoid near right)*

|  | dL | | dF | | d | | d | | γ | Δθ | ΔV |
|---|---|---|---|---|---|---|---|---|---|---|---|
| | F | | F | | F | | F | | MG | θGG | Incsped |
| | F | | F | | F | | F | | ML | θGP | Incsped |
| | F | | F | | F | | F | | Z | θZ | Incsped |
| If | F | ∧ | F | ∧ | F | ∧ | F | ∧ RL | Then | θDP | Incsped |
| | F | | F | | F | | F | | MR | θDG | Incsped |
| | F | | F | | F | | N | | ML | θGG | Decsped |
| | F | | F | | F | | N | | LL | θGP | Decsped |
| | F | | F | | F | | N | | Z | θZ | Decsped |
| | F | | F | | F | | N | | RL | θDP | Decsped |
| | F | | F | | F | | N | | RL | TDP | Decsped |

Figure 7.21. *Situation 4 (situation corridor)*

|  | dL | dF | | dR | | d | $\gamma$ | | $\Delta\theta$ | $\Delta V$ |
|---|---|---|---|---|---|---|---|---|---|---|
| | N | N | | N | | F | ML | | $\theta$M | Decsped |
| | N | N | | N | | F | LL | | $\theta$MG | Decsped |
| | N | N | | N | | F | Z | | $\theta$Z | Decsped |
| If | N | N | $\wedge$ | N | $\wedge$ | F | MR | Then | $\theta$RL | Decsped |
| | N | N | | N | | F | MR | | $\theta$ML | Decsped |
| | N | N | | N | | N | ML | | $\theta$ML | Decsped |
| | N | N | | N | | N | LL | | $\theta$ML | Decsped |
| | N | N | | N | | N | Z | | $\theta$Z | Decsped |
| | N | N | | N | | N | RL | | $\theta$RL | Decsped |
| | N | N | | N | | N | ML | | $\theta$RM | Decsped |

**Figure 7.22.** *Situation 5 (blocking)*

|  | dL | | dF | | dR | | d | | $\Delta\theta$ | $\Delta V$ |
|---|---|---|---|---|---|---|---|---|---|---|
| | N | | N | | F | | F | | $\theta$LR | Decsped |
| | N | | N | | F | | F | | $\theta$MR | Decsped |
| If | N | $\wedge$ | N | $\wedge$ | F | $\wedge$ | N | Then | $\theta$ Z | Decsped |
| | N | | N | | F | | N | | $\theta$ML | Decsped |

**Figure 7.23.** *Situation 6 (corner left)*

|  | dL | | dF | | dR | | d | | $\Delta\theta$ | $\Delta V$ |
|---|---|---|---|---|---|---|---|---|---|---|
| | F | | N | | N | | F | | $\theta$LL | Decsped |
| | F | | N | | N | | F | | $\theta$ML | Decsped |
| If | F | $\wedge$ | N | $\wedge$ | N | $\wedge$ | F | Then | $\theta$LL | Decsped |
| | F | | N | | N | | F | | $\theta$ML | Decsped |

**Figures 7.24.** *Situation 7 (corner right)*

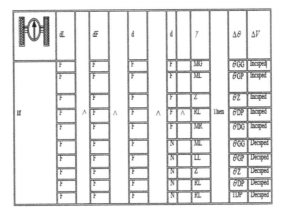

| | dL | | dF | | d | | d | | γ | | Δθ | ΔV |
|---|---|---|---|---|---|---|---|---|---|---|---|---|
| | F | | F | | F | | F | | MG | | θGG | Incsped |
| | F | | F | | F | | F | | ML | | θGP | Incsped |
| | F | | F | | F | | F | | Z | | θZ | Incsped |
| If | F | ∧ | F | ∧ | F | ∧ | F | ∧ | RL | Then | θDP | Incsped |
| | F | | F | | F | | F | | MR | | θDG | Incsped |
| | F | | F | | F | | N | | ML | | θGG | Decsped |
| | F | | F | | F | | N | | LL | | θGP | Decsped |
| | F | | F | | F | | N | | Z | | θZ | Decsped |
| | F | | F | | F | | N | | RL | | θDP | Decsped |
| | F | | F | | F | | N | | RL | | TDP | Decsped |

**Figure 7.25.** *Situation 8 (far obstacle: approaching the goal)*

This step concerns the development of rules, to define the expected behavior of the robot according to its intrinsic parameters: obstacles data, target data and the robot movement instructions. Every combination of input variable values results in an action to the output variables. In total we get 80 fuzzy rules.

*– Defuzzyfication*

The controller output is obtained by the defuzzification method called "weighted average". This step transforms the command values of the real area (physical variables). This choice is generally conditioned by a compromise between the implementation ease and calculation performance (Pelletier 2000). We have used the center of gravity method determined by the following relation:

$$z^* = \sum_{i=1}^{i=m} z_i * \mu(z_i) \bigg/ \sum_{i=1}^{m} \mu(z_i)$$

[7.5]

with

– m: number of rules;

– Z: variables of command;

– μ: membership function.

## 7.6. Simulation and results

To implement the control architecture developed and described in previous sections, in this part we have implemented a local planner based on sensory information in a constrained and unknown environment to navigate the robot to a final destination. The mobile robot must be able to make decisions about the movements to be made according to variations in the environment; the program implemented locates the robot, the target, and determines the position of the obstacles in relation to each moment during navigation. This program also allows the monitoring of places of evolution and transmits information about the environment to the robot. The implemented simulator is based on the hybridization between MAS and fuzzy logic, in order to benefit from the advantages of each methodology. Using programming tools (Borland 5 c ++), this implementation allows us to visualize the results of the navigation of the mobile robot in different environments.

Several navigation tests have been simulated for different configurations of the target and robot in different environments (simple and complex environments). Figures 7.26 and 7.27 show the path taken by the robot to reach its target; Figure 7.26 with environment 1 and environment 2 and Figure 7.27 with environment 4 and environment 5, which are more complex than environments 1 and 2.

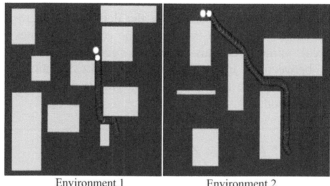

Environment 1                    Environment 2

**Figure 7.26.** *The robot, in environments 1 and 2, reaches the target (all obstacles are avoided). For a color version of this figure, see www.iste.co.uk/chelouah/optimization.zip*

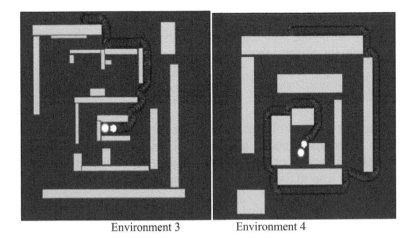

Environment 3          Environment 4

**Figure 7.27.** *The robot reaches the target in complex environments (environments 3 and 4) (all obstacles are avoided). For a color version of this figure, see www.iste.co.uk/chelouah/optimization.zip*

The navigation approach adopted deals with robot blockage situations. In the case of a deadlock situation, the fuzzy controller sends a deactivation message to the locomotion agent to stop the robot, as shown in Figure 7.28.

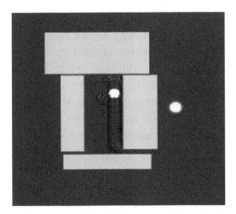

**Figure 7.28.** *The robot in a deadlock situation. For a color version of this figure, see www.iste.co.uk/chelouah/optimization.zip*

Through these figures, we note the performance and efficiency of the adopted approaches (MAS and fuzzy logic) in the mobile robot navigation in complex and changed environments. The robot always manages to reach its target without colliding with obstacles or with the walls of the environment, while choosing the shortest path.

## 7.7. Conclusion

The design of a control architecture is a central problem in a project of realization of an autonomous mobile robot. In the absence of a universal solution that eclipses all others, it is essential to detail and justify the design process that has lead to the proposed solution.

In this chapter, we presented a solution to this problem by developing a navigation control architecture based on the hybridization of two artificial intelligence approaches: MAS and fuzzy logic. More details have been given in this chapter about the inference mechanism. The overall behavior of the robot during its navigation is identified in two essential procedures: the obstacle avoidance procedure (there are seven situations: situation 1, …, situation 7) and the approaching goal (there is one situation: situation 8). These procedures are presented by some rules of navigation, using fuzzy logic as advanced tool for navigation.

The simulation results obtained are satisfactory because the robot manages to reach its target, despite the complexity of the environment in which it is located. This leads the way to the adaptation of our architecture developed for navigation in a dynamic environment (moving obstacles). The extension to distributed mobile robotics could be achieved because the chosen architecture is able to manage communications between other robots by adding specific agents, ensuring the link with other robots, which widens the field of application of mobile robotics. So design a multi-agent system organized by subsystems, where each robot is a subsystem multi agent.

## 7.8. References

Adv, J. (2018). Fuzzy logic as efficient tool to the navigation of mobile robot in an unknown dynamic environment. *Robot Systems*, 10(37), 1–7.

Ahmad, Z. and Ghanavati, M. (2012). Navigation of mobile robot using the PSO particle swarm optimization. *Journal of Academic and Applied Studies*, 2(1), 32–38.

Ahmadzadeh, H. and Masehian, E. (2015). Modular robotic systems: Methods and algorithms for abstraction, planning, control, and synchronization. *Artificial Intelligence*, 223, 27–64.

Alajlan, M., Koubaa, A., Chaari, I., Bennaceur, H., Ammar, A. (2013). Global path planning for mobile robots in large-scale grid environments using genetic algorithms. In *International Conference on Individual and Collective Behaviors in Robotics (ICBR'2013)*, Sousse, Tunisia.

Benbouabdallah, K. and Qi-dan, Z. (2013). A fuzzy logic behavior architecture controller for a mobile robot path planning in multi-obstacles environment. *Research Journal of Applied Sciences, Engineering and Technology*, 5(14), 3835–3842.

Buhler, H. (1994). *Réglage par la logique floue*. Presses polytechniques et universitaires romandes, Lausanne, Switzerland.

Capi, G., Kaneko, S., Hua, B. (2015). Neural network based guide robot navigation: An evolutionary approach. *Procedia Computer Science*, 76, 74–79.

Chaaria, I., Koubaa, A., Bennaceur, H., Ammar, A., Trigui, S., Tounsi, M., Shakshuki, E., Youssef, H. (2014). 5th International Conference on Ambient Systems, Networks and Technologies (ANT): On the adequacy of Tabu search for global robot path planning problem in grid environments. *Procedia Computer Science*, 32, 604–613.

Chaib-draa, B. (1994). Distributed artificial intelligence: An overview. In *Encyclopedia of Computer Science and Technology*, Ken, A., Williams, J.G., Hall, C.M. and Kent, R. (eds). Marcel Dekker Inc., New York.

Chaib-draa, B., Jarras, I., Moulin, B. (2001). Multi-agent systems: General principles and applications. In *Agent and Multi Agents System*, Briot, J.P. and Demazeau, Y. (eds). Hermes, Ottawa, Canada.

Darwish, H. and Joukhadar, A. (2018). Using the Bees Algorithm for wheeled mobile robot path planning in an indoor dynamic environment. *Journal Cogent Engineering*, 5(1), 1426539.

Dudek, G., Jenkin, M.R., Milios, E., Wilkes, D. (1996). A taxonomy for multi-agent robotics. *Autonomous Robots*, 3(4), 375–397.

Elfakharany, A., Yusof, R., Ismail, Z. (2020). Towards multi robot task allocation and navigation using deep reinforcement learning. *Journal of Physics*, 1447, January.

Engedy, I. and Horváth, G. (2009). Dynamic artificial neural network based mobile robot motion and path planning system. *6th IEEE International Symposium on Intelligent Signal Processing*, Budapest, Hungary.

Faisal, M., Hedjar, R., Al Sulaiman, M., Al-Mutib, K. (2013). Fuzzy logic navigation and obstacle avoidance by a mobile robot in an unknown dynamic environment. *INTECH International Journal of Advanced Robotic Systems*, 10(1), 1–7.

Farhad, B., Sepideh, N.N., Morteza, A. (2018). Mobile robots path planning: Electrostatic potential field approach. *Expert Systems with Applications*, 100, 68–78.

Ferber, J. (1995). *Les systèms multi-agents : vers une intelligence collective*. InterEditions, Paris, France.

Gul, F., Rahiman, W., Sahal, S., Alhady, N. (2019). A comprehensive study for robot navigation techniques. *Journal Cogent Engineering*, 6(1).

Holzmann, F., Bellino, M., Kolski, S., Sulzmann, A., Spiegelberg, G., Siegwart, R., (2005). Robots go automotive – The SPARC approach. *IEEE Intelligent Vehicles Symposium, Proceedings*, 478–483.

Iñigo-Blasco, P., Diaz-del Rio, F., Carmen Romero-Ternero, M., Cagigas-Muñiz, D., Vicente-Diaz, S. (2012). Robotics software frameworks for multiagent robotic systems development. *Robotics and Autonomous Systems*, 60(6), 803–821.

Khatib, O. (1986). Real-time obstacle avoidance for manipulators and mobile robots. *International Journal of Robotic Research*, 5(1), 90–98.

Latombe, J.C. (1999). Motion planning: A journey of robots, molecules, digital actors, and other artifacts. *The International Journal of Robotics Research*, 18(11), 1119–1128.

Lin, K., Li, Y., Sun, J., Zhou, D., Zhang, Q. (2020). Multi-sensor fusion for body sensor network in medical human–robot interaction scenario. *Science Direct, Information Fusion*, 57, 15–26.

Lozano-Pérez, T. (1983). Spatial planning: Configuration space approach. *IEEE Transactions on Computers*, C-32(2), 108–120.

Matoui, F., Boussaid, B., Metoui, B., Frej, G.B., Abdelkrim, M.N. (2017). Path planning of a group of robots with potential field approach: Decentralized architecture. *IFAC-PapersOnLine*, 50(1), 11473–11478.

Moreau, J. Melchior, P., Victor, S., Aioun, F., Guillemard, F. (2017). Path planning with fractional potential fields for autonomous vehicles. *IFAC-PapersOnLine*, 50(1), 11433–11438.

Moulin, B. and Chaib-draa, B. (1996). An overview of distributed artificial intelligence. In *Foundations of Distributed AI*, O'Hare, G.M.P. and Jennings, N.R. (eds). John Wiley & Sons, Chichester, UK.

Nguyen, D. and Widrow, B. (1989). The truck backer-upper: An example of self-learning in neural networks. *Proceedings of the International Joint Conference on Neural Networks*, 2, 357–362.

Pan, J. and Dinesh Manocha, D. (2015). Efficient configuration space construction and optimization for motion planning. *Engineering*, 1(1), 46–57.

Pandey, A. (2018). Different nature-inspired techniques applied for motion planning of wheeled robot: A critical review. *International Journal of Advanced Robotics and Automation*, 3(2), 1–10.

Pelletier, F.J. (2000). Review of metamathematics of fuzzy logics. *The Bulletin of Symbolic Logic*, 6(3), 342–346.

Qiongbing, Z and Lixin, D. (2016). A new crossover mechanism for genetic algorithms with variable-length chromosomes for path optimization problems. *Expert Systems with Applications*, 60, 183–189.

Reignier, P. (1994). Pilotage réactif d'un robot mobile : étude de lien entre la perception et l'action. Thesis, Institut national polytechnique de Grenoble, France.

Schwartz, J.T. and Yap, C.K. (1987). *Algorithmic and Geometric Aspects of Robotics*. Lawrence Erlbaum Associates, Hillsdale, NJ, USA.

Wijesoma, W.S., Khaw P.P., Teak, E.K. (2001). Sensor modeling and fusion for fuzzy navigation of an AGV. *International Journal of Robotic and Automation*, 16(1), 14–25.

Yahyaoui, K., Debbat, F., Khelfi, M.F. (2006). Conception d'une architecture de contrôle pour la navigation autonome d'un robot mobile. *Conférence Internationale sur l'Ingénierie de Électronique*, Université des sciences et technologie d'Oran Mohamed Boudiaf, Algeria, 28–29 May.

# 8

# Intrusion Detection with Neural Networks: A Tutorial

Alvise DE' FAVERI TRON

*Politecnico di Milano, Milan, Italy*

## 8.1. Introduction

### 8.1.1. *Intrusion detection systems*

Intrusion Detection is a key concept in modern computer network security. Rather than protecting a network against known malware by preventing the connection needed to enter the network, like in Intrusion Prevention Systems (IPS), Intrusion Detection is aimed at analyzing the current state of a network in real-time and identifying potential anomalies that are happening in the system, reporting them as soon as they are identified. This enables the possibility of detecting previously unknown malware (Mukherjee *et al.* 1994).

Intrusion detection systems are generally classified according to the following categories (Lazarevic *et al.* 2003):

− *Anomaly detection versus misuse detection*: in misuse detection, each instance in a dataset is labeled as "normal" or "intrusive" and a learning algorithm is trained over the labeled data. Anomaly detection approaches, on the other hand, build models of normal data and detect deviations from the normal model in observed data.

---

For a color version of all the figures in this chapter, see: www.iste.co.uk/chelouah/optimization.zip.

*Optimization and Machine Learning,*
coordinated by Rachid CHELOUAH and Patrick SIARRY © ISTE Ltd 2022.

– *Network-based versus Host-based*: network intrusion detection systems (NIDS) are placed at a strategic point or points within the network to monitor traffic to and from all devices on the network, while host intrusion detection systems (HIDS) run on individual hosts or devices on the network.

In this chapter, we will build an NIDS trained on labeled data which can recognize suspect behavior in a network and classify each connection as normal or anomalous.

### 8.1.2. *Artificial neural networks*

Artificial neural networks (ANN) are supervised machine learning algorithms inspired by the human brain. The main idea is to have many simple units, called neurons, organized in layers. In a feed-forward ANN, all neurons of a layer are connected to all the neurons of the following layer, and so on until the last layer, which contains the output of the neural network. This kind of network is a popular choice among Data Mining techniques today and has already been proven to be a valuable choice for Intrusion Detection (Reddy 2013; Subba *et al.* 2016).

Here we are building a feed-forward neural network trained on the NSL-KDD dataset to classify network connections as belonging to one of two possible categories: normal or anomalous. The goal of this work is to maximize the accuracy in recognizing new data samples, while also avoid overfitting, which happens when the algorithm is too attached to the data it learned and is not capable of correctly generalizing on previously unseen data.

### 8.1.3. *The NSL-KDD dataset*

The dataset used for training and validation of the neural network is the NSL-KDD dataset, which is an improved version of the KDD CUP '99 dataset (Dhanabal and Shantharajah 2015; Thomas and Pavithran 2018). This dataset is a well-known benchmark in the field of Network Intrusion Detection techniques, providing 42 features for each example and many anomalous examples. The dataset has been taken from the University of New Brunswick's website[1]. A detailed analysis of the dataset is provided in the next section.

---

1 https://www.unb.ca/cic/datasets/nsl. html.

## 8.2. Dataset analysis

This section provides a complete analysis of the NSL-KDD dataset.

### 8.2.1. *Dataset summary*

The NSL-KDD dataset is provided in two forms: *arff* files, with binary labels, and *csv* files, with categorical labels for each instance. Since the object of this work is to build a binary classifier, we will focus only on the *arff* files. The provided *arff* files contain a total of about 148,500 entries.

The train and test set were generated merging the provided *arff* files and splitting them with an 80:20 ratio.

Table 8.1 contains a summary of the most important attributes of the dataset.

| Dataset Summary | |
|---|---|
| Total rows | 148,517 |
| Columns | 42 |
| Duplicates | 629 |
| Null values | None |

**Table 8.1.** *Summary of the attributes of the NSL-KDD dataset*

### 8.2.2. *Features*

As for the features of this dataset, they can be broken down into four types (excluding the target column):

– 6 categorical;

– 5 binary;

– 15 discrete;

– 15 continuous.

Table 8.2 contains a list of all the features in the dataset, divided by their type. Note that this definition slightly differs from the one provided by Dhanabal and Shantharajah (2015), since here categorical and binary features are listed regardless of their format (text or numeric).

| Discrete | Continuous | Binary | Categorical |
|---|---|---|---|
| Duration | serror_rate | Land | Protocol_type |
| Src_bytes | srv_serror_rate | Logged_in | Service |
| Dst_bytes | rerror_rate | Root_shell | Flag |
| Hot | srv_rerror_rate | Is_host_login | Su_attempted |
| Num_failed_logins | same_srv_rate | Is_guest_login | Wrong_fragment |
| Num_compromised | diff_srv_rate | | Urgent |
| Num_root | srv_diff_host_rate | | |
| Num_file_creations | dst_host_same_srv_rate | | |
| Num_shells | dst_host_diff_srv_rate | | |
| Num_access_files | dst_host_same_src_port_rate | | |
| Num_outbound_cmds | dst_host_srv_diff_host_rate | | |
| Count | dst_host_serror_rate | | |
| Srv_count | dst_host_srv_serror_rate | | |
| Dst_host_count | dst_host_rerror_rate | | |
| Dst_host_srv_count | dst_host_srv_rerror_rate | | |

**Table 8.2.** *Features of the NSL-KDD dataset, divided by type*

The following sections will provide an in-depth analysis of this dataset, in order to get an intuitive understanding of the information described by each feature and the value distribution in both the train and test set.

At this stage, we are trying to get an insight on which are the important pieces of information that our NIDS will need in order to build precise and robust predictions.

### 8.2.3. *Binary feature distribution*

The binary features contained in this dataset are mainly related to characteristics of the network connection that is described in each row. Figures 8.1–8.5 show the number of "0"s and "1"s contained in the dataset for each of these features.

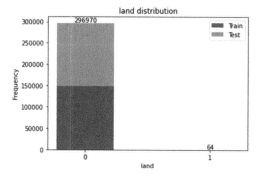

**Figure 8.1.** *Land category distribution*

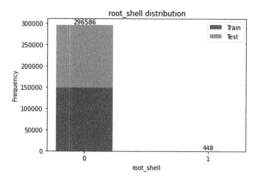

**Figure 8.2.** *Root_shell category distribution*

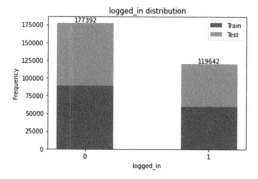

**Figure 8.3.** *Logged_in category distribution*

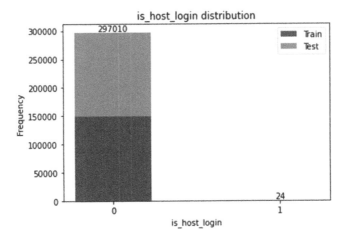

**Figure 8.4.** *Is_host_login category distribution*

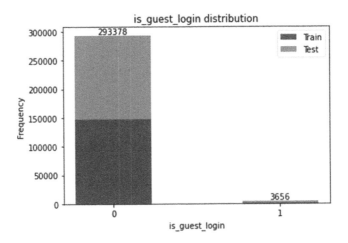

**Figure 8.5.** *Is_guest_login category distribution*

The target column ("class") is also a binary feature, which indicates whether a connection was classified as "normal" or "anomalous". Figures 8.6 and 8.7 show the number of normal and anomalous samples that were contained in the train and test sets. As we can see, the target variable (class) has a nearly even distribution of values throughout the dataset, meaning that there are a lot of anomalous examples that can be used for training.

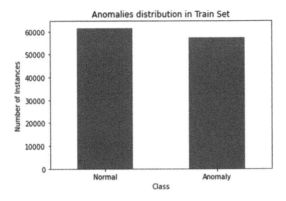

**Figure 8.6.** *Distribution of the target column values in the train set*

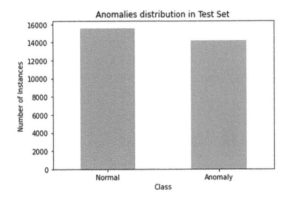

**Figure 8.7.** *Distribution of the target column values in the test set*

## 8.2.4. *Categorical features distribution*

The NSL-KDD dataset contains a few multi-class categorical features, which are used to label each connection with its protocol, service and other useful characteristics, for example, if the user tried to gain super-user access.

Figures 8.8 – 8.13 describe, for each categorical feature, how many occurrences of each label are present in both the train and the test set. Note that class, protocol type, service and flag features contain textual values, while all other categories are expressed by a number.

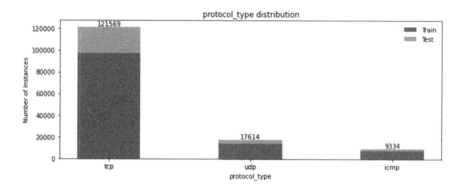

**Figure 8.8.** *Protocol type value distribution*

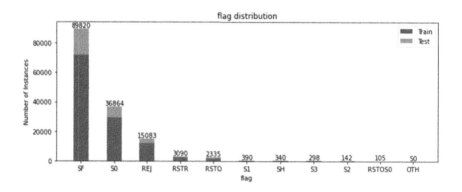

**Figure 8.9.** *Flag value distribution*

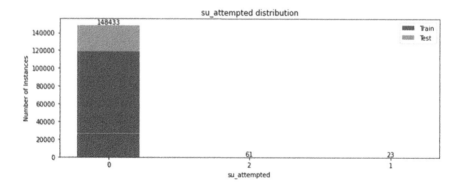

**Figure 8.10.** *Su attempted value distribution*

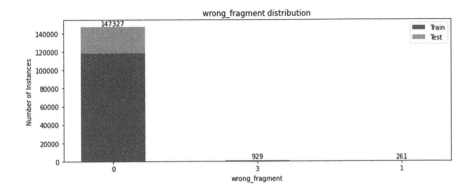

**Figure 8.11.** *Wrong fragment value distribution*

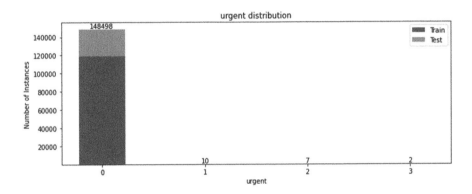

**Figure 8.12.** *Urgent value distribution*

We can see that some of the categories are not evenly distributed, with more than 99% of the sample belonging to just one class, for example, only 84 among more than 148,000 connections have tried to gain root access. This kind of analysis will be useful during the feature selection step, when we will try to identify which categorical feature carries more information about anomalies.

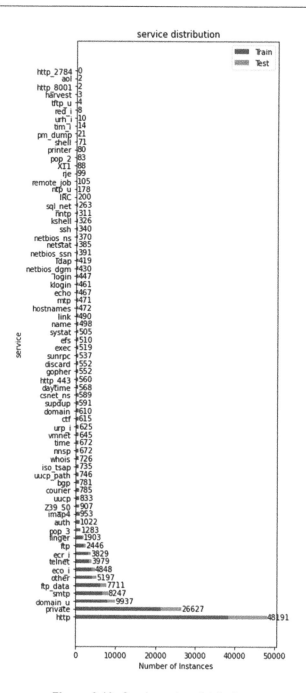

**Figure 8.13.** *Service value distribution*

## 8.2.5. *Numerical data distribution*

Numerical features have very different meanings in this dataset, and consequently different ranges. Continuous features are used for rates (e.g. error rates), which range from 0.0 to 1.0, and discrete features give information about the number of bytes in the packet, the connection duration, the number of reconnections and many other.

Figure 8.14 represents the normalized dataset: each column's value has been normalized between 0 and 1 to visualize how the different values of each feature are distributed.

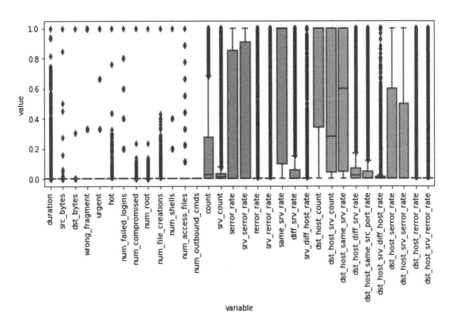

**Figure 8.14.** *Distribution of discrete and continuous features inside the normalized dataset*

Note that this normalization considers both the train and the test set, which is not a realistic scenario and is done only in this preliminary phase for data visualization purposes.

## 8.2.6. *Correlation matrix*

As a final step of the data analysis, we run a correlation analysis for all the features of the dataset. Figure 8.15 illustrates this correlation matrix.

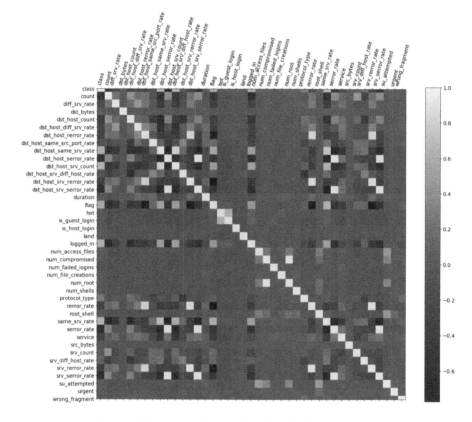

**Figure 8.15.** *Correlation matrix of all the features of the dataset. A lighter color means higher correlation*

Focusing on the class column, we can see how each feature is correlated with the target variable, either directly or inversely. This analysis can be extremely useful when performing feature selection to estimate how many important features are there in the dataset.

## 8.3. Data preparation

In this section, we will describe all the techniques used for cleaning and preparing the data for the learning phase.

### 8.3.1. *Data cleaning*

Since the NSL-KDD dataset is already an enhanced version of the older KDD '99 CUP dataset, little additional cleaning had to be performed: the set is already cleaned from redundant data and null values (Dhanabal and Shantharajah 2015).

The ratio between normal and anomalous entries is also good for machine learning purposes.

The only cleaning action that should be taken at this step, after loading the *arff* files and encoding strings in *UTF-8*, is to remove the *num_outbound_commands* column, which is filled with only "0"s.

### 8.3.2. *Categorical columns encoding*

After cleaning the dataset, the second step is to convert all categorical columns into one-hot encoded columns. This means that, for each distinct value of each categorical column, a new column is generated, containing "1" for the rows belonging to that category and "0" elsewhere.

This kind of encoding is the most popular choice when it comes to preparing data for ANN learning (Potdar *et al.* 2017). This is done to prevent the algorithm from interpreting categories as numbers, which can lead to problems such as the algorithm considering a category the mean of other two categories, which is clearly not what we want. The affected columns are:

– service;

– protocol type;

– super-user attempted;

– flag;

– wrong fragment;

– urgent.

The dataset resulting from this encoding contains 130 columns, of which one is the target columns.

Note that binary columns are not affected by the encoding. This is to avoid redundant columns, since binary features would have two corresponding encoded columns, in which one can be directly inferred by observing the other. Adding such columns would only increase the dataset noise and size, without adding useful information for the ANN.

### 8.3.3. Normalization

Having encoded the categorical columns, now the numerical columns must be treated.

Continuous features are already expressed with numbers from 0 to 1, so they all have the same scale. On the other side, discrete columns, which describe features such as the number of bytes exchanged and various counters, contain positive integers of different scales.

On this column we apply a normalization function, for two main reasons:

– To reduce all features to the same scale: when analyzing a particular instance in a classification problem, we are not interested in the absolute value that is contained in a feature, but instead we want to know what this value means *with respect to others*. This avoids the possibility of the neural network giving more weight to bigger numbers.

– To soften the impact of outliers: some of the recorded data in the dataset contain extreme values, for example, very long packets or very long connections. These extreme values represent exceptional cases, but, on the other hand, we want our ANN to be able to recognize primarily the most common cases.

For this reason, we decided to use *scikit-learn*'s *Normalizer*[2], which rescales the vector for each sample to have unit norm, independently of the distribution of the samples. The normalization process has been accomplished as follows:

– fit the model onto the train set;

---

2 https://scikit-learn.org/stable/modules/generated/sklearn.preprocessing.Normalizer.html.

– transform the train set;

– transform the test set (with the same normalization model).

Figure 8.16 shows the distribution of the numerical values in the train set after normalization, while Figure 8.17 illustrates the same transformation applied to the test set.

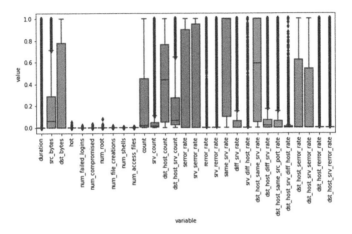

**Figure 8.16.** *Distribution of the values of each numerical feature in the normalized train set*

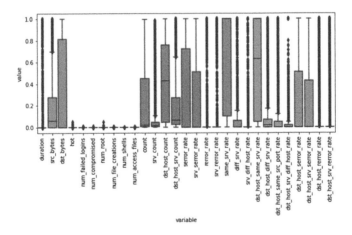

**Figure 8.17.** *Distribution of the values of each numerical feature in the normalized test set*

As an example of the behavior of this scaler, Figures 8.18–8.21 show the distribution of the values of two features before and after normalization.

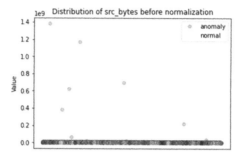

**Figure 8.18.** *Distribution of src_bytes before normalization*

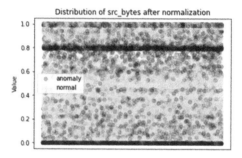

**Figure 8.19.** *Distribution of src_bytes after normalization*

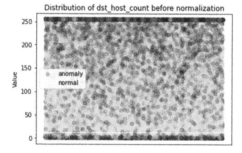

**Figure 8.20.** *Distribution of dst_host_count before normalization*

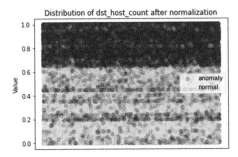

**Figure 8.21.** *Distribution of dst_host_count after normalization*

## 8.4. Feature selection

As a final step of our data preparation pipeline, we want to reduce the number of features over which the ANN should reason, that is perform feature selection. Feature selection in our case has two main purposes: reduce the problem complexity and reduce overfitting.

Since the one-hot encoding increased the number of features considerably, reducing the problem complexity can significantly impact speed and performance, especially during the ANN training phase.

By reducing the information on the train set, we also reduce the possibility of overfitting, since we are omitting specific information of the initial data while trying to concentrate only on the most useful features. However, if not correctly performed, feature selection can introduce some losses in terms of the accuracy of the final output.

Many algorithms are available today for performing feature selection (Huang 2015), each with different tradeoffs. For our IDS, we chose to try two commonly employed methods: *univariate selection* and *tree-based selection*.

### 8.4.1. *Tree-based selection*

Tree-based selection methods use decision trees to derive the *impurity* of each feature. This information can then be used to select important features in the dataset. In particular, a *random forest* of classification trees is built: the idea is to construct a great number of decision trees that see only a random extraction of the features of the initial dataset. Each tree will then construct its nodes, each of which will try to split the dataset into two sets of similar nodes. Calculating the impurity of the resulting sets for each feature, and averaging them out over the trees, we obtain the final importance of the variable.

To perform this kind of selection, we employ *ExtraTreesClassifier*, which is a classification algorithm provided by Python's *scikit-learn* library[3]. Figure 8.22 shows the ranking of the best features obtained when running the classifier on the train set.

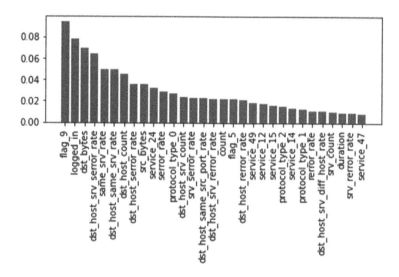

**Figure 8.22.** *Top features ranked by importance found by the ExtraTrees Classifier*

### 8.4.2. *Univariate selection*

Univariate feature selection is another common method for feature selection. It uses univariate statistical tests, such as *chi-squared* and *F* tests, from which we can obtain univariate scores and *p*-values. This method

---

3 https://scikit-learn.org/stable/modules/generated/sklearn.ensemble.ExtraTreesClassifier.html.

essentially differs from the tree-based method, since in the latter the forest is constructed randomly.

For our classification problem, the *chi-squared* statistical test is employed to measure the strength of the relationship of the feature with the target variable. The implementation used is provided by the *scikit-learn* collection[4]. Figure 8.23 shows the best 30 features found with univariate selection.

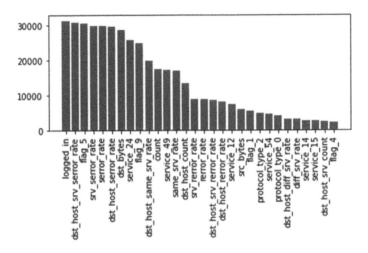

**Figure 8.23.** *Top 30 features ranked by importance found by univariate selection*

As we can see, the two methods have selected different sets of features. We will compare the results of these decisions in later sections.

## 8.5. Model design

### 8.5.1. *Project environment*

All results collected in this work have been generated building neural networks in *Python 3.6*. To build the ANN model, the *Keras* library has been employed, with *TensorFlow* as a backend. Therefore, many hyperparameters and specific implementations are provided by these frameworks.

---

4 https://scikit-learn.org/stable/modules/generated/sklearn.featureselection.SelectKBest.html#skl earn.feature_selection.SelectKBest.

## 8.5.2. *Building the neural network*

The approach for constructing the neural network for this work has been to try different combinations of layers and see how each model performs in terms of accuracy and loss, comparing these two metrics for the train and test set.

All neural networks have been implemented in *Keras*[5] using the sequential (i.e. feed-forward) model and dense (i.e. fully interconnected) layers. Following the work of (Kim and Gofman 2018), the tested models consist of both shallow networks and deep networks with up to four hidden layers.

## 8.5.3. *Learning hyperparameters*

When designing a neural network there are many hyperparameters that have to be set apart from the number of layers and neurons in each layer. In particular, the following parameters were chosen after some initial tests:

– Learning rate: In order to keep a good convergence without losing accuracy, this parameter has been set to 0.001. Other values tried were 0.01 and 0.0001.

– Optimization algorithm: *Adam*[6], one of the standard optimizers provided by *Keras*.

– Loss function: *Binary-crossentropy*. This was chosen since we are building a binary classifier.

## 8.5.4. *Epochs*

Each model was trained with a fixed number of epochs, which were empirically chosen to be 150.

In future developments, fixed epochs could be substituted by early stopping to speed up the learning phase: in this way, the training would stop

---

5 https://keras.io.

6 https://www.tensorflow.org/api docs/python/tf/keras/optimizers/Adam.

whenever the accuracy cannot be significantly improved, and this can happen much before the 150th epoch.

### 8.5.5. *Batch size*

Choosing the batch size implies a tradeoff between the speed of the learning phase and the accuracy of the model. A batch size of 1, sometimes called *online learning*, means that, for each epoch of the learning phase, the input data will be learned one entry at a time.

Having a batch size which is much smaller than the entire dataset but still greater than one, such as 16 or 32 (sometimes called mini-batch), means that more than one entry will be analyzed together in a single step of a learning epoch.

It has been shown in Keskar *et al.* (2016) that this solution might be preferable in general with respect to larger batches, so our choice has been to set the batch size to 16.

### 8.5.6. *Dropout layers*

Dropout regularization is a common and well-established method to prevent models from overfitting (Srivastava *et al.* 2014). This method consists of adding dropout layers to the neural network. These layers are interposed between the other layers of the network, and their effect is to inhibit the output of the previous layer with a certain probability. This is equivalent to randomly discarding some of the effects of the input during the training phase, which makes the model more robust and immune to overfitting.

The probabilities chosen are:

– Input layer: 0.5. A high dropout probability in the input layers means that not all features will be used for all the data, which is the primary idea when trying to avoid overfitting.

– Hidden layers: 0.2.

Other probabilities have been tried, such as 0.8 for the input layer and 0.5 for the hidden layers, but the results of the model were degraded. See section 8.6.4 for a more detailed analysis of the results.

### 8.5.7. *Activation functions*

For the hidden layers, different activation functions have been tried in the shallow versions of the network to verify their effect on the final classifier. The standard activation functions were tried: *relu*, *tanh* and *sigmoid*. Section 8.6.2 contains the results of the different experiments done with different activation functions.

The input and output layers were instead held at a fixed activation function: *relu* for the input and *sigmoid* for the output.

## 8.6. Results comparison

Different models have been tested to compare different solutions and find the best fit for this task. This section provides a comparison between the performances of each neural network model built.

Each model comes with a description of its shape (i.e. number of layers and units per layer), the training history (loss and accuracy in each epoch) and the results on the test set (confusion matrix).

For the learning and validation steps, the NSL-KDD dataset was divided into a train set containing 125,973 instances ($\approx$85%) and test set containing 22,544 instances ($\approx$15%). We also used 15% of the train set as dev set, in order to keep track and plot the accuracy and loss of each model during the training phase.

### 8.6.1. *Evaluation metrics*

The most common evaluation metrics for IDS, as reported by (Thomas and Pavithran 2018), are Attack Detection Rate (*DR*) and False Alarm Rate (*FAR*).

$$DR = \frac{TP}{TP+FN} \quad AR = \frac{FP}{FP+TN}$$

We can calculate these metrics from the confusion matrix, which is represented by the following terms:

– *True Positive* (*TP*): the instance is correctly predicted as an attack.

– *True Negative* (*TN*): correctly predicted as a non-attack or normal instance.

– *False Positive* (*FP*): a normal instance is wrongly predicted as attacks.

– *False Negative* (*FN*): an actual attack is wrongly predicted as a non-attack or normal instance.

False positives happen when a normal network activity is classified as an attack, and can waste the valuable time of security administrators.

False negatives, on the other hand, have the worst impact on organizations since an attack is not detected at all.

### 8.6.2. Preliminary models

As a preliminary step, three shallow networks consisting of just two layers (excluding the output node) were built with different activation functions. These neural networks have been trained with no dropout layers, no feature selection (all 128 features were used) and a smaller number of epochs (50). The idea is to look at the various results as well as learning curves and pick an activation function for later models. The results are reported in the following sections.

#### 8.6.2.1. Shallow network with "relu" activation

As a first attempt, we built a shallow network with two hidden layers and "relu" as activation function for the hidden layers' neurons. Figure 8.24 shows the learning curves of the model, plotted during the learning phase, while Table 8.3 contains information about the shape of the network and its results on the test set.

The results are already interesting, but we can see from the learning curves that the model starts overfitting fairly early.

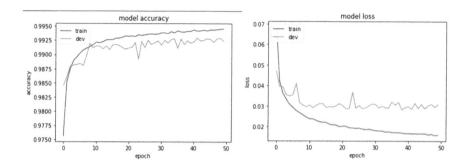

**Figure 8.24.** *Learning curves (accuracy and loss) of the first model (all features, no dropout, relu activation function for hidden layers)*

| Input Features | Input Dropout | Layer 1 | Layer 2 | Hidden Layers Dropout | DR | FAR |
|:---:|:---:|:---:|:---:|:---:|:---:|:---:|
| 128 | None | 30, relu | 10, relu | None | 99.20% | 0.93% |

**Table 8.3.** *Shape and results of the first model*

## 8.6.2.2. *Shallow network with "tanh" and "sigmoid" activation*

For comparison purposes, we also tried the same network with "tanh" and "sigmoid" as activation function for the second layer. Figures 8.25 and 8.26 show the learning curves of these models, while Table 8.4 contains the results.

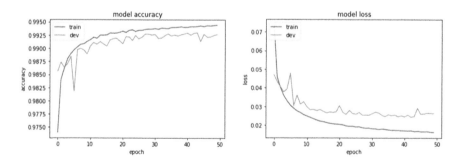

**Figure 8.25.** *Learning curves (accuracy and loss) of the second model (all features, no dropout, tanh activation function for hidden layers)*

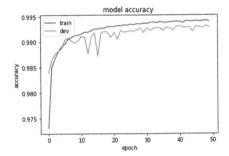
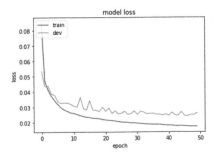

**Figure 8.26.** *Learning curves (accuracy and loss) of the third model (all features, no dropout, sigmoid activation function for hidden layers)*

| Input Features | Input Dropout | Layer 1 | Layer 2 | Hidden Layers Dropout | DR | FAR |
|---|---|---|---|---|---|---|
| 128 | None | 30, relu | 10, tanh | None | 99.44% | 1.05% |
| 128 | None | 30, relu | 10, sigmoid | None | 99.41% | 1.00% |

**Table 8.4.** *Shape and results of the second and third models*

### 8.6.2.3. Conclusions

After this preliminary phase, we can conclude that the generated models have a very similar accuracy. We choose to base the other models on the best we found in this phase, that is, use *tanh* as activation function for the hidden layers.

### 8.6.3. Adding dropout

Having decided the activation function, it is now the moment to decide the dropout probability associated with the dropout layers. Fixing the dropout rate too low would give us little benefit in terms of avoiding overfitting. On the other hand, having a dropout rate that is too high might introduce performance degradation in to the model.

Here we tried out three possible pairs of rates:

– aggressive dropout: input dropout 0.8, 0.5 for other layers;

– intermediate dropout: input dropout 0.5, 0.2 for other layers;

– low dropout: input dropout 0.3, 0.1 for other layers.

The results of these experiments are reported in Table 8.5.

| Input Features | Input Dropout | Layer 1 | Layer 2 | Hidden Layers Dropout | DR | FAR |
|---|---|---|---|---|---|---|
| 128 | 0.8 | 30, relu | 10, tanh | 0.5 | 99.12% | 4.54% |
| 128 | 0.5 | 30, relu | 10, tanh | 0.3 | 99.31% | 1.09% |
| 128 | 0.3 | 30, relu | 10, tanh | 0.1 | 99.17% | 0.88% |

**Table 8.5.** *Shape and results of the dropout models*

Looking at the learning curves we can see that the model is effectively overfitting less on the training set. Figure 8.27 shows the learning curve for the low dropout model.

This is an important result, since we want our model to be able to recognize previously unknown or unidentified violations in our systems, hence we cannot expect the training set to contain all the possible attacks.

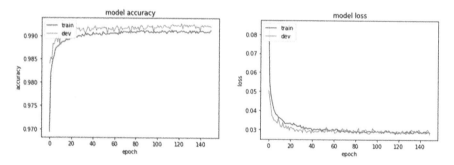

**Figure 8.27.** *Learning curves (accuracy and loss) of the low dropout model*

### 8.6.4. *Adding more layers*

Another typical choice that has to be made when designing a neural network is the number of layers and neurons in a layer.

Here we compare deeper models, that is, models with more layers, to the previously constructed ones, and we compare the results.

Table 8.6 shows the resulting accuracy and false alarm rate for the constructed models.

| Input Features | Input Dropout | Layer 1 | Layer 2 | Layer 3 | Layer 4 | Hidden Layers Dropout | DR | FAR |
|---|---|---|---|---|---|---|---|---|
| 128 | 0.3 | 80, relu | 30, tanh | 10, tanh | None | 0.1 | 99.29% | 0.90% |
| 128 | 0.3 | 80, relu | 30, tanh | 30, tanh | 10, tanh | 0.1 | 99.31% | 1.09% |

**Table 8.6.** *Shape and results of the deep models*

### 8.6.5. *Adding feature selection*

As a final step for our model design phase, we reduce our dataset using the techniques described in section 8.3.3 (*ExtraTrees Classifier* with a random forest and *univariate selection* using *chi-squared* statistical tests).

The resulting models are much lighter versions of the previous ones, which can be trained in less time.

Table 8.7 contains the results of the two selection algorithms in two different models: a shallow one and a deep one.

| Input Features | Selection | Input Dropout | Layer 1 | Layer 2 | Layer 3 | Hidden Dropout | DR | FAR |
|---|---|---|---|---|---|---|---|---|
| 31 | ExtraTrees | 0.3 | 30, relu | 10, tanh | *None* | 0.1 | 99% | 1.24% |
| 31 | ExtraTrees | 0.3 | 30, relu | 30, tanh | 10, tanh | 0.1 | 99.07% | 1.04% |
| 30 | Univariate | 0.3 | 30, relu | 10, tanh | *None* | 0.1 | 98.79% | 1.08% |
| 30 | Univariate | 0.3 | 30, relu | 30, tanh | 10, tanh | 0.1 | 98.61% | 1.02% |

**Table 8.7.** *Comparison between models trained on ExtraTrees Classifier selected features and on univariate selection selected features*

## 8.7. Deployment in a network

This section describes which steps should be made to deploy one or more of the produced models in a real network environment.

### 8.7.1. *Sensors*

To deploy an IDS in a real network, the first components we need are sensors that can record traffic and produce the tuples that will be then fed into the model. Sensor placement is a key factor for an IDS to be able to protect the network from invasion. For this task, the network architecture should be studied in detail, to observe all possible points of entrance.

Depending on how large and complex our network is, we can choose to deploy the whole system in a single device, as suggested by Kim and Gofman (2018), or implement multiple sensors, as done in Chen *et al.* (2010). In both cases, the most sensitive points to place the sensors are typically before and after each router or DMZ of the network. Figure 8.28 describes this situation.

In general, IDS sensors have two network interfaces – one for monitoring traffic and one for management. The traffic monitoring interface is unbound from any protocol, which means that the interface has no IP address and other entities cannot communicate with it. This guarantees that no attack surface is exposed on the network by the sensor itself.

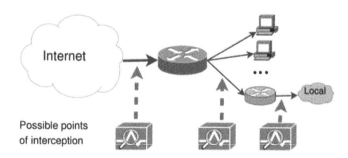

**Figure 8.28.** *Possible points of interception for an NIDS (source: Kim et al. (2012))*

### 8.7.2. Model choice

After deploying the sensors, we must choose which model to deploy. The model choice can depend on evaluation metrics like detection rate or false alarm rate but should also consider the model complexity. A higher model complexity can imply a higher cost for data acquisition and greater delays for the system's response.

This kind of analysis shall be done also taking into consideration the response time of each model, which is outside the scope of this work. For reducing the complexity, we can employ one of the feature selection methods previously described in this chapter.

### 8.7.3. Model deployment

Once the IDS is deployed in the network, we want it to work with streams of incoming data in a fully automated way. This implies several steps, which are described in Figure 8.29.

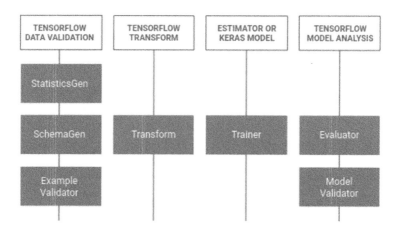

**Figure 8.29.** *Possible steps of the IDS once deployed in a real system (source: https://www.tensorflow.org/tfx/guide/serving)*

There are many possible solutions to achieving this automation which range from fully personalized solutions to fully COTS products. One simple possibility, since the models of this work have been trained using *TensorFlow*, is to use *TensorFlow Extend*[7], a collection of tools used for deploying ANN models in the wild. Figure 8.30 describes the components of the *TFX* framework, which range from data cleaning to *Keras* model validation.

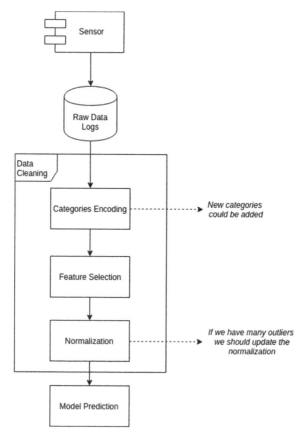

**Figure 8.30.** *Components of the TFX framework as described in the official guide*

On line deployment can be achieved by using *TensorFlow Serving*[8], which is a framework built to enable fast *TensorFlow* models' deployment

---

7 https://www.tensorflow.org/tfx.
8 https://www.tensorflow.org/tfx/guide/serving.

over REST APIs. *TF Serving* also has the ability to deploy a model to a *Docker* image and use *Kubernetes* to manage a cluster of these images running together. This offers a good solution in terms of scalability of the IDS, which can easily keep up with a possible growth of the network that it is protecting.

### 8.7.4. *Model adaptation*

Once it is online, the model should then be trained and updated with real data coming from the network. This is a time-consuming task, which requires the network to be in a temporary "safe" state in which the model can learn what the normal behavior of the system is.

After the training time, the IDS is ready to be used in the network environment. To extend the training time, a human supervisor can be assigned to check the entries that are signaled as anomalous and re-labeling them if necessary. The same model can also be periodically retrained with a larger dataset or with only the latest entries.

## 8.8. Future work

This work represents only a preliminary analysis of how an NIDS can be modeled and deployed using ANN and *TensorFlow*. Many improvements can be made to the models to achieve better performances, such as implementing early stopping instead of a fixed number of epochs and adapting the *Keras* model to work with *TPU*s (Tensor Processing Units), which can significantly improve the training time needed.

An in-depth analysis of a target network should also be performed to deploy the IDS in a real network. Problems such as the efficiency, delay and the sample collection in the new network environment are specific to each network and must be considered if we want to carry out the IDS deployment.

## 8.9. References

Chen, H., Clark, J.A., Shaikh, S.A., Chivers, H., Nobles, P. (2010). Optimising IDS sensor placement. *ARES '10 International Conference on Availability, Reliability and Security*, IEEE, 315–320.

Dhanabal, L. and Shantharajah, S.P. (2015). A study on NSL-KDD dataset for intrusion detection system based on classification algorithms. *International Journal of Advanced Research in Computer and Communication Engineering*, 4(6), 446–452.

Huang, S.H. (2015). Supervised feature selection: A tutorial. *Artificial Intelligence Research*, 4(2), 22–37.

Keskar, N.S., Mudigere, D., Nocedal, J., Smelyanskiy, M., Tang, P.T.P. (2016). On large-batch training for deep learning: Generalization gap and sharp minima. *CoRR* [Online]. Available at: https://arxiv.org/abs/1609.04836.

Kim, S., Nwanze, N., Edmonds, W., Johnson, B., Field, P. (2012). On network intrusion detection for deployment in the wild. *IEEE Network Operations and Management Symposium*, 253–260.

Kim, D.E. and Gofman, M.I. (2018). Comparison of shallow and deep neural networks for network intrusion detection. *2018 IEEE 8th Annual Computing and Communication Workshop and Conference (CCWC)*, 204–208.

Lazarevic, A., Ertoz, L., Kumar, V., Ozgur, A., Srivastava, J. (2003). A comparative study of anomaly detection schemes in network intrusion detection. In *Proceedings of the 2003 SIAM International Conference on Data Mining*, Society for Industrial and Applied Mathematics, 25–36.

Mukherjee, B., Heberlein, L.T., Levitt, K.N. (1994). Network intrusion detection. *IEEE Network*, 8(3), 26–41.

Potdar, K., Pardawala, T., Pai, C. (2017). A comparative study of categorical variable encoding techniques for neural network classifiers. *International Journal of Computer Applications*, 175(4), 7–9.

Reddy, E.K. (2013). Neural networks for intrusion detection and its applications. *Lecture Notes in Engineering and Computer Science: Proceedings of the World Congress on Engineering 2013*, International Association of Engineers, 2(205), 1210–1214.

Srivastava, N., Hinton, G., Krizhevsky, A., Sutskever, I., Salakhutdinov, R. (2014). Dropout: A simple way to prevent neural networks from overfitting. *Journal of Machine Learning Research*, 15(56), 1929–1958.

Subba, B., Biswas, S., Karmakar, S. (2016). A neural network based system for intrusion detection and attack classification. *Twenty Second National Conference on Communication (NCC)*, IEEE, 1–6.

Thomas, R. and Pavithran, D. (2018). A survey of intrusion detection models based on NSL-KDD data set. *2018 Fifth HCT Information Technology Trends (ITT)*, IEEE, 286–291.

# List of Authors

Rachid CHELOUAH
CY Cergy Paris University
France

Hocine CHERIFI
LIB
University of Burgundy
Franche-Comté
Dijon
France

Ahlem DRIF
Computer Sciences Department
Ferhat Abbas University
Setif 1
Algeria

Alvise DE' FAVERI TRON
Politecnico di Milano
Milan
Italy

Gustavo FLEURY SOARES
Brazilian Office of the Comptroller
General (CGU)
Brazil

Saoussen KRICHEN
Université de Tunis
Institut Supérieur de Gestion
de Tunis
LARODEC Laboratory
Tunisia

Belkharroubi LAKHDAR
University of Mascara
Algeria

Marwa MOKNI
MARS Laboratory LR17ES05
University of Sousse
Tunisia
and
ETIS Laboratory CNRS UMR8051
CY Cergy Paris University
France

Induraj PUDHUPATTU
RAMAMURTHY
CYTech
Cergy
France
and
University of India
India

Mohamed SASSI
PJGN IT Director
Gendarmerie Nationale
France

Ines SBAI
Université de Tunis
Institut Supérieur de Gestion
de Tunis
LARODEC Laboratory
Tunisia

SaadEddine SELMANI
Computer Sciences Department
Ferhat Abbas University
Setif 1
Algeria

Patrick SIARRY
Paris-East Créteil University
France

Khadidja YAHYAOUI
University of Mascara
Algeria

Sonia YASSA
ETIS Laboratory CNRS UMR8051
CY Cergy Paris University
France

# Index

Printed and bound by CPI Group (UK) Ltd, Croydon, CR0 4YY

27/10/2024

14580317-0002